Memories of the Mansion

Memories of the MANSION

THE STORY OF Georgia's Governor's Mansion

SANDRA D. DEAL, JENNIFER W. DICKEY, AND CATHERINE M. LEWIS

Published in cooperation with the University of Georgia Libraries and Kennesaw State University

The University of Georgia Press   ATHENS AND LONDON

© 2015 by the University of Georgia Press
Athens, Georgia 30602
www.ugapress.org
All rights reserved

Designed by Erin Kirk New
Set in Adobe Garamond Pro
Printed and bound by Thomson-Shore

The paper in this book meets the guidelines for
permanence and durability of the Committee on
Production Guidelines for Book Longevity of the
Council on Library Resources.

Most University of Georgia Press titles are
available from popular e-book vendors.

Printed in the United States of America

19 18 17 16 15 c 5 4 3 2 1

Library of Congress Cataloging-in-Publication Data

Deal, Sandra D.
    Memories of the mansion : the story of Georgia's Governor's Mansion
/ Sandra D. Deal, Jennifer W. Dickey, and Catherine M. Lewis.
        pages   cm
    "Published in cooperation with the University of Georgia Libraries
and Kennesaw State University."
    Includes bibliographical references and index.
    ISBN 978-0-8203-4859-9 (hardcover)
    1. Georgia Governor's Mansion (Atlanta, Ga.) 2. Architecture,
Domestic—Georgia--Atlanta. 3. Atlanta (Ga.)—Buildings, structures,
etc. I. Dickey, Jennifer W. II. Lewis, Catherine M. III. Title.
    F294.A83D43   2015
    975.8'231—dc23   2015004633

British Library Cataloging-in-Publication Data available

Contents

Foreword

My adventure as first lady of Georgia began when, at the age of thirty-six, I left my three-bedroom home in Augusta and moved with my husband, Carl Sanders, and my two elementary-school-age children into the fourteen-room Governor's Mansion in Ansley Park. The Granite Mansion, as it was known, had high ceilings, and the interior badly needed freshening. Previously, in the fall of 1962, after Carl was elected governor, I wanted to see the house that would soon become our home. I called First Lady Betty Vandiver and requested a tour of the mansion. On a rainy day, I flew to Atlanta with Carl and met my friend Betty. During our visit, one of the men who worked in the house told her the roof was leaking in two rooms upstairs, and without missing a beat, she told him to get the buckets. There was nothing of real value in the house except for an old piano, a very large rendering of the Old Governor's Mansion in Milledgeville by Wilbur Kurtz, which hung over the mantel in the living room, and the punch bowl and other pieces from the silver service formerly on the USS *Georgia*. There were very few linens and barely enough state china, silverware, or crystal glasses to set a table. On the flight home, I cried the whole way.

I simply could not believe it. Little had been added to the mansion over the years—no porcelain, no vases, and no paintings. Thank goodness for the secretary of state, Ben Fortson. He told me to fix the problem, so I called our good friend Dick Rich, the president of Rich's Department Store. He sent his best decorator over to the mansion and gave me some advice about what to purchase and what colors to paint individual rooms to match the existing furniture. We carefully chose the silverware, crystal, and china. This certainly helped, but there were other challenges we could not easily overcome.

We had a twelve-by-fourteen-foot kitchen and no ice maker, but we often were expected to feed three hundred to four hundred people for state functions. We could park only about ten cars on the property, so large events were a logistical nightmare. The caterers often had to set up tables in the yard by the kitchen area and then spend the entire event running in and out of the house to prepare and serve the meals. These events always seemed to happen on cold January nights and on hot August afternoons. It was simply exhausting to entertain a large group. None of the doors had locks, and my children were frightened by the noises made by the state troopers as they rattled each door during night security checks. One night, after we had lived there for about a year, the wallpaper in the guest bedroom just rolled up and fell off the wall. Squirrels and pigeons made strange sounds in the attic, and my children became convinced that we had ghosts.

The Sanders family in their Augusta home when Carl Sanders announced his candidacy for governor, 1962. *Courtesy Betty and Carl Sanders.*

There had been discussions for years about building a new governor's mansion. It was widely debated during the Vandiver administration. He appointed a study committee, but the committee never presented a plan to the legislature. After living there for a while, we certainly came to agree that the current house was not adequate. At one event, Mills B. Lane, a well-known banker, was walking out of the mansion when a large stone fell off the house and nearly hit him. That helped convince everyone that a new mansion was needed. Secretary of State Fortson became the main flag waver. He realized how much it cost to maintain the current mansion, to fix the old pipes and plaster, to mend the sagging roof, and to address the problems with parking. We could have employed a full-time repair crew just to keep the mansion from leaking.

Getting a new mansion approved and funded was not an easy process. In addition to my regular duties, much of my time as first lady was dedicated to planning and building a mansion of which our citizens would be proud. I wanted the new mansion on West Paces Ferry Road to make a statement and become a visible part of the history of our state. All the hard work of the architects, the Fine Arts Committee, and so many others resulted in a building that has served and continues to serve as an executive residence and as a home for our first families.

Each governor's wife brings her own personality, interests, and tastes to the house that she will call home. Though I never lived in the mansion, I am proud that my experiences in the Granite Mansion on the Prado in Ansley Park guided my vision of what was needed. I felt we should have a beautiful home and grounds, adequate parking, expansion space, guest rooms, entertainment areas, two kitchens, quality collections of antique furnishings, works of art, and a lovely Georgia marble fountain. The present mansion reflects all these goals. Each first family is a caretaker of the Governor's Mansion. It is a place where the family sleeps, entertains, and serves the public. The mansion has always been and will always be "the people's house." This book tells that story.

BETTY FOY SANDERS

Preface

Welcome to the beautiful Greek Revival mansion that has served as the Atlanta home for Georgia's governors since 1968. Designed by the Atlanta architect Thomas Bradbury, it sits on a hill surrounded by eighteen acres in the city's Buckhead neighborhood. Eight Georgia governors and their families have called this building home over the past forty-seven years. The mansion's outstanding collection of Federal period furnishings and decorative arts was inspired by items chosen by Jacqueline Kennedy as she redecorated the White House in the early 1960s. Most of the pieces of furniture on the first floor were created by American master craftsmen between 1800 and 1830. Resident governors and their families are privileged to share this special collection with the public during tour hours and with the numerous guests frequently entertained here. For me, serving as the official hostess of Georgia has been an honor and a pleasure. This book, with its history, pictures, and stories, is my way of saying thank you to the people of Georgia for such a privilege.

Georgia's seat of government, originally located in Savannah, has moved many times since Georgia, along with twelve other colonies, declared independence from Great Britain. Four cities—Savannah, Augusta, Louisville, and Milledgeville—served as official state capitals before the relocation of the capital to Atlanta in 1868. Before the construction of the current mansion, only the house in Milledgeville had been built for the exclusive use of the governor. During the first hundred years that the state government was based in Atlanta, Georgia's governors resided in houses that were acquired by the state to serve as the Executive Mansion; once, the official residence was in a private house on the outskirts of the city, and in another case in the Georgian Terrace Hotel. None of these makeshift solutions could satisfactorily accommodate the myriad public responsibilities of the state's top official. Finally, a century after the capital moved to Atlanta, a new governor's mansion, designed and built specifically to serve that purpose, opened on West Paces Ferry Road.

Exploring the Governor's Mansion and property was an experience that I will never forget. My curiosity was piqued when Nathan and I had the opportunity to move into the mansion and walk the grounds. I was astounded. Where did the

Sandra D. Deal.
Courtesy Christopher Oquendo.

columns that surround the tennis courts come from? Were they from a previous home? Who built the tennis courts and the two fountains? Who bought the beautiful "maidens of the seasons" that encircle one of the fountains? Who designed and built the terraces overlooking the fountain? Who built the swimming pool? Who was the Mrs. Smith who was born there, according to the mill grindstone? When did the furniture become part of the mansion's collection? There was so much to learn, and my curiosity got the better of me.

My predecessor, Mary Perdue, wife of Governor Sonny Perdue, had been kind enough to invite me to lunch, show me the family quarters, and tell me a little about the antiques that filled the house. Soon I began to ask questions of the employees and our wonderful volunteers, some of whom said they had served as docents for thirty years. I listened as they shared their knowledge and memories. I read and asked more questions. Joy Forth, the mansion manager, who had arrived three years before I did, helped me plan and invite all the previous governors and their wives for dinner. Most of them came, and I learned a little more, but not enough. Joy remembered that Kitty Farnham had been employed as the curator of the mansion and had completed the first inventory of the collection. We invited her to the mansion, and she kindly spent several hours teaching me about the house and its contents and provided me with even more materials to read.

I was particularly excited when I learned that former first lady Betty Sanders had served on the Fine Arts Committee that planned the mansion. Ember Bishop, my administrative assistant, made arrangements for us to visit with Mrs. Sanders. Although she answered many questions, I had more, so we visited the Georgia Archives. I continued to read and ask questions, and I eagerly shared what I had learned with the mansion's tour guides and anyone else who wanted to listen. Soon I concluded that what I really needed to do was to compile the information. I wanted to record the stories of the building and its contents, and also of the people who had lived here over almost a half century.

I learned so much about the mansion and its residents during the course of my research that I knew a book needed to be produced to preserve that history. I also quickly realized that I needed to engage professional historians to bring together all the rich stories of the mansion's past and the people who lived here. The Chancellor's Office of the University System of Georgia and Daniel S. Papp, president of Kennesaw State University, recommended that I invite Catherine Lewis and Jennifer Dickey, public historians at Kennesaw State University, to join me as coauthors. Well-known scholars who have published widely and are versed in Georgia history, they enthusiastically joined the team. They have been instrumental in bringing this project to fruition. Lisa Bayer and the University of Georgia Press soon signed on, and the book was in full swing. Many institutions in the state have helped us tell this story, including the Georgia Archives, the Atlanta History Center, Special Collections at the University of Georgia, and Georgia State University, just to name a few. I am particularly grateful to Mrs. Sanders for agreeing to write the foreword for this volume. She and her husband, Governor Carl Sanders, who was governor from 1963 to 1967, played a critical role in helping get the mansion built, even though they never lived here.

We had three goals when we began this project: recount the history of all the Georgia governor's mansions, with specific focus on the West Paces Ferry Road mansion; document the rich collections in the mansion and share these resources with readers; and share behind-the-scenes stories from the eight first families who, so far, have known it best. We have been very fortunate that all of them were willing to help us, and we are grateful for the time and energy that they have devoted to this project. Working on this book has brought my coauthors and me great joy, and we hope that our enthusiasm is contagious. This history belongs to the people of the state of Georgia, and we are delighted to have the opportunity to share it.

SANDRA D. DEAL

Memories of the Mansion

Introduction

All homes have a story to tell, and the Georgia Governor's Mansion is no exception. Opened in 1968, the mansion has been home to eight first families and houses a distinguished collection of American art and antiques. The mansion, which is often referred to as the "people's house," is open for tours nearly every week. Many people get their first glimpse into this building as children, and a field trip to the mansion is a treat that they seldom forget. Joe Frank Harris Jr., son of Georgia's seventy-eighth governor, Joe Frank Harris, recalled touring the mansion as a third grader, peeking into the kitchen, and thinking, "What would it be like to live in a place like this?" never imagining that one day he would do so. "When it happens," Joe Frank Jr. added, "you understand that it's a privilege, a blessing, and it's temporary. You are just a caretaker here for a very short period of time."[1] Many Georgia schoolchildren have been bedazzled by the glittering chandeliers, the shelves of historic books, the large portraits, and the vast array of vases and lamps. For some young guests, the mansion is the first museum they visit. Those who come as adults, either on formal tours or for public events in the ballroom, are often impressed by the splendor of the grounds as well as the elegance and beauty of the house and its contents.

The mansion is always on display, always serving the public. It is never just a home, but rather a state facility that conveys a sense of power, formality, and grandeur. But it has to serve, for four or eight years, as a private residence for the governor and the governor's family. Like any family home, the mansion is a place to raise children and teach them how to ride a bicycle or play baseball, to host weddings and holidays, to tend a garden, and to entertain family and friends. It is also a workplace for dozens of people who keep it running smoothly, whether through the hectic Christmas season, when thousands of people come for tours, or for state visits for foreign dignitaries. The mansion is never empty. In fact, there is no key to the front door because the mansion is always occupied, even in the absence of the first family, by a security team.

This book tells the story of the Georgia Governor's Mansion—what preceded it and how it came to be—as well as the stories of the people who have lived and worked here since its opening in 1968. Chapter 1 details the early history of the governors' residences in Georgia, from General Oglethorpe's tent near Savannah to the Granite Mansion in Ansley Park, which was the forerunner of the current mansion. Chapter 2 explains the process by which the current Governor's Mansion came to be,

Christmas card designed by Betty Sanders, ca. 1966. *Courtesy Betty and Carl Sanders.*

and chapter 3 offers readers a guided tour of the grounds and the building. Chapters 4 through 11 explore what it is like to live in the executive mansion through a look at the lives of the families who have called the mansion home. The family of Lester and Virginia Maddox were the first residents. They were followed by the families of Jimmy and Rosalynn Carter, George and Mary Beth Busbee, Joe Frank and Elizabeth Harris, Zell and Shirley Miller, Roy and Marie Barnes, Sonny and Mary Perdue, and Nathan and Sandra Deal. All the first families and many of their children have gladly shared their stories, as have many of the staff members and volunteers who keep the mansion running. The final chapter focuses on the role played by the staff members, who are often invisible to the public. Their work and dedication are vital to the facility's operation—something that First Lady Elizabeth Harris once described as being like "operating a small hotel where you have to host a dinner for 200 people every few weeks."[2]

First Lady Sandra Deal's love of history and deep interest in the mansion and in the people who have lived and worked there served as the inspiration for this book. Her efforts to bring this project to fruition deserve special recognition. Her vision and infectious enthusiasm made this project a labor of love. Like each first family before them, Nathan and Sandra Deal are committed to preserving the mansion for future generations and to making it accessible to the public. Every family that has lived here tells the same story—they were temporary caretakers of a precious resource. To that end, proceeds from the sale of this book will support Friends of the Mansion, Inc., the charitable organization dedicated to preserving the mansion and its fine and decorative arts collections. This book not only shares the stories of this extraordinary place and the people who have lived and worked here, but will also help ensure the preservation of this historic resource so that it may continue to serve the state and its people.

CHAPTER ONE

From the Tent to the Granite Mansion

Since its founding in 1733 as a British colony, Georgia has been led by more than a hundred men who were designated the chief executive—president, governor, or, in the case of the colony's founder James Oglethorpe, resident trustee. The residences of these chief executives have ranged from a tent on the bluff above the Savannah River to a modern, Greek Revival mansion in one of Atlanta's wealthiest suburbs.[1] During its long and illustrious history, Georgia has constructed only two buildings specifically to house its chief executive—the Executive Mansion in Milledgeville, first occupied in 1838, and the current Governor's Mansion in Atlanta, first occupied in 1968. Both of these mansions still stand; all the other residences of Georgia's chief executive, with the exception of the Georgian Terrace Hotel in Atlanta, in which Governor Thomas Hardwick lived during his time in office (1921–23), have been demolished. For many of these residences, there is little or no documentation. With this book, we hope to recover some of that lost history and to record the story of the current Governor's Mansion for future generations.

A Mobile Capital

During the colonial period (1733–76), Savannah served as the seat of government for Georgia and continued as the first capital of the state after the colonies declared independence from Britain. In addition to Savannah, Georgia has had four other official capitals—Augusta, Louisville, Milledgeville, and Atlanta—as well as several temporary capitals—Heard's Fort and Ebenezer—the last two necessitated by circumstances during the Revolutionary War.

Upon his arrival at Yamacraw Bluff in February 1733, General James Edward Oglethorpe established a new settlement, which he named "Savannah." Oglethorpe pitched his tent on the bluff above the Savannah River and proceeded to carve a town out of the wilderness, laying it out in a grid pattern. He negotiated a treaty with Tomochichi, the Yamacraw leader, who ceded to the trustees in England Creek lands from the Savannah to the Altamaha Rivers, inland from the coast as far as the tide flowed. Although few buildings or structures remain from the colonial era, Oglethorpe's imprint remains on the city that he founded: the town plan, organized around public squares, is still evident today. Oglethorpe, who never held the title of governor but rather that of "resident trustee," eventually built for himself a residence on St. Simons Island, where he lived until he returned to England in

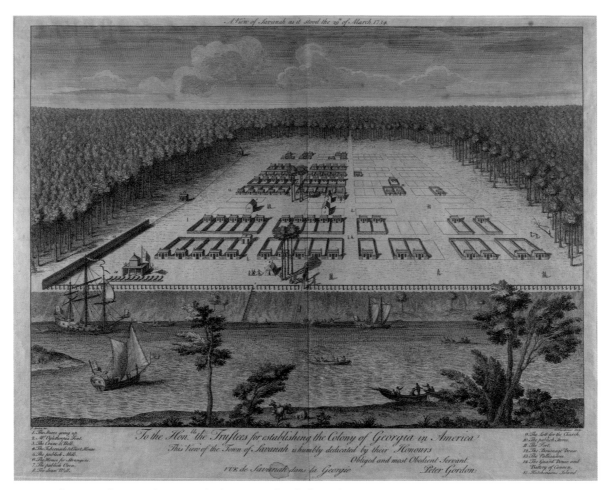

A view of Savannah, 1734, depicting the location of Oglethorpe's tent.
Courtesy Hargrett Rare Book and Manuscript Library, University of Georgia.

1743.[2] Governmental officials met in Savannah during the colonial period, even though official power resided with the trustees in England, whose decisions were subject to the king's consent and to approval by the Board of Trade.

The first structure that could be considered a governor's residence was General Oglethorpe's tent under four pine trees on the bluff at Savannah.[3] After occupying the tent for a year, he later moved into a "humble homestead" that included a cottage, garden, and orchard, where he planted figs, grapes, and oranges on fifty acres at Frederica on St. Simons Island.[4] Jack Spalding, who was born at Frederica, explained that the house was shaded by live oak trees, "but looked westward across the prairie (which was the common pasturage of the herds of the town) upon the entrenched town and fort, and upon the beautiful white houses, which had risen up as by the enchanter's will."[5]

The colony's charter gave the Georgia trustees control of the new colony for twenty-one years, 1733–54.

A year before the charter expired, the trustees gave up Georgia, and it became a crown colony in 1754.[6] The Board of Trade identified Savannah as the seat of government, where, in the words of the historian Edwin Lawson, the "royal governor, new legislative assembly, and courts established headquarters."[7] The royal governors of Georgia lived in Savannah, but the historical record is largely silent about where they resided. One early record mentions a house on what is now Telfair Square. Governor John Reynolds was listed as living on what is now Oglethorpe Square. In 1760, the General Assembly authorized the purchase of "a commodious dwelling" for a royal governor, at a cost of no more than five hundred pounds, but it is not known whether such a dwelling was acquired.[8]

When British troops occupied Savannah in 1778 during the Revolutionary War, the fledgling state government, which met sporadically, moved to Augusta. After the British captured Augusta, Georgia's government set up temporary headquarters in Heard's Fort

Choosing a Chief Executive

The method of choosing Georgia's governors and the length of their term of office have changed many times since the founding of the colony in 1733. Georgia's colonial governors were appointed, first by the trustees and later by the king. After Georgia and the other twelve colonies declared independence from Great Britain in 1776, the state adopted a set of Rules and Regulations, which specified that the legislature

would choose a president, who would serve for a period of six months. The state's first constitution, adopted in 1777, created the office of governor, whose occupant was to be chosen by the legislature each year to serve a one-year term. The 1789 state constitution extended the governor's term to two years, but the governor was still selected by the state legislature. A new constitution was ratified in 1798, but not until that document was amended in 1824 was the general electorate empowered to vote for the governor.

In 1825, George Troup (1823–27) became Georgia's first governor elected by popular vote. A new constitution drafted in 1865 set the governor's term at two years and limited the governor to two consecutive terms, although a former governor could run for reelection after a period of four years following the expiration of a second term. The 1865 constitution was replaced by the 1868 constitution, which specified a four-year term for the governor and did not prohibit reelection. Following the end of Reconstruction, a new constitution adopted in 1877 reverted to the system put in place by the 1865 constitution: a two-year term, a limit of two consecutive terms, and the chance to run for reelection four years after the expiration of the second term.

In 1917 the state legislature passed the Neill Primary Act, formalizing a practice known as the county unit system, which allocated votes by county in a manner similar to the procedure used by the Electoral College at the national level. A landmark U.S. Supreme Court decision, *Baker v. Carr*, in 1962 led to the suspension of the county unit system, which was finally ruled unconstitutional in 1963 by the Supreme Court's decision in *Gray v. Sanders*. Carl Sanders (1963–67) (who was not the litigant in the court case just mentioned) became the first Georgia governor to be elected by popular vote following the demise of the county unit system.

The Constitution of 1945 established a four-year term for the governor with no option for a second term until after the expiration of four years from the conclusion of the first term. An amendment to the Constitution in 1977 allowed a governor to serve two consecutive four-year terms. The Constitution of 1983 retained this provision and allowed any former governor who had served two terms to be eligible for election to the office of governor again after the expiration of four years from the conclusion of his last term.

Louisville, Georgia's capital from 1796 to 1806. This image of the former slave market dates from 1934. *Courtesy Library of Congress.*

(now Washington, the county seat of Wilkes County) in May 1780. During the remainder of the war, the capital moved from Heard's Fort to Augusta to New Ebenezer (near Rincon, in Effingham County) before finally returning to Savannah.[9] Not surprisingly, the Revolutionary War governors were transitory; one took refuge in North Carolina during the conflict. After the war, the capital rotated between Savannah and Augusta for two years in an effort to accommodate settlers who had spread inland. (Many civil matters now handled by the courts, including divorces, required legislative action in the late eighteenth century.) At a meeting in Savannah in February 1785, the General Assembly declared, "All future meetings of the Legislature shall be and continue at that place [Augusta] until otherwise ordered by the General Assembly."[10]

For many of the state's settlers, however, even Augusta was too far east, so the state legislature appointed a commission in January 1786 to find "a proper and convenient place" for the seat of government, one that, according to Jackson, would be more "centrally located and accessible to all [white] residents of the occupied sections of Georgia." The legislature further stated that the location should be "within twenty miles of an Indian trading post known as Galphin's Old Town, or Galphinton, on the Ogeechee River." The commission purchased a thousand acres in what is now Jefferson County and began developing the new capital, called "Louisville" in honor of King Louis XVI of France, who had supported Georgia during the Revolutionary War.[11] Although plans for the construction of Louisville, which included a statehouse and governor's mansion, were approved by the legislature, financial problems curtailed construction. Consequently, the state government continued to operate from Augusta for another decade.

The new capitol, a brick building in the Georgian style, was completed in March 1796, and the state legislature moved to Louisville. Because of financial difficulties and a general lack of enthusiasm for Louisville as a "permanent seat" of government, the governor's mansion was not built. In May 1803, the General Assembly began looking for a new capitol site, this time on the Oconee River, in an effort to accommodate the white settlers who were expanding along the western frontier of the state. Following a search lasting more than a year, the General Assembly passed in December 1804 an act authorizing construction of a new capital, to be called Milledgeville in honor of Governor John Milledge (in office 1802–6). Three years later, the new Gothic Revival capitol was ready for occupancy, and the state government left Louisville in October 1807 for Milledgeville.[12]

The historian James Turner notes that before the 1830s, "governors were not provided any lodgings by the state, but simply an allowance for rents in dwellings located throughout the city."[13] For the first thirty years that Milledgeville served as the state capital, Georgia's governors lived in a variety of residences, beginning with a "double log cabin overlooking Fishing Creek" into which Governor Jared Irwin (second term, 1806–9) and his wife moved in 1807. The log cabin served as the official residence of Governor Irwin and briefly as that of his successor, Governor David B. Mitchell (first term, 1809–13).[14] The state purchased a two-story clapboard-sided house from John Scott for $4,500 in 1809, and it was there in 1811 that Governor Mitchell hosted Parson Mason Locke Weems, who gained great fame as the author of the *Life of Washington*. In that same year, Mitchell hosted twenty-two Creek leaders for a dinner.[15]

Before 1821, the state acquired another mansion, located on Greene Street, to serve as the residence of the governor. It was there, in what became known as Government House, that Governor George M. Troup (in office 1823–27) hosted the Marquis de Lafayette in 1825. Legend holds that as Lafayette walked through the city, "young girls threw flowers in his path, and Revolutionary soldiers embraced him and wept."[16] Martha Lumpkin, the daughter of Governor Wilson Lumpkin (in office 1831–35), for whom the city of Atlanta was briefly named Marthasville, played under the oak tree in the front yard.[17]

Georgia's First Executive Mansion

By the term of Governor William Schley (1835–37), Government House had fallen into "a decayed and uncomfortable condition," according to the state legislature, which appropriated in 1835 fifteen thousand dollars for the construction of a new governor's mansion, to be built on the site of Government House.[18] In a design competition for the new mansion, the architect John Pell was awarded first prize, one hundred dollars, in January 1836. Pell's design would have proved prohibitively expensive to execute, however, so a second prize of one hundred dollars was awarded to another architect in April 1837. According to the *Journal of the*

House of Representatives from 1838, "Upon inquiry and examination, they became satisfied that this [Pell's] plan would cost near $70,000 and for this reason they reconsidered and adopted as their next choice, a plan proposed by an architect of eminence (Mr. Mclesky) [*sic*] under the decided conviction and expectation that the plan could be executed for $30,000."[19] The "architect of eminence" was, in fact, Charles Cluskey, an architect of some note in Georgia. A native of Ireland, Cluskey had immigrated in 1827 to the United States, plying his trade in New York before moving to Savannah in 1829. The Champion-McAlpin-Fowlkes and Sorrel-Weed Houses (both designed in 1835) in Savannah were two of Cluskey's notable designs, and the Old Medical College Building (1834) in Augusta, Cluskey's first major building, was considered a masterpiece of the Greek Revival style.[20]

Before construction could begin on the Cluskey design, Government House had to be demolished. Governor Schley and his successor, Governor George Gilmer (second term, 1837–39), took up residence in a house located at 311 West Greene Street while the new mansion was under construction.[21] The West Greene Street house was later used as the town residence of the author Flannery O'Connor and remains in the family's possession today.

The Gordon-Porter-Beall-Cline-O'Connor House, built in the 1820s and seen here in 1940. It served as the governor's mansion while the mansion in Milledgeville was under construction. *Courtesy, Georgia Archives, Vanishing Georgia Collection, bal068.*

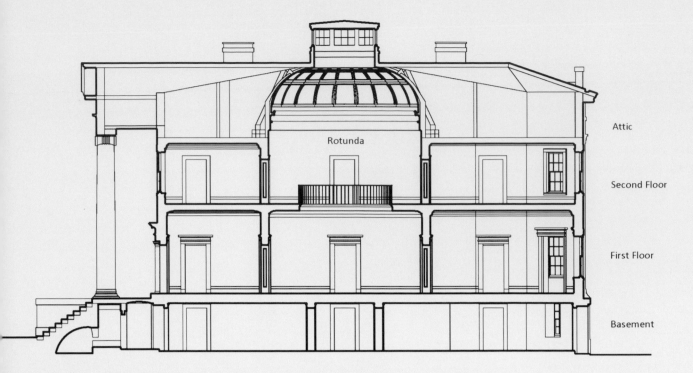

Rotunda

Attic

Second Floor

First Floor

Basement

East-West Section

Cross section for the Governor's Mansion in Milledgeville. *Courtesy Old Governor's Mansion.*

The family dining room in the Milledgeville mansion.
Courtesy Old Governor's Mansion.

The Old Governor's Mansion's domed rotunda.
Courtesy Old Governor's Mansion.

The state hired Timothy Porter of Farmington, Connecticut, to serve as the builder of the new mansion, and he arrived in the city in the fall of 1837 with carpenters, bricklayers, and twenty-eight boxes of tools, moldings, hardware, and Redford crown window glass.[22] The building was composed of pink stucco over brick and included a central rotunda and a grand Ionic portico.[23] Construction of the 21,912-square-foot mansion cost close to $50,000 (approximately $1.2 million in 2013 dollars).[24] The building was four stories tall, including the full basement, and was designed to serve as both a private residence for the governor and a public space where the governor could host the many gatherings that were expected of the state's chief executive. The ground floor, a daylight basement that served primarily as storage space and as the work area for the building's staff, included a banquet kitchen and a steward's bedroom. The second floor, the building's public space, featured a massive saloon (a large public room on the north side), a state dining room, the governor's office, and a parlor. The most spectacular feature of the building was the domed, skylit rotunda, which visitors entered on the second floor. On the third floor were the private quarters of the governor and his family, including six bedrooms. The fourth floor was the attic.[25] The mansion has long been regarded as one of the finest examples of the Greek Revival style in Georgia.

Construction of the new Executive Mansion, as it was known, was completed in the summer of 1839. Governor Gilmer never moved into the mansion, since he was in the final months of his term as governor when it was ready for occupancy and the mansion was not yet fully furnished.[26] On November 21, 1839, the *Savannah Daily Georgian* reported:

> An appropriation of two thousand dollars has just been passed by both houses of the Georgia Legislature to further furnish the Governor's House. Apropos of that, I have not seen anywhere a more imposing building. It is built on the summit of one of those hills which afford such a commanding site for public buildings in Milledgeville. It is one of the first buildings, after the Statehouse, which strikes the eye of the stranger as he enters upon that amphitheatre in which the city lies. The Mansion portico, fronting west, is a fine specimen of architecture; it is chaste and of the Ionic order; the capitals are of fine granite quarried within two miles of this place. The interior corresponds with the exterior.

The great reception room is said to be the finest in the United States comparable to the East Room of the White House. Altogether it is a credit to the State of Georgia, that she has provided such a splendid Mansion for her governor.[27]

Governor Charles J. McDonald (1839–43) was the first governor to live in the new mansion and was the first to host a wedding in there. On May 5, 1843, the McDonalds' daughter, Mary Ann, was married in the saloon. An account of the event tells an unfortunate tale of "one guest, Billy Springer, who weighed five-hundred pounds, crash[ing] to the floor when the spindly legs of a sofa broke beneath him."[28]

Over the years, the Executive Mansion was home to many colorful occupants and played host to some memorable events. During Governor George Crawford's administration (1843–47), the noted British geologist Sir Charles Lyell visited the mansion while traveling throughout the Southeast. Lyell, well known for keeping meticulous journals, noted in one entry that

Governor Charles James McDonald (served 1839–43). *Courtesy, Georgia Archives, Vanishing Georgia Collection, geo034.*

muddy footprints had been left on the governor's newly installed Axminster carpet. Lyell's description of the carpet was so thorough that the State of Georgia used the diary entry to help reproduce the carpet years after his visit.[29] One night when inmates from the state penitentiary, across Hancock Street, kept Governor George W. B. Towns (1847–51) and his family awake, he "blasted them with indignation and condemnation they had never listened to before or since."[30] The governor and his family never had to complain again. Governor Howell Cobb (1851–53) was known for hosting a lavish inauguration party that attracted Unionists, Whigs, and Democrats, who all "mingled kindly and socially, and spent the evening together in a most cordial and good humor."[31] During Governor Herschel Johnson's tenure (1853–57), one guest "took from his pocket a jack-knife and applied it vigorously to his teeth while gazing at his image with apparent satisfaction."[32] First Lady Elizabeth Grisham Brown worried about the cost of entertaining during her husband's tenure (1857–65). To save money, she raised vegetables in a garden on the grounds.[33] One attendee at a social function hosted by Governor Brown described the scene:

> The reception given by Governor and Mrs. Brown to a vast crowd of guests on Wednesday evening was quite the event of the season. Some half dozen large rooms in the Executive Mansion were thrown open, and all were filled. The lights shown brilliantly, and so did the ladies. Occasionally the lovers of music had a song at the parlor piano. Such a press of human beings! Gentlemen chatted in groups to themselves, then promenaded with the ladies. The supper was magnificent. Such piles of good things, loading the several tables, rarely meet the eye.[34]

During the Civil War, the Executive Mansion was occupied by General William T. Sherman from November 22 to 24, 1864, during his March to the Sea. Four days before Sherman's arrival, a citizen of Milledgeville wrote, "Everything in the Executive Mansion was in the wildest uproar. The halls and rooms were filled with men, removing furniture and everything valuable from the Mansion and Mrs. Brown, pale and hurried, was everywhere in the same instant."[35] The Brown family fled to Macon just ahead of Sherman's arrival. Years later in his memoir, Sherman reflected on the government's retreat: "The people of Milledgeville remained at home except the Governor (Brown), the state officers, and Legislature, who had ignominiously fled, in the utmost disorder and confusion, standing not on the order of their going, but going at once—some by rail, some by carriages, and many on foot."[36]

Although the mansion was vandalized during the occupation by Sherman and his troops, it was not

The Old Governor's Mansion, which was occupied by Union forces in 1864. *Courtesy Old Governor's Mansion.*

burned. The Browns returned a few days after Sherman's departure and replaced the furnishings. After the Confederacy surrendered, Governor Brown was arrested at the Executive Mansion on May 9, 1865, by federal troops and taken to Washington, D.C. A week later, President Andrew Johnson allowed him to return to Georgia under the condition that he resign the governorship. President Johnson appointed former U.S. representative James Johnson, a Unionist who had opposed secession, governor of Georgia (June–December 1865). Governor Johnson oversaw the drafting of a new constitution for the state and was succeeded by former Georgia attorney general Charles L. Jenkins (1865–68), who had run unopposed that November.[37]

Jenkins quickly made long-overdue repairs, installing gas lighting and purchasing new furnishings, in anticipation of the inaugural ball. A popular governor, Jenkins opened the mansion to the public, hosting receptions and "welcoming all citizens, rich and poor, high and low." It seemed that good times had returned to the Executive Mansion following the years of war, but they proved short-lived. When the Georgia state legislature refused to ratify the Fourteenth Amendment, Congress imposed Radical Reconstruction on the state in 1867, much as it did throughout the South. General John Pope arrived in Atlanta in April 1867 to establish his headquarters for overseeing the military occupation of the Third Military District, which included Georgia, Alabama, and Florida. Pope decided that Georgia's next constitutional convention should be held in Atlanta, not Milledgeville. Representatives began meeting in Atlanta to draft a new constitution in December 1867. When Governor Jenkins refused to pay the bill for the convention, he was removed from office in January 1868 by General George Meade, who had replaced Pope as head of the Third Military District. Meade appointed Brigadier General Thomas H. Ruger (January–July 1868) the provisional governor of Georgia. Ruger was the last resident governor to live in the Milledgeville Executive Mansion.[38]

The new state constitution was ratified in March 1868. Among its provisions was the permanent relocation of the state capital to Atlanta. According to J. C. Bonner, a historian at Georgia College and State University, the decision to move the capital to Atlanta created "a ruckus in Milledgeville." Unsurprisingly, residents there fought hard against the change: "Earlier, local citizens met and wrote a long letter to the 40th Congress trying to get

it to remove the clause that would make Atlanta the capital. . . . They said Georgia couldn't afford the move, that it would bankrupt the state. But the clause stayed in and the constitution passed."[39] After furnishings of the Executive Mansion in Milledgeville were moved to a new, temporary residence for the governor in Atlanta during the summer of 1868, the Milledgeville mansion was "gloomy, deserted, funereal," according to a visitor who stopped by after the building was vacated.[40]

The Executive Mansion, now known as the Old Governor's Mansion, remained in state hands after the capital was moved to Atlanta, but the state was not always a good caretaker. For a while, according to legend, the mansion was used as a flophouse.[41] The Middle Georgia Military and Agricultural College began using it as a barracks to house cadets in 1879. The building was transferred to the Georgia Normal and Industrial College (created by an act of the Georgia legislature on November 8, 1889, and renamed Georgia College at Milledgeville in 1967) in 1891 to serve as the residence of the college's president—a role the mansion played until 1987.[42] In the mid-1960s, the mansion was restored and refurnished under the direction of a committee appointed by Governor Carl Sanders, which included Henry D. Green, Frank E. Bone, and John D. Harris.[43] The historic mansion was opened to the public in 1967, and the building was designated a National Historic Landmark in 1973. In the 1990s, the state began a major effort to restore the mansion to its antebellum glory. Following completion of the almost nine-year, $10 million project in 2005, the Old Governor's Mansion was opened to the public as a historic house museum.[44]

The first governor elected under the new state constitution was the Republican Rufus Bullock (1868–71). Bullock moved into rented quarters in Atlanta in a three-story building owned by Charles Larendon on the east side of Peachtree Street between Harris and Baker Streets. In 1870, the state purchased for $100,000 the house of John H. James to serve as the governor's mansion in Atlanta. James was a former whiskey salesman who had become one of the city's most prominent bankers; his house, designed by the architect W. H. Parkins, was described by the *Atlanta Constitution* as "one of the best-equipped and most magnificent homes in the city."[45] James happily sold his home to the state and soon built himself another residence on Peachtree Street on a lot that was later purchased by the Capital

The Old Governor's Mansion hosting an event for the Georgia College for Women, 1938.
Courtesy Kenan Research Center at the Atlanta History Center.

The Old Governor's Mansion, Milledgeville. *Courtesy Old Governor's Mansion.*

City Club. The former James mansion, located at Cain (now Andrew Young International Boulevard) and Peachtree Streets, was a red brick, Italianate building with a sixty-foot-tall tower. An elaborate wrought-iron fence surrounded the building.

In 1870, Governor Rufus Bullock became the first governor to live in the new official residence. Seventeen governors occupied this mansion over the next half century, including the former vice president of the Confederacy, Alexander H. Stephens, who died there in 1883 just after taking office. Presidents Rutherford B. Hayes (in 1877) and Grover Cleveland (in 1887) visited the mansion. Dr. Floyd W. McRae, one of the founders of Piedmont Hospital, performed an appendectomy at the mansion on Governor William Y. Atkinson (1894–98).[46] The historian Franklin Garrett noted the significance of the mansion: "[It] became symbolic of the era of post-bellum progress in Atlanta. Within its historic walls the destinies of a people were shaped, and in its spacious rooms the beauty and chivalry of two generations graced its floors."[47] When in 1893 the Blue and Red Rooms in the mansion were redecorated, a trade publication at the time described the changes as follows: "The two great drawing rooms on either side of the reception hallway are fresh and beautiful with the new tints, graceful draping and handsome furniture. . . . The contract for furnishing the mansion was awarded to J. M. High & Co., of Atlanta, Ga., over all competitors. This firm [has] furnished many other fine residences in the city and throughout the State. . . . They have one of the largest dry goods and carpet establishments in the South."[48]

Rufus Brown Bullock, Georgia's Reconstruction governor, 1868–71. *Courtesy, Georgia Archives, Small Print Collection, spc17-033.*

View of Peachtree Street from the Hotel Aragon, 1895, showing the governor's mansion with the tower near the center of the image. *Courtesy Special Collections and Archives, Georgia State University Library.*

Penny postcard depicting the mansion on Peachtree Street, ca. 1909. *Courtesy Georgia Governor's Mansion.*

Governor Hugh Dorsey, governor during World War I (1917–21). *Courtesy Richard B. Russell Library for Political Research and Studies, University of Georgia.*

View of the parlor, known as the "Red Room," at the mansion on Peachtree Street, 1894. *Courtesy Kenan Research Center at the Atlanta History Center.*

Governor Hugh M. Dorsey (1917–21) was the last governor to occupy the mansion on Peachtree Street. The Dorsey family kept a cow and a vegetable garden on the property. Dorsey's wife, Adair, remembered some of the expectations that came with being first lady: "During sessions of the legislature, it wasn't unusual for my husband to telephone that he was bringing a dozen guests home for lunch. I was usually prepared to feed 15 at our midday table."[49] During one Memorial Day parade, the governor and his wife stopped to offer a ride to several veterans who had marched down Peachtree Street. Adair Dorsey recalled, "We couldn't get rid of them. They came home with us. They stayed to dinner. A couple spent the night. Some of them corresponded with the governor for the rest of his years in office. Whenever they came to Atlanta, they visited us. If they were passing the mansion and felt like sitting down, they came in and sat on the porch rocking."[50] The Dorseys had a number of distinguished guests, including General John J. Pershing, soldiers from Camp Gordon, and Calvin Coolidge and his wife, before Coolidge was elected vice president.

Although the Dorseys flung the door open wide and welcomed numerous visitors to the mansion, the building itself did not present the best image of the state's chief executive. The Atlanta historian Franklin Garrett explained, "For some years prior to Dorsey's time, the old home was becoming untenable as a residence."[51] By Dorsey's last year in office, the mansion on Peachtree Street had become so run-down that the governor moved to his private home on Water Works Road (now Ridgewood Road). Dorsey's successor, Governor Thomas W. Hardwick (1921–23), took up residence in the Georgian Terrace Hotel at the corner of Peachtree Street and Ponce de Leon Avenue. The old James mansion was demolished in 1923, and the next year the Henry Grady Hotel was built on the site. The hotel was demolished in 1974 to make way for the Westin Peachtree Plaza.[52]

Hardwick's successor, Governor Clifford M. Walker (1923–27), and his family moved into a rented house at 1540 (now 1798) Peachtree Street, and a search began for a permanent residence for the governor. In 1924 the state rented a house in a relatively new suburban development on the north side of Atlanta. The Granite Mansion, as it was called, had been built in 1910 by Edwin P. Ansley to serve as his residence in the new Ansley Park neighborhood, which he developed. Located at 205 The Prado, the house, designed by the preeminent Atlanta architect A. Ten Eyck Brown, had thirteen rooms, five baths, and a red-and-white-tiled veranda enclosed in granite columns. The home was owned by J. N. McEachern when the state rented it to serve as the governor's residence.[53] After renting the house for a year, the state purchased it, along with three additional acres of land, for $100,000 in 1925.[54] Governor Walker was the first governor to live in the Granite Mansion.

Eleven governors and their families lived in the Granite Mansion over the next forty-five years.[55] Both Eugene Talmadge (1933–37, 1941–43) and his son, Herman (1947, 1948–55), kept cows and goats on the grounds. Dr. Herbert Reynolds and his wife, Nannie, lived next door to the governor's mansion and had fond memories of the seventy-year-old governor Lamartine G. Hardman (1927–31) playing marbles with their two sons. Mrs. Reynolds recalled, "The Hardmans were very neighborly. They melted into the life of Atlanta and he just went along in a normal sort of way, like anybody else. Governors were different in those days. They didn't have all this advertising we do today, and there was no publicity about the governor and the governor's wife. Governors just lived the life of others. Now they are terribly publicized."[56] The Reynolds family also played tennis with Governor Richard B. Russell.[57] Mrs.

Reynolds also remembered that Miss Mitt, as Governor Gene Talmadge's wife was fondly called, was a kind of proto-environmentalist: "[She] used to fuss at me because I put my leaves out on the street for the trash man. She said every leaf should be dug into the soil."[58] Mrs. Reynolds recalled how Betty Talmadge, the wife of Governor Herman Talmadge, once saved her life: "One day the church called to say there were no flowers for Sunday and I went out in the yard with a ladder to cut some Burford holly covered with red berries. It was bitter cold and the wind was blowing hard. I set the ladder up on the governor's side of my holly, climbed up and took off like a sail. When I came to, Betty Talmadge was hanging over me. I don't know what would have happened to me if she hadn't come by. She was a precious neighbor."[59]

Emma Hardman, the wife of Governor Lamartine G. Hardman, did her part to beautify the mansion's grounds by planting a "Georgia garden" featuring plant specimens native to the state. She worked with the landscape architect W. H. Harvey from the State College of Agriculture in Athens to make improvements to the property, declaring, "I wanted to interest the people of the state in their property. I remembered how much pleasure the entire country has received from the cherry trees presented to Mrs. Roosevelt by the Japanese government, trees which she planted in Washington's public park along the Potomac, and I hoped that some day the people of this state would take

The Granite Mansion, 1950s. *Courtesy Georgia Governor's Mansion.*

Governor Eugene Talmadge, Henry Ford, and
Clara Bryant Talmadge in the Granite Mansion, 1935.
*Courtesy Kenan Research Center at the Atlanta
History Center.*

From left: Wilbur Kurtz, William F. Rodgers (MGM
executive), David O. Selznick (producer), Clark Gable,
and Governor E. D. Rivers at the *Gone with the Wind*
festivities at the mansion, December 15, 1939. *Courtesy
Kenan Research Center at the Atlanta History Center.*

as much pride in their garden here in Atlanta."[60] The
Georgia Experiment Station at Griffin shipped crepe
myrtles, deodar cedars, and silvertip spruce to the mansion. Each of the twelve Georgia congressmen sent a
plant representing his district. Representative Charles
G. Edwards of Savannah and Representative Charles
R. Crisp from Americus both sent *Podocarpus japonica*.
Representative E. E. Cox of Camilla chose an English
dogwood, and Representative Leslie J. Steele of Decatur
contributed a forsythia bush. To round out the garden,
Emma Hardman brought several hundred plants from
her home in Commerce. She explained the reasons for
her selections: "Practically everything was raised here in
Georgia, is typical of the state's production and is a gift
from the state or individual Georgians."[61]

Governor Ellis G. Arnall (1943–47), in an interview
with Devereaux McClatchey, reflected on his time in
the Ansley Park mansion:

[The years] 1943–1947 were meaningful and happy years
for me and my family. During those years we lived in the
Governor's Mansion in Ansley Park. The Mansion was an
imposing granite-stone home and was said to be built on
the highest spot in Atlanta. Our son, Alvan, six years old,
moved with us into the Mansion and our daughter, Alice,
was born while we occupied the Governor's Mansion.

We found the residents of Ansley Park to be hospitable,
gracious and friendly. . . . When we moved into the
Mansion, Mrs. Arnall and I had difficulty finding our
way home since frequently we lost our way by reason of
our lack of knowledge of the streets, circles, and curves
in Ansley Park. But, in time, we [be]came familiar with
the area and had no difficulty in getting to the Mansion.
We frequently had children's parties at the Mansion and
the children cavorted and frolicked on the lawn. We
placed play equipment there and had a roller coaster to
go downhill. When the Old Governor's Mansion on The
Prado was demolished, it saddened us greatly. The new
Governor's Mansion on West Paces Ferry Road is attrac-
tive and beautiful, but the "real" Governor's Mansion
in my mind and heart is still located on the hill on The
Prado in Ansley Park where some of the finest people I
have ever known reside.[62]

Although Arnall had fond memories of living in
Ansley Park and of the Granite Mansion, not all of
its residents felt the same. The mansion was not large
enough for many state functions. In 1957, the *Atlanta
Journal and Constitution* published an article titled
"That Miserable Mansion," in which Frank Daniel
describes it as a "monstrosity" and "just a pile of rub-
ble."[63] Former first lady Mattie (Miss Mitt) Talmadge
called the mansion a "horror" that was not a "'fit' place

The Granite Mansion was purchased by the state in 1925 to serve as the governor's mansion. *Courtesy Kenan Research Center at the Atlanta History Center.*

Governor Ellis Arnall's wife, Mildred, and her sister, Margaret Slemons, in the Granite Mansion, Atlanta, Georgia, January 31, 1943. *Copyright* Atlanta Journal-Constitution. *Courtesy Georgia State University.*

to live." By the early 1960s, Governor Ellis Arnall and his successor, M. E. Thompson, who resided in the mansion from 1947 to 1948, agreed that the state needed a new mansion, and "the sooner the better." All the former residents of the Granite Mansion were reportedly delighted when in June 1961 Governor Ernest Vandiver appointed a committee to study the idea of building a new official residence.[64]

When state senator Carl Sanders was elected governor in 1962, he inherited the debate that was raging about whether a new governor's mansion should be built. Sanders's wife, Betty, visited the mansion on a rainy day during which water poured in through the leaky roof. She recalled, "I was just astounded with everything that I saw." She noted the many defects of the place: "The house had no treasures in it whatsoever except a painting, one piano, and the silver from the [USS] *Georgia* battleship. There was no china, no crystal, no silverware. People had taken the silverware. It had Governor's Mansion on it, so they just took it home with them after functions. I couldn't believe it."[65]

Upon moving into the Granite Mansion, Sanders set about making improvements. As she recalled, "The mansion had not been freshened in several years, and the interior needed freshening badly." The secretary of state, Ben Fortson, who was well aware of the costs associated with maintaining the current mansion and had long advocated for the construction of a new one, told Sanders to "fix it." She promptly called Dick Rich of Rich's Department Store and put the wheels in motion to update the interior of the house. "I told [Rich] my predicament," said Sanders, "and then I went out there and bought all the silver, the china, the crystal, the glasses, and whatever. He offered me his best decorator to meet me at the mansion. He sent him out to tell me what color to paint the walls and what to do about upholstery." The cost of the much-needed "freshening" of the interior was almost $17,000, but that was just a fraction of the cost of the total repairs to the building for the year, which topped $82,000, much of which went to fix damage caused by the leaking roof.[66]

The repairs made in 1963 might have stopped the leaks, but only temporarily. Two years later, on February 8, 1965, the *Atlanta Journal* reported that the roof fell in on Governor Sanders and his family on the second-floor sun porch. First Lady Betty Sanders took several

Christmas decorations at the Granite Mansion, 1945. *Courtesy Kenan Research Center at the Atlanta History Center.*

The Sanders family at their inauguration, 1963. *Courtesy Betty and Carl Sanders.*

journalists on a tour through the mansion, which she likened to "an old shoe," noting plaster cracks, rain leaks, squirrels in the attic, and sagging ceilings. She explained the dire situation: "No matter how much you spend on this house now, there's always going to be something else that you'll have to do. It's reached the point of no repair."[67]

By this time, the state had begun moving forward with plans for a new mansion. Prompted largely by state representative J. B. Fuqua, the legislature passed a bill authorizing the State Office Building Authority to issue $1 million in bonds for the purpose of building a new residence for the state's governors. But Governor Vandiver did not move forward on construction before he left office in January 1963.[68] Governor Sanders, not wanting to get caught up in the political maelstrom that swirled around the subject of the mansion, publicly stated, "I'm going to be happy to live in whatever type of home is provided me by the people of Georgia."[69] But

in April 1963, a state commission approved a basic plan for a "new 25-room Georgian-type home for Georgia governors" that was expected to cost $750,000.[70] Among the advocates for the new mansion was C&S Bank president Mills B. Lane, who had nearly been struck on the head by a stone that fell from the side of the Granite Mansion as he was leaving an event there.[71] Lane, along with many other state leaders, believed that the current mansion was "inadequate" and that a new mansion "would serve a triple purpose—a home, a state exhibit with the public invited to some sections, and the provision of badly needed executive office space." Conceding that the total cost of $1 million for the land and the new building seemed "like a lot of money," Lane nonetheless offered a rationale for the expenditure: "In view of the multi-purposes, it would be extremely modest. It would be a showplace to put the South's best foot forward— an investment in Georgia's future."[72] Lane's assessment proved to be prophetic.

CHAPTER TWO

A New Mansion

As debate continued in the General Assembly throughout 1963 about the suitability of spending $1 million on a new mansion for the governor, newspapers from across the state kept Georgians informed about all the developments. A site for the new executive residence had been selected in late 1962—Woodhaven, the eighteen-acre Buckhead estate of former Atlanta mayor Robert Maddox. The ninety-two-year-old Maddox, who had agreed to sell the property to the state for $250,000, hoped that much of the formal landscaping, which had been designed and nurtured by his late wife, Lollie, would be preserved. "The gardens are owned by the state now," commented Mayor Maddox in November 1962, adding, "They tell me the state is going to maintain them. I'm glad."[1] But the fifty-year-old Tudor-style house, located at 391 West Paces Ferry Road, was slated for demolition. Maddox commented that although he hated to see the house torn down—"It's a beautiful old house," he noted—he recognized that the dark and rambling mansion in which he had lived for the past half century was not well suited to serve as the executive mansion.[2]

The search for a site for the new mansion had been going on for some time. Betty Foy Sanders, wife of Governor Carl Sanders, recalled riding around with Secretary of State Fortson to look at houses in the area to see whether there might be something suitable already in existence. They visited the Nunnally mansion, a 1937 sixteen-room house on Blackland Road that was made famous when Clark Gable and Carol Lombard posed in front of it while in town for the 1939 film premiere of *Gone with the Wind*. The house, which had long offered Atlantans a cherished impression of North Georgia grandeur, and its lot were determined to be inadequate. They also visited the Swan House, the Inman family home from the late 1920s, which was designed in the Second Renaissance Revival style by the Atlanta architect Philip Shutze (the house is now part of the Atlanta History Center). The Swan House was certainly more beautiful than the Granite Mansion and could have been acquired for a mere $450,000. But according to Betty Sanders, because the Swan House had "bad plumbing and a small kitchen," improvement over the Granite Mansion would be slight: "You were walking into the same situation that we were already in." Ben Fortson was more blunt in his assessment. "We don't need any damn Italian villa as a governor's mansion."[3]

The Maddox property proved to be exactly what Fortson wanted. He explained, "We bought it—for $250,000—because it was the largest tract of undivided land we

Woodhaven, the home of Robert Maddox, ca. 1933. *Courtesy Peachtree Garden Club.*

could find in an area of the city that's not going down." The legislature had approved the sale of up to $1 million in bonds, but Fortson felt confident that everything could be done for "well below that figure." The new governor's residence had to "be a beautiful house, one that represents Georgia's past and its future," said Fortson, who wanted the new residence to "be a symbol of our people, our hopes, aspirations and growth."[4] Because the legislature was out of session in late 1962, when Woodhaven was identified as the perfect site for the new mansion, banker Mills Lane donated $25,000 in earnest money to begin acquisition of the land and went on to buy the property on behalf of the state for $250,000.[5] Legislators quibbled about the mansion for more than a year, but the state finally acquired the property from Lane in March 1964.[6]

Acquisition of the land for the new mansion did not resolve the contentious debate surrounding construction costs. Although Secretary Fortson repeatedly assured the public that the new mansion, which

was being designed by the architect Thomas Bradbury, would cost well under $775,000, the amount remaining of the $1 million bond issuance, bids received by the state in December 1964 far exceeded the budget. The low bid was $1.1 million for construction of the Greek Revival brick structure.[7]

Throughout the year, Bradbury repeatedly reworked the plans for the building, at one point reducing it to just over eighteen thousand square feet. The final design that was sent out to bidders included twenty-four thousand square feet distributed over three floors. The ground floor, or basement, included a grand ballroom suitable for hosting the large gatherings required of the state's chief executive. The main floor featured a state dining room and state living room, along with a library and several smaller rooms for use by the first family, as well as a kitchen and several bathrooms. A circular stairway led to the family and guest quarters on the top floor, which included six bedrooms, eight bathrooms, and offices for the governor and first lady. The brick

Thomas Bradbury

Abraham Thomas Bradbury (1902–92), trained as an architect and lawyer, became, according to the *New Georgia Encyclopedia*, one of Georgia's best-known midcentury architects of modernist government buildings. Educated at the Georgia Institute of Technology, Bradbury worked throughout the South for a number of firms, including Hentz, Adler and Shutze for a short time during the Depression. During World War II, he established his own company, A. Thomas Bradbury and Associates. Bradbury designed the Agriculture Building and the Law and Justice Building, both near the Georgia Capitol. He was the lead architect for the 1957 renovation of the capitol, and soon after worked on buildings at Georgia Tech and the Georgia Mental Health Institute (now part of Emory University). The Governor's Mansion, a neoclassical building with columns intended to evoke southern charm and grandeur, was a departure from Bradbury's modernist style. Throughout the 1960s, Bradbury returned to designing minimalist, modernist structures, such as the Georgia Archives, as well as other buildings around the capitol. He sold his firm and retired in 1978.

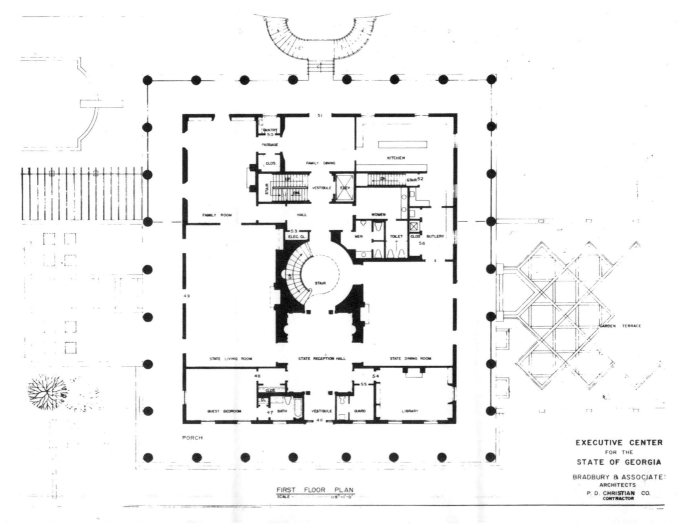

Plan for the first floor. *Courtesy Kenan Research Center at the Atlanta History Center.*

Construction of the new mansion, 1967. *Courtesy Kenan Research Center at the Atlanta History Center.*

Construction of the new mansion, 1968.
Courtesy Kenan Research Center at the
Atlanta History Center.

mansion was surrounded on all sides by a twelve-foot-wide veranda supported by thirty white columns, each twenty-four feet high.[8]

In May 1965 the state again advertised for construction bids for the mansion but once again faced high costs. Although the submission by the P. D. Christian Company, $1,045,000, was about $89,000 lower than the previous lowest bid, it was still much higher than anyone had anticipated.[9] State auditor Ernest Davis pondered this predicament for several weeks before deciding to go ahead with the project. He awarded the contract on July 2, 1965, declaring, "The contractor can start work today if he wishes."[10] P. D. Christian Jr., who owned the company, noted that a strike by operating engineers would have to be resolved before construction could begin.[11] The project seemed to be cursed as strikes by heavy-machinery operators and ironworkers further delayed construction. By May 1966, Davis announced that the building was scheduled for completion in November.[12] When that date came and went, the projected occupancy date was moved to February 1967.[13]

Meanwhile, Davis had begun contemplating how to furnish the mansion, something for which there was no provision in the budget. In late 1964, he contracted with the W. E. Browne Decorating Company, an Atlanta interior design firm, to serve as consultants during the architectural design phase. Norman Pendley and David Richmond Byers III of that firm remained actively involved in the mansion project through to its completion. Byers had studied architectural history at the University of Virginia and was well known for his expertise on historic architecture and decorative arts, especially of the Federal period.[14] Concurrently, Davis and First Lady Betty Sanders began reaching out to "interested and knowledgeable citizens" from around the state to serve on "a Mansion Advisory Committee to review the plans for the grounds and landscaping as well as to counsel with the decorator on interior features." The committee was to "assist in obtaining appropriate antiques and other items of historical value that Georgians may wish to make available to the new Mansion."[15]

On July 14, 1966, Governor Carl Sanders issued an executive order creating the Fine Arts Committee, which was charged with "making recommendations for the appropriate furnishing and interior decoration of the new Governor's Mansion." According to the order, "The interior decorations and furnishings of the Mansion should reflect the same qualities as its exterior architectural design and landscaping"; it further noted that "the combined talents, creative abilities, energies and ideas of distinguished Georgians, professionally qualified in the field of interior decoration and design" would be necessary "to insure that the Governor's Mansion be appropriately furnished, decorated, and appointed."[16] Clearly the new, million-dollar mansion was not going to be outfitted in the same haphazard way as the mansion in Ansley Park. The new residence would be a showplace.

An editorial in the *Atlanta Journal and Constitution* noted in November 1966 that the new mansion was "a monumental sort of place" that "should be a tourist attraction and visited by droves of school children as an historical shrine for generations to come." The editorial added that all worries about furnishings for the mansion had been "calmed last summer by the announcement of a number of committees of people of good taste and discernment." The editorial particularly saluted Sanders's appointment of Henry D. Green as chairman of the Executive Fine Arts Committee, noting that Green was "the leading authority on Piedmont antiques" and was "a man who knows what is right for a Governor's Mansion of the State of Georgia." The editorial concluded that Green and the rest of the committee should be "free to do the right thing by this Mansion so that this generation and those to come will be proud of it."[17] Green and the subcommittees under him were given free rein to assemble for the mansion an unparalleled collection of antique furnishings, fine art, and decorative objects, many of which are highlighted in the next chapter.

Henry Green and the Fine Arts Committee worked tirelessly to bring together an extraordinary collection. Edna Thornton chaired the furniture and furnishings committee. A prominent member of that group was Edward Vason Jones, an architect and collector from Albany, Georgia, who brought valuable expertise in the area of Federal design. The Atlanta historian Franklin Garrett chaired the books, manuscripts, and memorabilia committee, and was assisted by Holcombe T. Green, a bibliophile and scholar of Georgia history. Anne Lane, wife of C&S Bank executive Mills B. Lane, led the gardens and grounds committee, on which Edward Daugherty, an Atlanta landscape architect, also served. Edward Shorter, director of the Columbus (Georgia) Museum of Arts and Crafts, chaired the paintings and

Henry D. Green

When Betty Sanders and Ernest Davis began looking for someone to chair the Fine Arts Committee for the new Governor's Mansion in 1966, Henry D. Green was the natural choice for the job. As noted in the *New Georgia Encyclopedia*, Green was a pioneer in the effort to recognize and preserve the history and material culture of Georgia. Born in Camilla, Georgia, in 1909, Green moved with his family to Atlanta at an early age. He attended the Georgia Institute of Technology, where he studied civil engineering. Although his professional career was in the highway-paving business, Green's greatest love was history as told through material culture. He began collecting antique furniture and decorative arts when he was a young

man, and in 1952 he helped organize *Southern Furniture, 1640–1820*, the first major exhibition of furniture made in the southern states. Held at the Virginia Museum of Fine Arts in Richmond, the exhibition was sponsored by the museum, Colonial Williamsburg, and *Antiques* magazine. Green later curated an exhibition of southern furniture and decorative arts, *Furniture of the Georgia Piedmont before 1830*, for the High Museum of Art in 1976; he served on the advisory committee for *Georgia's Legacy: History Charted through the Arts*, an exhibition held at the Georgia Museum of Art in 1985.

Always sharing his knowledge and contributing his services without charge, Green played a leading role in the restoration and furnishing of numerous historic sites and structures across the state, including several buildings in the historic district of Jekyll Island. He was part of a three-person committee appointed by Governor Carl Sanders to oversee the restoration and furnishing of the Old Governor's Mansion in Milledgeville in the early 1960s. A tireless advocate for preservation, Green gave strong support to the National Trust for Historic Preservation, the Georgia Trust for Historic Preservation, the Williamsburg Antiques Forum, the Georgia College Foundation, and the Coastal Georgia Historical Society. He received numerous awards for his efforts to promote and protect the artistic legacy of the South, including the Distinguished Service Award from Georgia College in Milledgeville. According to a biographical sketch by Dale Couch, Green's support helped the Georgia Museum of Art develop a decorative arts program that includes a broad collection of objects, and led to the establishment of the Henry D. Green Center for the Study of the Decorative Arts at the museum in 2000.

sculpture committee, and was assisted by Gudmund Vigtel, director of Atlanta's High Museum of Art.[18]

The first business of the Fine Arts Committee was to define its vision for the mansion's furnishings. Under Henry Green's strong leadership, and with knowledgeable input from Edward Vason Jones and David Richmond Byers, the committee agreed to focus on collecting American furniture of the Federal period, along with appropriate European and Asian period accessories. Notably, this was the same period featured by First Lady Jacqueline Kennedy in her restoration work at the White House (1961–63) and publicized by her in the 1962 televised walking tour of the White House, which was reportedly watched by eighty million Americans. Members of the Fine Arts Committee traveled extensively to gather art, furnishings, and carpets to outfit the new residence. Invoices record that items were purchased from leading American dealers, including Ginsburg & Levy, Israel Sack, Hirschl & Adler, J. A. Lloyd Hyde, and others. When proposing items for the approval of the committee, Green would always remind committee members, "Don't worry about the cost. Tell me if it is quality!"[19]

In addition to her leadership in creating the Fine Arts Committee, Betty Sanders was responsible for the creation of one of the most beautiful and best-loved outdoor features on the property—the marble fountain located directly in front of the mansion. She decided

State dining room, 1968. *Courtesy Kenan Research Center at the Atlanta History Center.*

State drawing room, 1968. *Courtesy Kenan Research Center at the Atlanta History Center.*

Family dining room, 1968. *Courtesy Kenan Research Center at the Atlanta History Center.*

that the "dazzling new Executive Center," as the mansion was being called, warranted a "fountain of classic design featuring the Greek key motif," but she realized that the projected $20,000 cost was beyond the state's budget. Determined to see the fountain built, she launched a one-woman art show to raise the money. Sanders had majored in fine arts at the University of Georgia and had studied painting with Lamar Dodd, a nationally known artist and head of the University of Georgia School of Art. Sanders had devoted a great deal of time and energy to the continued study and practice of art and to support of artistic causes throughout her time as first lady. She selected twenty-five of her works and sent them on a tour around the state under the exhibition title *Portrait of Georgia*. All funds raised by the tour went toward the fund for the Fountain of Progress, the name Sanders had decided upon for the fountain that would grace the front lawn of the mansion.[20]

The grounds of the new mansion were extensive, and the effort to shape them into what the *Atlanta Journal* reporter Elizabeth Sawyer described in April 1968 as a "Dixie Jewel" fell into the hands of the Atlanta landscape architect Edward L. Daugherty. He worked closely with Thomas Bradbury and Anne Lane, chair of the Garden and Grounds Committee. In addition to the Fountain of Progress, two veranda gardens were built. Cost overruns dictated that plans for an outdoor swimming pool be delayed, so grass was planted in the area and an arbor with wisteria and trumpet vine was constructed adjacent to the grassy plot. The pool was constructed in 1980 during Governor George Busbee's tenure.[21] Describing the view of the grounds on the east side of the mansion, Sawyer wrote, "The east veranda garden opening off the state dining room is designed to be a warm, enclosed intimate space for sitting—typical of 'Old South' gardens. It is abundant with crab apple trees and hydrangeas and is screened with Carolina Jasmine and Cherokee rose vines tumbling over the railings. A low boxwood hedge outlines the zig-zag design of brick and grass."[22] Designed by James Wiley of Edward L. Daugherty's office, the garden is a comfortable family retreat. The west garden was ringed with English boxwood and planters of yaupon holly. The Garden of Terraces, made famous by the lavish parties thrown by Robert Maddox's family, was retained but slightly modified. The stone columns that were part of the peristyle surrounding the original tennis courts were kept. A number of other features were included in the design, including a "cutting garden" along Woodhaven

Betty Sanders on the sun porch of the Granite Mansion, ca. 1965. *Courtesy Betty and Carl Sanders.*

Road and twenty-four cast-iron, gaslight lamps of pre–Civil War origin.[23]

A building known as the red barn, which had served as a garage while the Robert Maddox family lived on the property, was also retained. Troy Strickland, who had come to work for Robert Maddox in 1930 as a groom for his horses, was still living in the barn above the garage in September 1967. When Governor Lester Maddox was told about the sixty-nine-year-old Strickland, he made a suggestion: "He might be a good caretaker for the thing. I don't see any reason for him to move. If it's all right with everybody concerned and if he wants to stay, I'll sure cooperate and work with them." The red barn, which was "somewhat dilapidated," was remodeled to "make it fit into the surroundings a little better," and it remains on the property today.[24] For many years it served as the sleeping quarters for the state troopers who were stationed on the property.

Among the changes that Governor Maddox requested was the addition of an entrance gate, a seven-foot-high brick and wrought-iron fence, and a guardhouse, which were designed by Edward Vason Jones.[25] When asked about these changes, Governor Maddox "said it was for protection of the physical property against damage by the thousands of visitors expected to view the

Edward L. Daugherty

Edward L. Daugherty, a native Atlantan, studied architecture at the Georgia Institute of Technology and landscape architecture at the University of Georgia and the Harvard Graduate School of Design. He was awarded a Fulbright Scholarship to study town planning in England in 1951. Upon his return to Atlanta, he began his practice in landscape architecture.

According to the Cultural Landscape Foundation, Daugherty was among the "first and most important of a new generation of practitioners in the southeast following World War II." His career has spanned more than six decades and has included work for such notable organizations as the Atlanta Historical Society, the Atlanta Botanical Garden, the Cathedral of St. Philip, the High Museum of Art, Georgia Tech, and the Georgia Governor's Mansion.

Daugherty served on the Atlanta Urban Design Commission and the licensing board for landscape architects in Georgia. He lectured for ten years at Georgia Tech, teaching a course on landscape architecture in the urban environment. A member of the American Society of Landscape Architects (ASLA) since 1954, he served on its Board of Trustees for six years and was made a Fellow in 1971. In 1987 he received the Atlanta Urban Design Commission Award of Excellence for lifelong contributions to landscape architecture in Atlanta. The Georgia Chapter of the ASLA gave him its award for Outstanding Professional Practice in 1995. He received the ASLA Medal in 2010.

Laying brick for the mansion's east garden, September 1967. *Courtesy Kenan Research Center at the Atlanta History Center.*

Construction of the mansion's east garden, 1968. *Courtesy Kenan Research Center at the Atlanta History Center.*

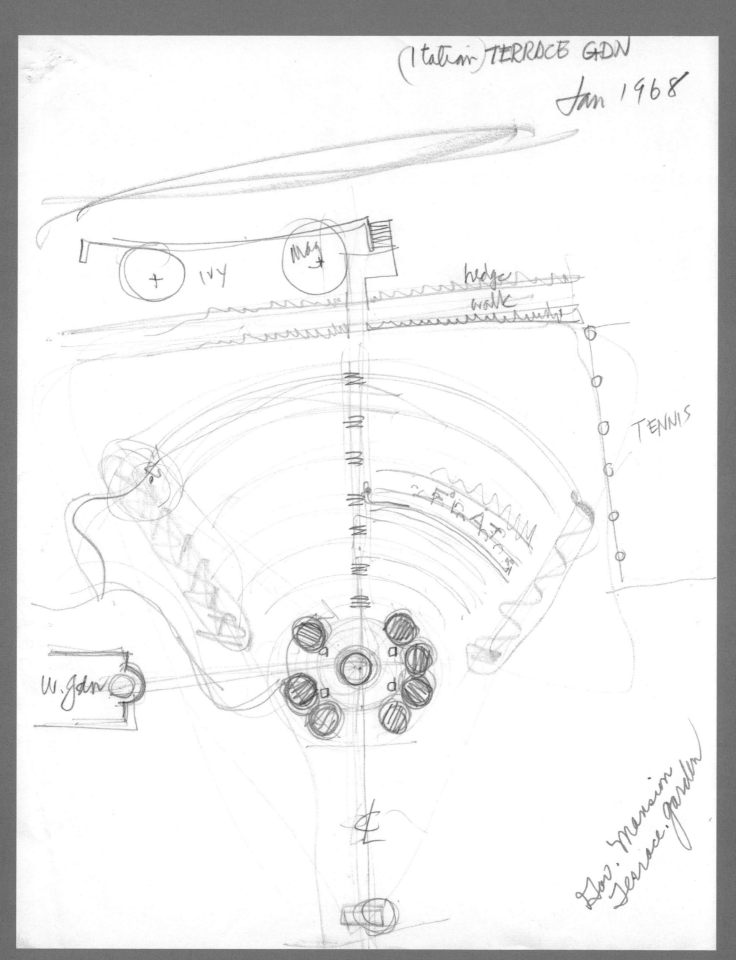

Edward Daugherty's hand-drawn plan for the terrace garden, January 1968.
Courtesy Kenan Research Center at the Atlanta History Center.

Security gate, 1970s. *Courtesy Kenan Research Center at the Atlanta History Center.*

mansion upon its completion."[26] The fence, which took several months to complete, ran 987 feet across West Paces Ferry Road, 848 feet down Woodhaven, and 959 feet across the back of the house. The front gate was 8 feet high, with limestone coping in the shape of an urn at the top. All thirty-four brick piers were capped with limestone. The fence alone added $116,503 to the cost of the mansion.[27]

In the summer of 1967, before the mansion's completion and before the first family moved in, Governor Maddox invited two hundred Georgia Democratic county committee chairmen and legislators for a behind-the-scenes tour. When asked whether he was related to Robert Maddox, the former Atlanta mayor on whose land the mansion sat, Governor Maddox answered, "No, but I told them to just leave the mailbox up and scratch out his first name and write 'Lester' above it. We've got to save all we can."[28] The governor toured the terraced gardens and recessed parking lots, which he told his guests, were included "so it won't look like a used car lot around here."[29] Thomas Bradbury, the architect, joined the tour and said, in reference to the landscaping, that it would take three years "to really get this thing to look beautiful." Phil Gailey, writing for the *Atlanta Constitution*, recounted the scene: "Maddox, pointing out the mansion's highlights with the zeal of a real estate agent, led his guests through every room in the big house, including the separate bathrooms of the governor and first lady. He seemed proudest of the governor's bathroom, complete with gold faucets and a steam bath."[30] After the tour, one guest said of the

mansion, "We need this thing for prestige. Some people think we still go barefooted in Georgia."[31]

The mansion did turn out to be an impressive residence, and in December 1967 the Maddoxes became the first official residents. The front door was "8.5 feet tall and framed by leaded, beveled plate glass and hand-carved molding," with bronze doorknobs decorated with State of Georgia seals.[32] In a feature story published in 1984, *Southern Living* magazine described the mansion as "a showpiece for rare antiques and exquisite interior décor," adding, "Marble floors, crystal chandeliers, and colorful carpets provide a royal backdrop for the furniture, one of the finest collections of Federal-period fine art and antiques in the country."[33] Kitty Farnham, a graduate of the Winterthur Program at the University of Delaware, was named curator of the mansion in 1967. She inventoried the collection and prepared a photographic record of each piece. Reflecting on the collection many years later, Farnham commented, "What was amazing to me was the overall high quality of the collections. Then and now, almost 50 years later, it is the quality of the art and furnishings that makes our mansion a distinguished and dignified place in which to conduct the state's business."[34] After Lester Maddox disbanded the Fine Arts Committee in July 1968, Secretary of State Fortson continued working with Henry Green and several others to complete the interior design.[35] Farnham remained a consultant and advised subsequent first ladies about the mansion's collection for the next four decades.[36]

The Maddoxes believed the mansion was the "People's House" and made sure it was open to everyone. The staff offered tours in order to encourage widespread visitation. One newspaper article reported, "The tours are conducted by women who are volunteers, well-versed in the mansion's antiques and history. Whether you are six years old or an elderly antique dealer, you get a tour on your level." One docent, Mrs. Joel Maloof, welcomed young guests: "We have no problems with the children. They usually are so good. The only thing I worry about is that (pointing to a rare French porcelain vase with a portrait of Benjamin Franklin on its side). They think he's a hippie and want to touch it."[37]

After the new mansion opened, the state began efforts to sell the Ansley Park mansion for $170,000. Secretary Fortson thought the state should hold on to the property as an investment, but that proved to be impractical.[38] But no one came forward with an offer that even remotely approached the state's asking price. The Ansley

Front view of the governor's mansion, 1968. *Courtesy Kenan Research Center at the Atlanta History Center.*

Park Civic Association expressed an interest in the property, but could not raise the money to acquire the house. It was finally sold to David J. Harris, an attorney, for $100,000. Harris planned to demolish the residence and divide the approximately three-acre site into four lots for resale. He retained the two-story carriage house, terraced gardens, and tennis courts for his own use.[39] Before the house went under the wrecking ball, Harris hosted a "Phooey Party" in honor of Governor Maddox and invited a few guests to smash windows in the fifty-nine-year-old mansion with axe handles.[40]

The Governor's Mansion on West Paces Ferry Road has become "a showplace to put the South's best foot forward," just as Mills Lane once predicted. The grounds and gardens have developed much as Thomas Bradbury once forecast. And in spite of the loss of more than fifty trees to a tornado that ripped several columns off the mansion in 1975, the grounds retain a mix of rolling lawns, gardens, and wooded areas that provide residents at least a modicum of respite from the pressures of living in the public eye. Significant changes to the mansion and grounds have been few over the decades since it opened. Most notably, a major renovation of the kitchen, along with the construction of additional storage areas and improvements to the heating and air conditioning system and the garage area, was undertaken during the Sonny Perdue administration. The most recent addition to the property is the so-called mini-mansion, completed under Nathan Deal's administration. The two-story brick building behind the mansion serves as headquarters for the Georgia State Patrol, which provides the governor's security force.

The outstanding collection of furnishings and fine arts so carefully assembled by the Fine Arts Committee still graces the Governor's Mansion. Indeed, the collection has appreciated over the past decades to the point that it is more valuable than the building in which

Presidential suite, 1968. *Courtesy Kenan Research Center at the Atlanta History Center.*

Family sitting room, 1968. *Courtesy Kenan Research Center at the Atlanta History Center.*

Main staircase, 1968.
*Courtesy Kenan Research
Center at the Atlanta
History Center.*

it is displayed. Georgia's governors and first ladies have worked hard to preserve the collection. In 1974, Governor Jimmy Carter introduced legislation to create a fine arts committee of knowledgeable Georgians to advise on the protection and care of the mansion collections. The following year, under Governor George Busbee, the Georgia General Assembly approved the formation of the Executive Center Fine Arts Committee within the Georgia Building Authority. Committee members are appointed by the governor and serve rotating terms.[41] A continuing problem was that no state funds were budgeted or otherwise allocated for the care of the furnishings and art. To remedy that situation, in 2005 First Lady Mary Perdue created a tax-exempt charitable foundation, Friends of the Mansion, Inc., to raise funds for the upkeep of the collection.

The Deals have continued the pattern established by Lester and Virginia Maddox in 1968 of opening the mansion to the public; and like many first ladies before her, Sandra Deal prides herself on greeting many of the visitors personally at the front door. Her keen interest in the history of the mansion, its contents, and its grounds fueled her desire to communicate that history to the public with this book.

CHAPTER THREE

Behind the Velvet Ropes

As the first residents of the Georgia Governor's Mansion, Lester and Virginia Maddox set a precedent of opening the mansion to the public for regularly scheduled tours, and that tradition has continued through today. The public tours, which offer visitors a look at many of the fine furnishings and objects that are a part of the mansion collection, are limited to the main floor of the building. Other areas, such as the basement, which contains a ballroom and service areas; the second floor, where the guest rooms and first family's living quarters are located; and the attic, where Lester Maddox once kept a pool table, are generally unseen by the public. What follows is a tour of some of the highlights of the mansion—its grounds as well as the building and the art collection and furnishings. Readers will get a peek behind the velvet ropes into some of the areas not normally visible to the public.

The Grounds

Visitors to the Georgia Governor's Mansion are often as awed by the grounds and gardens that surround the Greek Revival residence as they are by the building and its outstanding collection of furnishings and decorative arts. The entry drive to the Governor's Mansion winds past the octagonal guardhouse, located at the security gate, to the front of the residence. A traffic circle provides turnaround space for vehicles and encircles the white marble Fountain of Progress, which was made possible by Betty Sanders when she raised $20,000 for its construction through a statewide tour of her own art. From the front steps of the mansion, visitors can look out over the fountain, past the three flagpoles installed by Lester Maddox in 1968, across a vast expanse of the well-groomed green lawn toward West Paces Ferry Road. Such an open view was not possible when the mansion first opened. The property was much more heavily wooded when it was owned by the Robert Maddox family. While some trees were removed during construction to accommodate expansion of the roadways and installation of the fountain, a tornado in 1975 cleared out many trees on the property, enough so that it became possible to land a helicopter on the front lawn. The concrete heliport, located southeast of the fountain, was added during the Deal administration.

The roadways throughout the property follow much the same path as the ones that existed during the Robert Maddox residency. According to Edward Daugherty, the landscape architect who directed the development of the site for the new mansion,

Betty Sanders by the fountain, 1995.
Courtesy Betty and Carl Sanders.

"there was a logical, practical, sympathetic road system that would not adversely affect the siting of the house."[1] Daugherty was among those who advocated for the new mansion to be built on roughly the same spot as the Robert Maddox house in order to preserve as much of the historic landscaping as possible. The existing roadways were widened and paved, but the landscape was preserved. Additional parking lots were created in places where the parked cars would not be visible from West Paces Ferry Road or the front porch so that during large events, the property would not "look like a used car lot," as first resident Lester Maddox once explained.[2]

The basic form of the terraced amphitheater garden on the west side of the mansion has been preserved from the Robert Maddox era. Although the plantings in this garden have been simplified for maintenance purposes, the five rolling terraces created by Lollie Maddox in the early 1900s remain one of the outstanding features of the landscape. During the residency of the Robert Maddox family, the terraced garden was the setting for

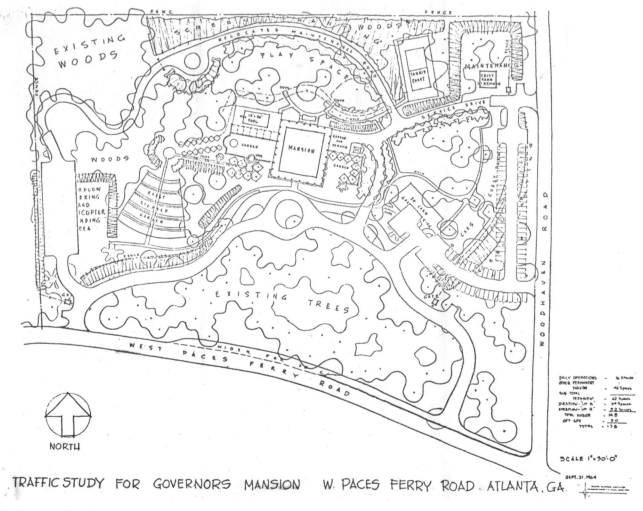

Traffic study for the new mansion, 1964. *Courtesy Kenan Research Center at the Atlanta History Center.*

Aerial view of the mansion, 1970. *Courtesy Kenan Research Center at the Atlanta History Center.*

"dancing recitals, opera parties, and garden club meetings."[3] The fountain installed by Lollie, surrounded by rings of boxwood and statues representing the four seasons, remains the focal point of the garden. Restoration of the garden began during the Jimmy Carter residency. A boxwood-lined path links the fountain to an arbor with two wooden swings—a spot that was a favorite of Governor Zell and Shirley Miller and the place where Joe Frank Harris Jr. proposed to his girlfriend, Brooke Gurley.[4]

Another notable landscape feature includes a tennis court surrounded by stucco-covered columns near the southwest corner of the property. The court and the columns date to the Robert Maddox era. Originally made of clay, the tennis court was renovated during the Carter administration, when it was extended to regulation size and paved. The columns, which once supported a chain-link fence and were topped with wooden beams draped

Tennis Court, 2014. *Courtesy Christopher Oquendo.*

with roses, are now an unadorned accent surrounding the tennis court.[5]

Near the tennis court is a small garden dedicated to Robert and Lollie Maddox by their daughter, Laura Maddox Smith. In the garden, a millstone with a dedication plaque in its center is embedded in a small paved space furnished with benches and urns filled with evergreen shrubs. Smith was born and raised on the property. She married Edward Smith in 1938, and the couple moved into a house on the adjacent property to the north of her family's home. Smith was invited by Betty Sanders to serve on the Fine Arts Committee, and she did so as an adviser on the gardens and grounds.

A wooded area on the northwest corner of the property is laced with winding paths, some of which have been paved with bricks and slabs of granite and concrete embedded with pea gravel left over from mansion renovations made during the Perdue administration. Hidden in the woods is a gazebo constructed by the grounds staff. A wooden bridge crosses over a picturesque stream that runs through the property. Several benches made of slabs of granite, built by trusties, state prisoners in a rehabilitation program who make up the grounds crew at the mansion, offer visitors a shady place to rest along the paths.

The roadway circling the property passes by the mansion compost site and the gasoline pump where the state patrol officers fuel the vehicles used to transport the governor and first lady. The road continues behind the mansion past a children's playscape added by Mary Perdue and a rose garden that was begun by Rosalynn Carter in the early 1970s. Elizabeth Harris expanded the rose garden, and a plaque in the newer section reads, "This garden is dedicated to the glory of God in honor of Elizabeth Carlock Harris, 1983."

Farther along the driveway are the brick residence of the state patrol, the red barn, a greenhouse, and the dog pen. The facility for the state patrol, known as the mini-mansion, was added during the Deal administration to accommodate the security team that is always present on the mansion grounds. Before construction of this building, the troopers lived in the red barn, which contained a garage downstairs and living quarters upstairs during the Robert Maddox era. The barn was renovated to accommodate the troopers when the mansion was built. The children of several governors resided temporarily in the red barn over the years. Today it houses office space for the grounds crew and

Terrace Garden, 2014. *Courtesy Christopher Oquendo.*

Bench in the mansion woods, 2014.
Courtesy Christopher Oquendo.

Playscape built during the Perdues' tenure,
2014. *Courtesy Christopher Oquendo.*

Red barn, 2014. *Courtesy Christopher Oquendo.*

other mansion-support functions. The greenhouse is filled with plants and flowers that are used for seasonal decorations of the mansion. An indoor-outdoor dog pen located near the greenhouse serves as the residence for the canine troopers, Atom and Fred, who help patrol the grounds.

Across the road from the greenhouse are a garden and a small orchard from which the mansion chef gets fruit and vegetables for the first family. The orchard has apple, fig, peach, pear, and plum trees. The organic garden is filled with carrots, cucumbers, lettuce, okra, peppers, peas, squash, tomatoes, watermelon, and zucchini. Muscadine vines run between the rows of peas and lettuces. Across from the garden is the grave of Marie Barnes's dog, CC, the only marked grave on the property.

Other significant landscape features include the west garden, a perennial garden located on the southwest corner of

C.C.'s grave site, 2014. *Courtesy Christopher Oquendo.*

the mansion, and a swimming pool located on the northwest corner. The west garden at veranda level was designed as a more formal extension of the state drawing room. Its largely paved surface is used for large-scale entertainments. Groups of small boxed evergreen trees accentuate the axial symmetry and lead west to a view of the terraced gardens inherited from Lollie Maddox. The original plan called for a fountain in this area modeled on one in the Villa Medici in Rome, but it was never built. The garden is now covered with an open-sided tent, which makes it usable year-round and during inclement weather. To the south, down eight circular steps, is the perennial garden, designed by Dan Franklin. The garden features an open grass lawn framed by flower beds and shrubbery. On the south end of the garden, the shrubbery bows out into a niche that contains a small arbor and a statue.[6] The swimming pool, which was constructed during the Busbee administration, is at the basement level of the mansion. Brick columns on the south side of the pool support an arbor draped with wisteria. The pool is surrounded by a pea-gravel concrete patio edged with red brick and surrounded by flowers and a row of shrubs on three sides. The pool itself, which includes a children's pool, is edged with red brick.

Inside the Mansion: The Main Floor

Public tours of the mansion begin on the front porch across from the white marble Fountain of Progress with its Greek key design. Classical elements from the fountain are echoed in the ironwork of the balconies, over doors and windows, and in some of the interior detail. Made of mahogany and surrounded by beveled-glass sidelights and a fanlight, the front door has carved Greek key, honeysuckle, and oak-leaf moldings around it that reflect patterns found in Asher Benjamin's publications from the 1830s.[7] Benjamin was a well-known author and American architect whose work spanned the Federal and Greek Revival styles. The doorknob features the state seal of Georgia. First Lady Sandra Deal takes great pride in welcoming on the front porch almost everyone who comes to tour the mansion. As the docent Beth Wassell noted, "Mrs. Deal is always so impressive the way she greets everyone. A busload of children will come, and she will shake every hand."[8]

Visitors enter a small vestibule where they see a bronze state seal inlaid into the polished Tennessee marble floor. This area opens into the state reception hall, a sparingly furnished square room that serves as a gathering and greeting space for visitors. Among the treasures in this room is an English octagonal podium table that dates from 1800 and is made of Carpathian elm burl with rosewood veneer crossbanding. The table is usually adorned with fresh flowers, which are often displayed in a large silver punch bowl, a piece from the silver service made for the battleship USS *Georgia* in the early twentieth century. Like most states in the union, Georgia donated a set of silver, including

a punchbowl, cups, candelabra, and ancillary pieces to the U.S. Navy to be housed in the officers' quarters of the battleship named after the state. The *Georgia* was launched in 1904 and decommissioned in 1920, and the silver was then returned to the state. The silver was used at the Granite Mansion in Ansley Park and has been on display at the current mansion since its opening. Other notable pieces in the reception hall include bronze busts of George Washington and Benjamin Franklin modeled after 1778 sculptures by Jean-Antoine Houdon, a French neoclassical sculptor known for his portraits of political leaders of the Enlightenment.

The reception hall serves as the nexus of the first floor. From it visitors have access to the library, located on the southeast corner of the mansion; a guest bedroom on the southwest corner; the state dining room on the east; the state drawing room on the west; and the soaring circular staircase that leads to the family quarters on the second floor. The staircase, located north of the reception hall, immediately catches the eye of everyone who comes in the front door. A massive bronze and lead-crystal chandelier hangs in the round room where the staircase is located. It is a blend of an Italian chandelier that dates from 1790 and a modern reproduction. The chandelier was salvaged from the Progressive Club, a Jewish social club founded in 1913, following a fire. It has graced the stair hall of the mansion since its opening.[9] The fixture can be lowered by a crank located in the attic—something the staff does once a year for cleaning.

Other treasures in the stair hall include the American artist Samuel King's copy of a portrait of George Washington in his general's uniform, a painting of the Georgia historian Major Hugh McCall, a pier table, and a French porcelain vase. The original portrait of Washington was painted by Charles Willson Peale in 1776. In 1777, John Hancock asked King to paint a replica of Peale's painting and then presented the copy to the comte d'Estaing in appreciation for the French admiral's support of the colonies against the British in the American Revolution. Hanging over the stairs is the portrait of McCall, author of the first history of Georgia, published in 1811. A copy of his

Georgia State Seal in the entry hallway, 2014. *Courtesy Christopher Oquendo.*

Front door, 2014. *Courtesy Christopher Oquendo.*

Main lobby, 2014. *Courtesy Andrea Briscoe.*

Punch bowl from the battleship silver set. *Courtesy Christopher Oquendo.*

two-volume *History of Georgia* was donated to the mansion by the Daughters of the American Revolution. The work, a favorite of Sandra Deal's, is kept in a glass-fronted bookcase in the family living room on the first floor. The American Empire mahogany pier table is attributed to Charles-Honoré Lannuier, a French immigrant to New York City who became one of the most renowned cabinetmakers in America in the early nineteenth century. The rarest piece in the mansion collection is the French porcelain vase, which dates to about 1800. On the vase is a portrait medallion of Benjamin Franklin, shown without a wig and in simple clothing, just as he appeared in the late 1770s when he was the colonies' minister to France. The image on the vase is a variant of a portrait of Franklin painted by the French artist Charles-Amédée-Philippe van Loo.

Benjamin Franklin vase, 2014. *Courtesy Christopher Oquendo.*

Main staircase, 2014.
Courtesy Christopher Oquendo.

The ladies' powder room on the main floor, 2014. *Courtesy Christopher Oquendo.*

Library

In the southeast corner of the first floor is the cherry-paneled library, which houses a distinguished collection of Georgia-related books. The library was initiated under the mansion's original Fine Arts Committee, which collected hundreds of volumes, including works by prominent Georgia authors such as Joel Chandler Harris, Erskine Caldwell, Flannery O'Connor, Sidney Lanier, and Margaret Mitchell. Among the original acquisitions was a first edition of *Gone with the Wind*, which is kept on display inside a Plexiglas case in the family living room. A wide range of nonfiction books about such subjects as history, natural history, Georgia institutions, medicine, industry, architecture, and fine arts, as well as many biographies of outstanding Georgians, was part of the original collection. In subsequent years the library has continued to grow through gifts from authors, publishers, and citizens. Expanding the library was of special interest to First Lady Elizabeth Harris.

Books in the mansion library, 2014.
Courtesy Christopher Oquendo.

Library, 2014. *Courtesy Christopher Oquendo.*

She publicized the collection in her travels around the state and was responsible for attracting donations of many additional volumes. The Deals have had the catalogue of the Georgia library updated so that its contents are accessible online.

In an effort to allow visitors to see the mansion's collection of portraits of American presidents, some of which previously hung upstairs in the foyer of the presidential suite, Mrs. Deal moved the portraits of James Madison, painted by an unknown artist in the early nineteenth century, and Andrew Jackson, painted by the American artist Ralph E. W. Earl in 1830, into the library. Also in this room is a large framed needlepoint portrait of General George Washington at the Battle of Trenton, an image copied from a 1792 oil painting by the prominent American artist, John Trumbull; Trumbull's painting hangs in the Yale University Art Gallery. A small statue of Jimmy Carter represents the only U.S. president ever elected from Georgia. Carter was the second Georgia governor to live with his family in the mansion. A prized piece of furniture in the library is the elegant Philadelphia-made mahogany card table with carved dolphin supports. It reportedly belonged to Octavia Walton LeVert, granddaughter of George Walton, one of Georgia's three signers of the Declaration of Independence and the state's fourth governor.

Guest Bedroom

Located in the southwest corner of the first floor is a guest bedroom. A late nineteenth-century French wallpaper panel, *Psyche Showing Her Jewels to Her Sisters,* hangs over an American-made alcove bed (ca. 1815) carved with Egyptian motifs. The rug is a reproduction of the early nineteenth-century English needlework rug that originally covered the floor of the room. When the original rug became severely tattered, it was taken apart and the sections that were salvageable were made into needlepoint cushions.

First-floor bedroom, 2014. *Courtesy Christopher Oquendo.*

The state dining room, located on the east side of the reception hall, is used regularly for formal dinners. The room houses several outstanding pieces of furniture, paintings, and decorative-art pieces of note. The mahogany accordion table (ca. 1810) is the centerpiece of the room. Attributed to the Boston workshop of the cabinetmaker John Seymour, the fourteen-foot-long table can expand to seat eighteen or can be folded up to seat six for more intimate meals. The classical klismos-form curly maple chairs are modern English replicas of early nineteenth-century American chairs from the home of former Governor Edward Telfair. (The klismos form is an ancient Greek design featuring a concave back and curved legs.) Telfair was the first governor to serve under the Georgia Constitution of 1789. The silver candelabra and silver serving pieces that often grace the table are part of the USS *Georgia* silver service set. Like the punch bowl in the front reception hall, the tray is adorned with symbols of Georgia—pinecones and magnolias—as well as the state seal. A mahogany sideboard, made in Philadelphia between 1820 and 1835, stands against the north wall of the dining room. On the south wall are two card tables attributed to the prominent American cabinetmaker Duncan Phyfe, who worked in New York City in the early nineteenth century. The mantelpiece in the room was crafted in England of white and green Italian marble. The regency convex mirror above the fireplace was made in Ireland in 1810.

Two large paintings hang in the state dining room— Benjamin West's *The Preparation of Psyche* (1763) and Severin Roesen's *Nature's Bounty* (ca. 1850). West was the first American artist to achieve an international reputation. He trained in Italy and lived most of his life abroad, settling in London, where he dramatically influenced American painting and trained other famous American painters such as Charles Willson Peale, Rembrandt Peale, John Trumbull, and Gilbert Stuart. King George III named West his royal history painter. West helped establish the Royal Academy and became its second president. *The Preparation of Psyche* depicts the Greek myth of Psyche and Cupid. Roesen, who immigrated to the United States in the middle of the nineteenth century from Germany, was well known for his still lifes reflecting the "bounty of America." A similar Roesen still life hangs in the White House.[10]

Silver on the state dining room table, 2014.
Courtesy Christopher Oquendo.

Cups from the mansion's china collection, 2014.
Courtesy Christopher Oquendo.

State dining room, 2014. *Courtesy Christopher Oquendo.*

State Drawing Room

On the west side of the reception hall is the most elaborately furnished room in the house—the state drawing room—where governors formally receive honored guests. Most of the official photographs taken during such visits are made in this room. The room, which measures almost forty feet by twenty-five feet, is often compared to the Red Room in the White House because the same red Scalamandré silk fabrics were used in both. After many decades of service, the silk draperies in the state drawing room were in shreds, primarily from sun damage. The original Scalamandré fabric was no longer in production, but the Scalamandré firm reproduced the pattern for the mansion and made enough fabric to re-create the drapes and re-cover several pieces

of furniture. The original drapes in this room and all other rooms of the mansion were designed by David Richmond Byers III, who derived their designs from early nineteenth-century French pattern books.

Several pieces in this room, including a mahogany Pembroke table (1800) and a mahogany scroll-arm sofa (1800), are attributed to the New York City workshop of Duncan Phyfe. A pair of Regency gilt gesso and carved-wood wall sconces were made in England around 1815; each depicts an eagle holding a globe in its beak. The carpet is a replica of the original Aubusson carpet from the early nineteenth century. Lacey Champion Carpets of Fairmount, Georgia, created the replica after the antique carpet had been so badly damaged by the large

State drawing room, 2014. *Courtesy Christopher Oquendo.*

Mirror in the state drawing room, 2014. *Courtesy Christopher Oquendo.*

George Washington clock, 2014. *Courtesy Christopher Oquendo.*

number of visitors over the years that it could no longer be repaired. First Lady Shirley Miller, wife of Governor Zell Miller, and her staff used to work on their hands and knees repairing the carpet after tours and large events.[11]

Paintings in this room include *Barn Interior*, a rustic scene by the American artist Alvan Fisher, and portraits of Lieutenant and Mrs. John Marston of Philadelphia, painted by the American artist John Neagle (1796– 1865). Neagle, known for his portraits of Gilbert Stuart, James Fenimore Cooper, and Henry Clay, served as

director of the Pennsylvania Academy of Fine Arts. On the mantel is a French-made, gilt bronze mantel clock with a bust of George Washington that dates from 1805. The inscription on the clock celebrates Washington as "First in War, First in Peace, First in the Hearts of His Countrymen." An interesting ceramic piece is the Chinese export porcelain punch bowl, commonly referred to as a hong bowl because it depicts the trading pavilions, or hongs, in Canton, China. The flags of France, England, and Holland are featured on the bowl, which is from about 1785.

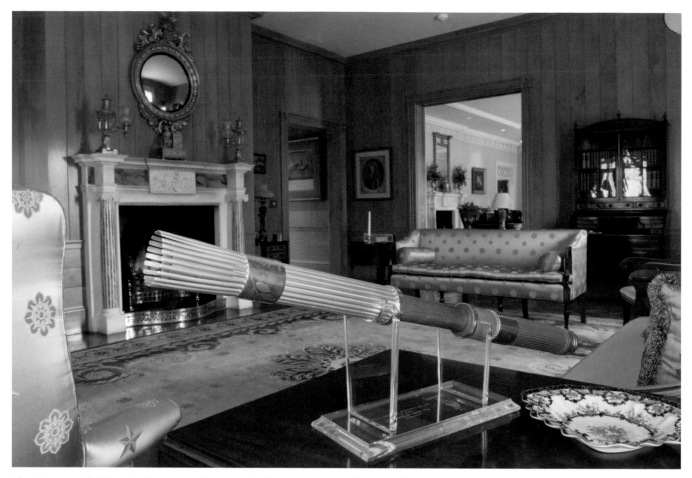

The Centennial Olympic Games torch in the family sitting room. *Courtesy Christopher Oquendo.*

Family Living Room

Located between the state drawing room and the family dining room in the northwest corner of the mansion, the family living room was intended as a gathering space for the first families. Although this butternut-paneled room is less formal than the adjacent drawing room, it does include several fine pieces. The giltwood convex mirror was made in Philadelphia and dates to about 1800. Perched on top is an eagle flanked by pierced acanthus leaves, a classical motif depicting a flowering plant native to tropical and warm temperate regions. The mahogany bird's-eye maple sewing table was one of Mary Perdue's favorite furnishings. The table was made in New York around 1820; its hanging fabric bag, for storing handcraft work, pulls open as a lower drawer. Above the table is a banjo clock made in Concord, Massachusetts, in about 1790; on its face its maker inscribed "warranted by T Whiting Concord." The neoclassical white marble mantel adorned with goats and a single Cupid is from England and dates from the late eighteenth century. This room also houses two modern treasures—a 1936

signed first edition of Margaret Mitchell's *Gone with the Wind* and an Olympic torch from the 1996 Centennial Olympic Games torch relay.

First edition of *Gone with the Wind.*
Courtesy Christopher Oquendo.

Family Dining Room

Between the family living room and the kitchen is a small dining room used by the first families for private dinners and small affairs. The mahogany double-pedestal table dates from 1800. The chairs, made in about 1825, are elaborately carved with grapes and grape leaves. They were once owned by Jim Williams, the Savannah antiques dealer made famous in the 1994 book *Midnight in the Garden of Good and Evil*. The small sideboard is one of the few antique pieces in the house that was possibly made in Georgia. Over it hangs a landscape painting, *View of the Berkshires*, that was a particular favorite of First Lady Elizabeth Harris. This scene was painted by Thomas Doughty, a native of Philadelphia; his signature and the date "1839" can be seen along the lower edge of the painting. Doughty was an artist of the Hudson River School. Another Severin Roesen still life, from around 1850, hangs on the northwest wall of the family dining room. Also worthy of note is the small landscape *Marsh in a Thunderstorm*, painted by the American artist Martin Johnson Heade in about 1860, which hangs to the right of the outside door.

Family dining room, 2014. *Courtesy Christopher Oquendo.*

Preparing for Valedictorian Day, 2014. *Courtesy Christopher Oquendo.*

Kitchen

The kitchen is the heartbeat of most homes, and the Georgia Governor's Mansion is no exception. Renovated during the Perdue administration, the kitchen features quartz and marble countertops and a center island for food preparation. Budget cuts during original construction in the 1960s resulted in a kitchen that was outfitted with "low, commercial-grade equipment."[12] Although such a configuration was inadequate for the food preparation requirements at the mansion, it was certainly an upgrade from what had been available in the Granite Mansion in Ansley Park. For forty years, mansion chefs made do with the 1968 kitchen, but by the middle of the Perdue administration, a renovation had become long overdue. Much of the original equipment no longer worked properly, and the layout of the space was less than ideal. Additionally, the kitchen did not meet current building codes.

The renovation, which began in early 2008 and was completed in July 2009, created a modern, efficient, aesthetically pleasing kitchen from which the staff can feed the thousands of guests who attend events at the mansion each year.[13] Holly Chute, who served as the mansion's chef for more than thirty years, proudly notes that she can bake four hundred cookies at once in the twin convection ovens. The mansion's manager, Joy Forth, adds that the commercial-grade equipment is much more complicated to operate than the old electric stove that was once there. "You have to have expertise to operate all this equipment," Forth explains.[14] In addition to the convection ovens, the kitchen includes two gas ovens, a six-burner gas stove top, a griddle, a deep fryer, a toaster oven, an industrial-size Hobart mixer, a Viking refrigerator-freezer, and two industrial-size refrigerators. The renovation included the addition of a family dining space within the kitchen, which doubles as an additional work surface during big events. Mary Perdue also implemented a feature that has become a favorite of the staff—the kitchen candy drawer.

Second Floor

As originally designed, the second floor of the mansion had six bedrooms and eight bathrooms as well as an office for the first lady, a study, and a family room. There were separate bedrooms for the governor and first lady, but Lester Maddox famously quipped that he and his wife needed only one. And that has since been the case for every first family. The space designated as the first lady's bedroom has become the governor's and first lady's bedroom, although each has continued to have his and her own bathroom. The bedroom is furnished largely with twentieth-century pieces, although a large George IV mahogany bachelor's bureau (ca. 1820) graces one wall. A Louis XVI trumeau mirror (ca. 1775) that features an applied giltwood bowknot and musical trophies on its wide frieze hangs on the west wall. The Deals were awakened suddenly one night when a piece of the ornamentation broke off the mirror and dropped to the floor next to the bed. The mirror has since been repaired.

The space originally designated as the governor's bedroom has long served as the family room. Furnished with a sofa, chairs, and the governor's recliner, this is where the first family can relax and watch television. A notable feature of this room is the mantel, a Greek Revival–style piece that was salvaged from Woodhaven, the Robert Maddox home that once stood on the property. Although most of the furniture in this room is from the late twentieth century, there are a few antiques, including a George III–style bureau bookcase with glazed doors that feature a shield-shaped panel with an eagle crest, and a Chippendale-style mahogany serpentine chest of drawers.

Adjacent to the family room is a paneled room originally meant to be a study for the governor. Today

Mirror in the governor and first lady's bedroom, 2014. *Courtesy Christopher Oquendo.*

Mantel in the second-floor sitting room, 2014. *Courtesy Christopher Oquendo.*

it serves as office space for the first lady and her staff; the governor maintains a desk there as well. The furnishings are twentieth-century pieces, except for an early nineteenth-century portrait of Thomas Jefferson that hangs on the east wall.

The guest bedroom in the southwest corner was originally designated as the aide's room because of its proximity to the presidential suite, the mansion's primary guest room. A notable piece in the aide's room is the banjo clock (ca. 1800) with two eglomise panels, one depicting an eagle and shield and the second featuring American and British fighting ships. (An eglomise panel is glass with a painted picture on the back, which shows through.) Other pieces of interest include a late Federal cherry and bird's-eye maple chest of drawers and a small worktable (ca. 1800).

The largest and most elaborately furnished room on the second floor is the presidential suite, which includes a sitting room, balcony, bedroom, dressing room, and bath. It is reserved for state and royal guests. The mahogany four-poster bed, dating from about 1795, was made in Pennsylvania. An American Chippendale-style mahogany slant-front desk and bureau and a similar chest of drawers are other notable pieces in this room. The desk (ca. 1795) is supported on two claw-and-ball front feet and two ogee brackets in the rear. A Regency mahogany inkstand (ca. 1810) sits atop the desk. The room also contains a George III mahogany breakfront chest and bookcase that dates to 1780, and a Federal mahogany sofa (ca. 1800) made in Massachusetts.

The guest lounge, which serves as a sitting area between the presidential suite and the circular staircase, has a white marble floor and is furnished with a Federal scroll-arm sofa (ca. 1820) and a pair of mahogany game or console tables, one from New York and one from Boston, that date from 1800–20. The guest lounge also contains a Federal lady's writing desk (ca. 1800). The desk is made of mahogany with bird's-eye maple panels on the drawers and features a green tooled-leather writing surface. On the wall hangs Joseph Mallord William

Aide's room with banjo clock, 2014. *Courtesy Christopher Oquendo.*

Presidential suite, 2014. *Courtesy Christopher Oquendo.*

Foyer outside the presidential suite, 2014. *Courtesy Christopher Oquendo.*

Carter Bedroom, 2014. *Courtesy Christopher Oquendo.*

Turner's *View of the Cathedral of Christ Church, and part of Corpus Christi College*, a hand-engraved print on paper that dates from 1811. (The painting it is based on is from 1803–4.) James Basire was the engraver. Turner was a renowned English Romantic printmaker, landscape painter, and watercolorist.

The room on the southeast corner of the second floor was originally designated as an office for the first lady. When Shirley Miller moved her office into the basement, she created the "Carter Bedroom" in this space, furnishing it with pieces used by Governor Carter and his wife, Rosalynn, when they lived in the mansion from 1971 to 1975. The centerpiece of this room is the mahogany four-poster bed that dates to around 1800.

Along the east side of the second floor is a series of bedrooms furnished with a mix of twentieth-century and Federal-period pieces. These rooms serve as guest bedrooms, primarily for family members. A closet located between two of the bedrooms has been converted into a "wrapping-paper closet," a favorite feature of Marie Barnes during her time in the mansion. Here are stored boxes and wrapping materials to allow the first lady and her staff to package and wrap hostess gifts efficiently.

Wrapping-paper closet, 2014. *Courtesy Christopher Oquendo.*

Attic, 2014. *Courtesy Christopher Oquendo.*

Attic

The attic, which is accessed by a staircase from the second floor, has a concrete floor and is filled with a combination of mechanical equipment, such as duct-work, and assorted supplies and equipment. During the Maddox administration, the attic also housed a pool table. Among the treasures found in the attic today are the original window treatments from throughout the mansion, which were wrapped and placed in storage over the years whenever they were replaced, as well as rows of tablecloths, boxes of stationery, and seasonal decorations. As might be expected, Christmas decorations, organized by color, take up a significant amount of space. As mentioned previously, in the center of the attic is a crank that allows the maintenance staff to lower the stairwell chandelier for cleaning.

Ground Floor

Approached from the south side, the mansion appears to be a two-story building. From the north side, however, the ground floor, or basement level, of the mansion is visible. Guests who attend events held in the mansion ballroom often enter the building through the basement. The basement contains both public and private spaces, including work areas for the support staff and a large ballroom designed to accommodate the many state functions hosted by the first family. An elevator serves all three floors. A narrow service staircase connects the service areas of the basement to the kitchen on

the main floor, and a wider staircase, located across from the elevator, runs from the basement to the second floor.

Ballroom

The ballroom, which is seventy-three feet long and forty feet wide, can hold up to four hundred seated guests. During the Carter administration, the High Museum of Art lent paintings on a rotating basis for visitors to enjoy. Today the paintings that hang in the basement are on loan from the Georgia Capitol and feature fourteen portraits of previous governors, including Button Gwinnett (1777), George Walton (1789–90), John Milledge (1802–6), and John Slaton (1913–15). One of the most beloved works in the mansion's collection is a Wilbur Kurtz painting of the Old Governor's Mansion in Milledgeville. Kurtz, a well-known Atlanta artist who worked for the Works Progress Administration (WPA), was asked by L. L. Perry, the agency's director of information and publications, to do the painting in 1938. After Kurtz was "dropped from the WPA," he continued working on the painting, assured by Perry that he would be paid for his efforts. Kurtz completed the painting while in California, where he was serving as a technical adviser on the film version of *Gone with the Wind*. Inspired by what he saw on the movie set, Kurtz added a figure representing Ashley Wilkes (whose likeness is based loosely on Leslie Howard) astride his horse, being bid farewell by Melanie Wilkes (based loosely on Olivia de Havilland) in front of the Milledgeville mansion.[15] In the hallway adjacent to the ballroom is a mahogany tall-case clock with an arched cupboard door flanked by fluted columns. The American-made case houses a German-made clock with a silvered dial and arabic numerals.

Reception Area

On the north end of the ballroom is a small reception area. The space is used for smaller events and for photographs taken with the governor and first lady during larger events, such as the Valedictorian Day gathering. Docents gather there each Tuesday, Wednesday, and Thursday morning for refreshments before hosting public tours. A mahogany three-pedestal table that was made by Sacks Fine Furniture in the twentieth century and served as the dining table in the Granite Mansion occupies the space. A large portrait depicts Catharine Cecil, Countess of Egmont (1719–52), who was the daughter-in-law of the 1st Earl of Egmont, first president of the Trustees of Georgia. It was painted by the renowned British portrait painter Thomas Hudson.

Ballroom, 2014. *Courtesy Christopher Oquendo.*

Service Areas

Adjacent to the ballroom are numerous service areas from which the staff provides support for the mansion and its residents. This rabbit warren includes the floral room, complete with a walk-in refrigerator where flowers are stored to prolong their life between events, plus a catering kitchen, a laundry room, a pantry, a walk-in refrigerator and freezer, mechanical rooms, and security offices. A dumbwaiter in the floral room communicates with the kitchen on the first floor. The basement also includes a suite of rooms that served as living quarters for one of the sons in both the Carter and Busbee administrations. During the Perdue and Deal administrations, the suite has housed the office of the mansion manager. A renovation during the Perdue administration added a large storage area on the east side of the mansion beneath the east patio. Before the creation of this storage space, the only significant storage in the building was in the attic. Creation of the additional storage area at ground level has greatly enhanced the speed with which mansion staff can set up major events and clean up afterward.

Since its opening in January 1968, the Governor's Mansion has undergone three major renovations—waterproofing of the exterior walls that surround the ground floor, the addition of the basement storage space, and an upgrade of the kitchen. The basic form

Hallway on the ballroom level, 2014. *Courtesy Christopher Oquendo.*

and configuration of the building, however, have remained the same for almost half a century. According to the mansion's manager, Joy Forth, "The timelessness of the mansion is wonderful. The way the mansion was designed makes it so functional. We can entertain two people or 200."[16]

Despite all the controversy that surrounded its construction in the 1960s, the mansion has proved to be a good investment. It continues to house the first family and to serve as a showplace for the state. Each family that has lived here has made the mansion its home, and each family has also graciously opened its doors to the public. The following chapters explore what life was like in the mansion for each of these families.

The Maddoxes on the formal staircase, ca. 1968. *Courtesy Virginia Maddox Carnes.*

CHAPTER FOUR

Opening the People's House

THE MADDOXES

A trip to the Governor's Mansion when Lester and Virginia Maddox lived there was never dull. As one journalist explained, "Important visitors to the splendid new Governor's Mansion on Atlanta's swank North Side are as likely to find Maddox not in his office, but in the front yard romping with his basset hound."[1] Lester and Virginia, the new mansion's first residents, lived there for three years and set a tone that endures. Although the mansion is a temporary residence for the governor and his family, its main function is to serve the people of Georgia. Since the Maddoxes opened the doors wide to the citizens of the state, every succeeding governor has replicated their hospitality.

Born to a working-class Atlanta family on September 30, 1915, Lester Garfield Maddox left high school in 1933 to begin full-time work at Atlantic Steel, his father's place of employment. Three years later, he married Virginia Cox of Birmingham, Alabama. During World War II, Maddox worked in several industries, including the Bell Bomber factory in Marietta. He opened the Pickrick, a restaurant serving home-style fare at 891 Hemphill Avenue, in 1947 near Georgia Tech. Maddox became known for his "Pickrick Says" advertisements, which ran in the *Atlanta Journal*. Maddox ran unsuccessfully for mayor of Atlanta against William B. Hartsfield in 1957; four years later, he ran again and lost to Ivan Allen Jr.

Maddox's stand on segregation made the Pickrick a target for civil rights activists. When three African American patrons attempted to enter the Pickrick on July 3, 1964, Maddox and a group of his supporters, all of whom were carrying pick handles (often referred to in the media as axe handles), met them in front of the restaurant. The next day, newspapers across the country carried a photograph of the incident, and Maddox eventually chose to close the Pickrick rather than abandon his support for segregation.[2] He then embarked on a campaign for the office of governor and was elected in November 1966. Maddox was sworn in on January 11, 1967.

Although construction had been under way since 1965, the new executive residence on West Paces Ferry Road was not yet ready for occupancy, so Lester and Virginia moved into the Granite Mansion on The Prado in Ansley Park. Neither of them knew the house well, even though Lester had catered three events there while he owned the Pickrick restaurant. Touring the house after he was elected, Lester noted, "I wanted to be Governor of Georgia, but somehow, not in my wildest imagination,

The Maddox family outside the Pickrick restaurant, ca. 1951. *Courtesy Virginia Maddox Carnes.*

Lester and Virginia Maddox, ca. 1966. *Courtesy Virginia Maddox Carnes.*

Governor Maddox with Alabama governor George Wallace and first lady Lurleen Wallace in the Granite Mansion, 1967. *Courtesy Larry Maddox.*

did I ever think that me and my wife would be occupants of this house."[3] Even though the roof leaked and squirrels scampered through the attic, Virginia said of the mansion, "I'm learning to like it. I'm even growing fond of it."[4] Larry Maddox, the couple's youngest son, who was nineteen when his father was elected governor, remembered that he and a friend climbed into the attic and used Larry's BB gun to shoot at the light bulb above one of the windows in the mansion as a prank. As he explained later, "The light bulb was so far away I did not realize it was chipping the window."[5]

In his first press conference, Lester set the tone for his administration as it related to the mansion: "All visitors to the governor's mansion will get a cool sip of cow's milk or a soft drink if they're thirsty, but no alcohol."[6] Lester had opened the governor's office to the public with the establishment of People's Day, a time when any citizen of the state could have an audience with the governor in his office. He designated the first and third Wednesday of each month for this purpose, and as his biographer Bob Short noted, "People's Day was a roaring success."

Building on the principle of giving the people access to their elected officials, Lester and Virginia opened the Granite Mansion to "anyone and everyone who wanted to come."[7] Among the most unexpected guests were four prisoners who escaped from a work camp about eighty miles from Atlanta in April 1967. The African American men (Booker T. Gary, MacArthur Davis, Douglas May, and Henry Lewis Jackson) walked through a reception line with four thousand other guests, including, just by chance, Dr. Martin Luther King Sr., at an open house at the mansion. Governor Maddox listened for about twenty minutes to their complaints concerning conditions at the camp and promised "the most thorough investigation ever conducted by the department of corrections." He continued, "If what they say is true then we need to shut down that camp."[8] The men were accompanied by Gary's mother, who had read about the reception and decided it would be a good place to gain an audience with the governor.[9] This incident triggered one of Maddox's main legacies—prison reform.

As the time drew near for the Maddoxes to move into the new mansion, the Democratic Women of Georgia became concerned about Virginia's being able "to come up with suitable linens for the bigger, grander new mansion." The group set about gathering three thousand

dollars worth of trading stamps to help remedy the situation. Inspired by the example of Lurleen Wallace, wife of Alabama governor George Wallace, who reported that she was gathering books of stamps in order to purchase a vacuum cleaner for the Alabama governor's mansion, Marguerite Schott led a similar campaign in Georgia. As Schott related to the newspaper columnist Celestine Sibley, "A few conversations, a few telephone calls, and little postcard correspondence . . . 750 stamp books!"[10] The effort took on a life of its own when Fred Wilkerson, who worked for one of the trading-stamp companies, became interested in the effort. Wilkerson arranged for the head buyer of his company to meet with Virginia Maddox and help her select "a lace banquet cloth, of 'White House' design, a Belgian damask banded in satin in a Louis XIV motif, many smaller damask and linen cloths and some just for use of the Governor's family and for smaller parties."[11]

After spending a year in the Granite Mansion, the Maddoxes moved into the new Executive Center, as the new residence was called at the time, on December 31, 1967. Lester declared, "Georgia's state house is the finest in the nation. It doesn't belong to the Democrats or the Republicans or the Lester Maddoxes. It belongs to the people of Georgia."[12] Among the last-minute additions to the mansion before the Maddoxes moved in were the security fence and gate. Although he welcomed visits from the public, Lester was unhappy about the lack of security that was to be afforded him and his family at their new home. "The new mansion and the mansion grounds were left wide open to any Tom, Dick or Harry that wanted to come in," he observed, adding, "Can you show me a governor who would want to live in a state house that did not have a security fence?"[13]

At the Granite Mansion, which had no fence, pranksters periodically crept onto the lawn and posted "For Sale" signs, and people just came up to knock on the door. As Captain Steve Polk, Maddox's chief of security, explained, "You'd be surprised how many people there are who, when they drink too much, want to see the governor or the governor's mansion."[14] Remembering an incident when a would-be assassin had breached the grounds of the Granite Mansion during the tenure of Governor Carl Sanders, Lester allocated $116,000 for the addition of a fence and gatehouse at the new mansion. Although he was criticized for spending the money, Lester pointed out that he had eliminated such luxuries as a tennis court and a swimming pool from the

State troopers with the first family, ca. 1970.
Courtesy Virginia Maddox Carnes.

you are cordially invited

to a special Preview Showing

of

Executive Center

Wednesday, January 24th

at ten o'clock in the morning

391 West Paces Ferry Road

Atlanta, Georgia

Invitation to preview the mansion,
January 24, 1968. *Courtesy Kenan Research
Center at the Atlanta History Center.*

plans in favor of the security fence, adding, "I don't have time to go swimming."[15]

Even without a swimming pool or usable tennis court, the Executive Center was quite a showpiece, and no one appreciated this more than the Maddoxes. "I think it will pay for itself many times over," declared Lester. The first party held in the mansion, in late January 1968, honored more than seventy people who had been involved in getting the mansion built, including state officials, architects, members of the Fine Arts Committee, and former first lady Betty Sanders, who declared, "I am so excited I can't stand it." The architect of the mansion, Thomas Bradbury, noted, "It looks better than I even imagined! I've watched it grow like a baby. This room [the drawing room] is so breathtaking I'm getting chill bumps. I love it better than the White House!"[16] Sylvia Ferst echoed Bradbury: "It's prettier than the White House, but I hope saying so doesn't get me in trouble with Mr. Johnson." At the event, Lester spoke to the distinguished crowd: "Most of us can never think back to a moment as happy as this one. Virginia and I want to thank you on the committee for all you've done—carrying the weight, making the decisions,

relieving us of the responsibility when we were so busy moving from house to mansion, and from mansion to mansion. I think it will pay for itself many times over. The first person to have breakfast here was the chairman of an industrial plant who was ready to block a $70 million industrial complex. . . . We brought him out here and served him ham and eggs in the back of the unfinished mansion and got him not to block the complex."[17]

Bruce Galphin, writing for the *Atlanta Constitution*, noted, "Atlanta has no museum of decorative arts, but this could well serve as one."[18] Writing about the mansion shortly before it was opened to the public for the first time, the *Atlanta Journal* columnist Celestine Sibley observed, "It sounds grand and I won't blame the Maddoxes if they find such elegance oppressive at first. After all, many men in high public office have chosen to live very simply in their private lives. Remember Sen. Walter George's remodeled sharecropper's shanty? And President Roosevelt's plain little cottage at Warm Springs with the oilcloth and dime store knives and forks in the kitchen? But as the Fine Arts folks say, this is an important building, too, and should reflect credit on the state."[19]

Lester Maddox in the mansion's kitchen, 1968.
Courtesy Library of Congress.

Lester inspecting the mansion's collections,
1968. *Courtesy Library of Congress.*

During the first few weeks in the mansion, Lester and Virginia began to notice a few problems. A roof leak had caused the parquet floors to buckle in one of the upstairs bedrooms; when visitors rang the doorbell, the state trooper had to run from the security office in the basement at the back of the house up a flight of stairs and across the entire expanse of the main floor to the front door, a journey that often took several minutes. As Steve Ball, writing for the *Atlanta Journal and Constitution*, explained: "That arrangement, like the buckling parquet floor and the leaking roof, is just another one of the things that will eventually be adjusted at the $2 million mansion."[20] These problems delayed the opening of the mansion for public tours until February 1968. In July, newspapers reported that Lester could not get hot water in any of the mansion's bathrooms and was forced to boil some on the stove and carry pots upstairs to take "a part-time bath."[21] To complicate matters further, the family also discovered that the elevator did not work.

Lester was equally concerned that the mansion did not have a flagpole. When he asked that one be added, he was told by the Georgia Building Authority that the new mansion "is no little school house and we don't fly flags like that anymore."[22] Extolling the virtues of patriotism, Lester said, "In keeping with our desire to display the flag at the mansion, and believing that most Georgians would want the flag so displayed, rather than the one flag I originally requested, I have ordered three large flag poles placed at the new Governor's Mansion. . . . We are looking to the good people of Georgia who would like to see the flags displayed at the mansion to finance this project by sending a contribution to the governor's mansion or to the governor's office."[23] Optimistic that he would receive the support he requested, Lester asked the National Guard to dig holes for the three poles. The flagpoles were soon installed and began flying an American flag flanked by Georgia state flags.

Events at the West Paces Ferry mansion were rarely formal; instead, they focused on welcoming average people. In May 1968, the Georgia Commission on Aging held its second annual governor's reception at the new mansion with more than a thousand visitors. In its first year, the event had been hosted at the Granite Mansion, which could barely accommodate the large numbers. For the 1968 reception, a group of women from Cartersville borrowed a high school bus and

Legislators and their wives arriving for the annual legislative dinner, ca. 1968. *Courtesy Virginia Maddox Carnes.*

Johnny Cash kissing Virginia Maddox, 1970. *Courtesy Virginia Maddox Carnes.*

Lester riding his bicycle backward at the Capitol, ca. 1970. *Courtesy Virginia Maddox Carnes.*

joined the receiving line. Much to the disappointment of the guests, the governor, whose flight back to Atlanta had been delayed by weather, was late in arriving at the event. As Dora Lawson remarked, "I would have liked to shake his hand. I met the first lady, though. She was real nice." Lawson was impressed by the new mansion, but added, "It's too fancy for poor folks like us."[24] The group was treated to Coca-Cola and cookies in the west garden wing.

Lester and Virginia invited a range of guests to come visit in both mansions. Vice President Hubert Humphrey came to the Granite Mansion, as did Alabama governor George Wallace. Johnny Cash, who was in town to do a concert in North Georgia as a favor to a local sheriff, visited the new mansion, as did the actor Danny Thomas.[25] In December 1969, Lester invited anyone in the state who had received a new bicycle for Christmas to come join him for an afternoon of bicycle riding on the mansion grounds.[26] He was well known for his cycling stunts, including his ability to ride his bicycle backward while sitting on the handlebars. Larry Maddox explained that his father learned the trick

when he was a child and decided it was more efficient to ride it backward when delivering newspapers. One year, Nelson Rockefeller, the former governor of New York, sent Lester a motorcycle, joking that he would like to see the governor try to ride that backward.[27]

Although the Maddoxes appreciated their new home and the outstanding job that the Fine Arts Committee had done furnishing it, their euphoria about living there was soon dampened by the lack of privacy. The mansion was open to the public six days a week, and the Maddoxes regularly hosted events there. Virginia once said that living there was "like living in a glass bowl—with the whole family on the inside looking out and the whole world on the outside looking in."[28] In addition to the guests and visitors who were invited, members of the Fine Arts Committee also were frequently at the mansion. According to the committee chair, Henry Green, "furnishings at the mansion were 75 percent completed, bookshelves 25 percent filled, grounds about half finished and only 25 percent of the mansion's art work selected" when Lester issued an executive order terminating the services of the committee on June 30,

1968. Although appreciative of the work that the committee had done, Lester stated, "This function is no longer needed. The mansion is completed. We've been in the house some seven months."[29]

The *Atlanta Constitution* reported that Lester disbanded the organization because of "an undercurrent of discontent on the part of the governor in which he complained privately that some committee members had breached the privacy of the mansion's living quarters." According to unconfirmed reports, one

State trooper with the player piano from the Pickrick, 1968.
Courtesy Library of Congress.

committee member saw the governor in his underwear, and another was found rummaging through one of Virginia's bureaus in search of a serial number for an inventory.[30] Green, who was surprised by the termination, noted, "We would have tried to correct anything that didn't suit him." In place of the Fine Arts Committee, Maddox appointed the Executive Center Committee, which was composed of Secretary of State Fortson, state auditor Ernest B. Davis, and state budget officer Wilson B. Wilkes.[31]

Among the furnishings that the Maddoxes brought to the mansion themselves were a television set, family pictures, and a well-worn player piano that had been at Lester's Pickrick restaurant. They loved the family living quarters, and were awed by the bathrooms with gold-plated fixtures, the steam bath, and the long white dressing room filled with generous closets. When first informed that there were separate bedrooms for the governor and first lady, Lester responded, "This must be planned for some other governor. I get along with my wife!"[32] The mansion was very different from what they were accustomed to, as Virginia noted: "Our home was contemporary, but I learn to like this more each day."[33]

The Maddoxes had four children, two of whom lived in the mansion for at least part of their father's tenure as governor. The oldest daughter, Linda Maddox Densmore, and the oldest son, Lester Maddox Jr., lived in the suburbs with their families. Linda and her husband, Don, had three children when Lester became governor—Tanya, Tamara, and Tori—and another child, Tara, born in 1970. They visited the mansion often. Virginia Maddox, always known as Ginny, was twenty-five when her father became governor. She was working for DuPont and continued living with her parents until she married George Carnes. Ginny's and George's wedding, held on November 20, 1970, was the first wedding held at the governor's mansion. Ginny recalled, "The ceremony was in the state drawing room, and it was just immediate family. It was not a large enough event to use the ballroom. The reception was held in the drawing room as well." Her husband, George Carnes, added, "There was a pool table upstairs and we played pool in the attic the day of the wedding. It was very informal."[34]

The Maddoxes' youngest son, Larry, lived with his parents in the Granite Mansion before moving with them into the new residence. Larry and his new bride continued to live in the mansion after getting married

Mac the goose with his water bowl, 1968.
Courtesy Library of Congress.

noon, Monday through Friday, and 3:00 to 5:00 p.m. on Sundays. Virginia met visitors at the door each morning and allowed groups to have teas at the mansion. As she explained, "I don't feel right if I'm not there to greet them. And they seem to appreciate it so much."[37] On Sundays, Lester often greeted visitors on the ground floor of the ballroom, where he entertained them with his upright player piano.[38]

As reporter Elizabeth Sawyer noted, "It takes a heap of living to make a house a home—especially if the house is a place like the splendid mansion built for Georgia's governor and his family." Sawyer added that in the eighteen months of her residency, Virginia had "made the Greek Revival–style building and its dignified and historical furnishings seem like home—not only to the Maddox family but to everyone in the state who has been there." More than 150,000 guests had come through the house in its first year, and Virginia had been there to greet them all.[39] The rooms on the main floor were open and visitors were given a brochure to help them complete the self-guided tour. Virginia placed two guest books in the circular-stair hall for visitors to sign, and noted that people came from all fifty

in Tulsa, Oklahoma, in 1969. He and his wife welcomed their daughter, Tracy Lynn, in October of that year. When Tracy Lynn was barely a year old and just learning to walk, she fell down the kitchen stairs that led to the garage. Miraculously, she was not injured.[35]

The family brought with them a basset hound named Pickrick, but they soon had another animal resident at the mansion. In 1968, three high school students, Jim Patton, Steve Bishoff, and George Knight, gave Lester a goose that he named Mac. The goose was given the run of the grounds, including the marble fountain that graced the front lawn. Much to the consternation of the Fine Arts Committee and the public's amusement, Lester had a special ramp constructed for Mac so that he could easily get in and out of the fountain. The Associated Press reported that the fully grown gander would likely enjoy getting to know the fountain's other resident, a frog named Leaping Lester II.[36]

The Maddoxes wanted to share their new home with the public and kept active visiting hours: 10:00 a.m. to

Open house at the mansion, 1968.
Courtesy Virginia Maddox Carnes.

Virginia and Lester in the mansion garden, ca. 1970. *Courtesy Virginia Maddox Carnes.*

states and from Australia, England, Belgium, Finland, Japan, and the Philippines.[40]

Lester frequently joked about living in the "finger bowl" section of West Paces Ferry Road, referring to the wealth of their neighbors, but he and Virginia worked hard to make the mansion comfortable. Alongside the formal and elaborate landscaping coordinated by the Fine Arts Commission, they established a garden fifty yards from the mansion's east wing. They planted watermelon, squash, okra, and corn on the grounds. Virginia regularly used the fruits and vegetables in meals for the family or for small gatherings. She often cooked for guests. At one event in June 1969, reporters asked why she did not meet them at the front door. Embarrassed, she whispered, "I had to finish the biscuits."[41] Apparently, the official chefs and kitchen help could not match her skill when it came to preparing southern fare.

Lester, Virginia, Larry, and the mansion staff once played a joke on Mike Stitt, the mansion's cook, who had worked at the Pickrick restaurant. According to Larry, "Mike started the garden on West Paces Ferry Road, and he couldn't grow anything. Each year the governor was given the largest watermelon grown in the state, and that gave us an idea. We decided to slip it into the garden. When Mike walked down to see how his plants were doing, we stayed behind and watched from the kitchen window with binoculars. He saw that prize watermelon, and I thought he was going to have a heart attack."[42] Lester added, "You should have seen Mike running back with that big watermelon. He nearly fell out of his skin when he saw it."[43] Virginia, also in on the joke, watched the whole episode from the window.

Virginia planned and cooked for most of the mansion events, large and small. Though she often had kitchen help, she was clearly in charge. One morning she prepared over a hundred biscuits for a legislative breakfast. In addition, she had responsibilities related to management of the family's furniture business, which they opened after closing the Pickrick. "I still have to do my work at the furniture store. I do the books and send out bills, and it takes quite a bit of time, as it's 'way across town," she reminded the reporter Mary Utting.[44] After managing the busy social schedule of the mansion by herself for almost two months, she hired a part-time secretary in February 1968.

Virginia Maddox by the new fountain, ca. 1968. *Courtesy Virginia Maddox Carnes.*

Lester Maddox's Portrait

Governor Lester Maddox Portrait, Bruce Halfley, artist, 1992. *Georgia Capitol Museum Collection, Courtesy of Richard B. Russell Library for Political Research and Studies, The University of Georgia Libraries.*

The official portrait of Lester Maddox that hangs in the Capitol in Atlanta reflects his personality and what was important to him. It includes a framed photograph of his beloved wife, Virginia, with two peaches by his right hand. Behind him on the table is a piece of fish wrapped in a copy of the *Atlanta Constitution*. He had a long-running, legendary battle with the newspaper, often calling it "the fishwrapper." According to Bob Short's biography of Maddox, *Everything Is Pickrick*, the governor said of the placement of the paper in the painting: "The artist wanted to put it out front, but I wanted the fishwrapper near my rear end because that's where it belongs."

For Larry Maddox, the mansion was a place where a young man could get into trouble. Recounting one of his most memorable events, Larry explained:

One day, Trooper Sonny King and I were playing football on the mansion grounds. He threw the ball over my head and broke the window of my brand new 1968 Oldsmobile 442. I started picking the glass off my car, but it was scratching the paint. So I came up with the brilliant idea that I was going to drive around the grounds to blow off the glass. I got up to 92 miles per hour, lost control of the car, hit a tree and rolled it three times. I was bleeding on my face from the small glass fragments, and Dad was out of town. He missed all my fun. The troopers wanted to take me to Piedmont Hospital, but I did not want to get into trouble so I thought I'd go pick up a girl I was dating who was studying nursing at Georgia Baptist Hospital. I got back to the mansion, and here comes Dad and Mom. Dad had outsmarted me. I thought having the girl there would keep him from getting so mad. Boy, was I wrong.[45]

Because the state constitution at that time precluded Maddox's running for a second term, he and Virginia moved out of the mansion in 1971. On Lester's last day in office, Georgians turned out for a public farewell to the governor and first lady. Hundreds of cars created a traffic jam on West Paces Ferry Road. They were filled with people—young and old, rich and poor, black and white—who said they "just wanted to shake his hand." The state patrol estimated that more than five thousand people came to the mansion that blustery day in

Governor Sonny Perdue welcoming Lester Maddox to the mansion, 2003. *Courtesy Larry Maddox.*

Lester Maddox lifting Governor Zell Miller on his eightieth birthday at the mansion, 1995, with Maddox's daughter, Linda Maddox Densmore, looking on. *Courtesy Kenan Research Center Atlanta History Center.*

January. One woman explained why she was there: "I've been waiting for two hours, but I wanted to see Lester. I'm going to stay here till they run me off."[46]

Not yet ready to end his political career, Lester ran for lieutenant governor and served under Jimmy Carter while also operating a gift shop and a Pickrick restaurant in Underground Atlanta and a Pickrick in Sandy Springs. He enjoyed a brief career in show business as part of a musical and comedy team, "The Governor and His Dishwasher," which toured with Bobby Lee Fears, one of Lester's former employees. They played in clubs in Florida, California, and New York through 1977.[47] Lester ran again for governor in 1974, but lost to George Busbee. In 1976, Maddox ran for president as the nominee of the American Independent Party, losing to fellow Georgian Jimmy Carter. That same year, he opened the Lester Maddox Realty Company and subsequently

experienced a long struggle with health problems, including a heart attack and cancer.[48] Determined to make a comeback, Maddox ran for governor one final time, in 1990, losing to his old employee and friend Zell Miller. Though he never held public office again, he did get to return to the mansion for special occasions. In September 1995, Governor Miller invited Lester to the Governor's Mansion for his eightieth birthday party. Former governors Joe Frank Harris and Carl Sanders and the singer James Brown were on hand to cut the cake with Maddox and two thousand friends. Two years later, Virginia passed away on June 24, 1997. Shortly before Lester died, Governor Sonny Perdue invited him back to visit the mansion; when the elevator door opened, Perdue warmly greeted him with "Welcome home, Governor."[49] Lester died on June 25, 2003, marking the end of an era in Georgia history.

The Carter family—Rosalynn, Amy, Jimmy, Jack, Jeff, and Chip—at the mansion, c. 1971.
Courtesy Richard B. Russell Library for Political Research and Studies, University of Georgia.

CHAPTER FIVE

A Long Way from Plains

THE CARTERS

Jimmy Carter is the only Georgian to have served as both governor (1971–75) and president of the United States (1977–81). A native of Plains, Georgia, James Earl Carter Jr. (fondly known as "Jimmy") is the son of small-town farmers James Earl Carter and Lillian Gordy. After attending school in Plains, Jimmy attended Georgia Southwestern College and Georgia Tech before receiving a prestigious appointment to the U.S. Naval Academy in Annapolis, Maryland.[1] He graduated with a naval commission and served at sea on two battleships and two submarines before being assigned to duty as commander of a crew that helped build the second nuclear-powered submarine, the USS *Seawolf*.[2] Immediately after graduating from Annapolis, he married Rosalynn Smith in Plains on July 7, 1946. They had three sons while Jimmy was serving in the navy—John William, James Earl III, and Donnell Jeffrey— and their daughter, Amy Lynn, was born after they returned to Plains.

Rosalynn was also a native of Plains, and as Jimmy recalled, "I was her next-door neighbor when she was born."[3] Rosalynn, who was friends with Jimmy's younger sister Ruth, graduated as valedictorian of her high school class. Rosalynn's father, Wilburn Edgar Smith, a farmer who also owned and operated the first auto shop in the county, had died when she was thirteen. Her mother, Frances Allethea Murray Smith, had always been a stay-at-home mother and seamstress, but a few years after her husband died she began working in the post office and worked there until retirement. During Jimmy's time in the navy, he and Rosalynn lived in Virginia, Connecticut, Hawaii, and California. Following the death of his father in 1953, Jimmy resigned from the navy so that he and Rosalynn could return to Plains and manage the family farm and peanut business. They became active members of the community, and Jimmy served on the local library, school, and hospital boards.[4]

Jimmy's civic activism led him into politics, and in 1962 he was elected to the Georgia Senate from the fourteenth district. While Jimmy was away from home during legislative sessions, Rosalynn oversaw the family business. After four years in the senate, Jimmy ran for governor in 1966. He finished third in the Democratic primary. The winner was Lester Maddox. Four years later, Jimmy ran again. The whole family campaigned in what was later called their "Hi Neighbor" strategy. Lillian joined Rosalynn, Jimmy, and their sons, crossing the state to help drum up

Rosalynn and Jimmy Carter on their wedding day, 1946. *Courtesy Kenan Research Center at the Atlanta History Center.*

Rosalynn Carter's childhood home, 219 South Bond Street, Plains, ca. 1989. *Courtesy Library of Congress.*

Carter Peanut Warehouse Complex, Plains, Georgia, ca. 1989. *Courtesy Library of Congress.*

Jimmy Carter in Plains, July 30, 1966. *Courtesy Special Collections and Archives, Georgia State University Library.*

votes.[5] Rosalynn and Jimmy estimated that they alone shook the hands of more than six hundred thousand Georgians in 1970.[6] While campaigning, Jimmy made 1,800 speeches.[7] That level of dedication helped secure his election as Georgia's seventy-sixth governor. The family moved from Sumter County to the mansion on West Paces Ferry Road in January 1971. Jimmy said of the move, "It was quite a transformation for us from Plains to Atlanta."[8]

The mansion was still new, and not all the kinks had been resolved. The roof leaked, and the heating and air conditioning system did not work properly. In spite of these glitches, however, the Carters were enthusiastic about moving into their new home. Reflecting on the contentious debate that had unfolded about funding for the mansion when he was serving in the legislature, Jimmy commented, "When I was in the Senate, I voted against it. But I'm glad it was built."[9]

Rosalynn began preparing for life in the mansion before she and her family became residents. She had never been inside the new Governor's Mansion and later recalled, "[I] had not had time in the hectic months of campaigning to even consider what my responsibilities as the governor's wife might be."[10] In an effort to learn more about her new home, she arranged to meet with Virginia Maddox, Governor Maddox's wife, to take a tour and glean insider information about life in the mansion. Remembering her first visit to the site, Rosalynn stated, "I was nervous that first day as I drove up to the entrance gates and was stopped by the state patrolmen. I associated state patrolmen with traffic accidents and speeding tickets, but these men were cordial and directed me up the circular driveway to the front door, where I was met by more state patrolmen."[11] After making it through the many levels of security, Rosalynn sat down with Virginia in the small parlor and began discussing the mansion operations. She was dismayed to learn that Virginia did all the cooking for her family and the small events they hosted, did not have an administrative assistant or receive mail at the mansion, and kept the mansion open for tours six days a week. The sheer amount of work seemed daunting. She also heard from Virginia that the state troopers served both as tour guides and as security inside the house, because visitors "would pick up everything they could as souvenirs"; and she was not exaggerating, "They had even

Jack, Chip, Jeff, and Rosalynn Carter playing miniature golf during Jimmy's first gubernatorial campaign, August 3, 1966. *Courtesy Special Collections and Archives, Georgia State University Library.*

Rosalynn and Jimmy Carter greeting
Lieutenant Governor Maddox
and his wife, Virginia, c. 1971.
Courtesy Virginia Carnes Maddox.

taken the handles off the fixtures in the downstairs bath-room." On her drive home, Rosalynn recalled, "I didn't know what I was going to do when I left her that day. I didn't want to spend all my time taking care of that big house."[12]

Soon after her visit with Virginia Maddox, the Carters attended a conference in North Carolina for newly elected governors, hosted by Governor Robert W. Scott and his wife. The new first families "all had similar questions that needed answers."[13] Some of the lessons were learned outside the formal sessions. Rosalynn recalled an incident at one of the formal dinners:

> I looked carefully at everything, absorbing it for the time
> when I would be the one entertaining. It made me ner-
> vous just to think about it. And when the bowl of warm
> water with flower petals arrived, I had no idea what to
> do with it. My instincts told me it was a finger bowl, but

this was my first experience with one. I waited, carefully watching the governor next to me. Nonchalantly I followed suit, lifting the bowl and small doily underneath from my plate and setting them aside as though I had been using finger bowls all my life.[14]

Over the next several days, Rosalynn and Jimmy learned a great deal about how to operate the executive residence. Rosalynn attended sessions on invitations, correspondence, and even telephone etiquette. The Carters, who had already learned the importance of managing the phone, requested an unlisted number for the mansion. Rosalynn pointed out, "The telephone never stopped ringing," even in the middle of the night, when "inebriated friends would call."[15]

Meeting with other first ladies and learning about their executive residences boosted Rosalynn's confidence by confirming that Georgia's mansion was a showplace with few equals in the nation. The ballroom could seat four hundred for dinner, and the mansion had pleasant overnight accommodations that could suit even royal tastes. She discovered that the southern states tended to have the most lavish mansions, remarking, "In Massachusetts, for instance, there is no mansion at all; the governor lives in his own home. The wife of the governor of Arizona told me that they lived in a high-rise apartment building and did all their entertaining in hotels."[16] Rosalynn left the conference "feeling much better," she said: "I was not alone in being overwhelmed by my new circumstances; the other new governors' wives shared my feelings. And best of all, we had learned there were no set rules."[17] Armed with advice from their peers, the Carters made their own way. Rosalynn reflected, "The transition from the simpler life of being a wife and mother in Plains and working in the peanut warehouse to being the First Lady of Georgia was a difficult one. The move to the White House later was much easier for me compared to this initial move."[18]

After the inauguration on January 12, 1971, the Carters opened the doors of the mansion for a public reception. The crowds poured in, and the Carters "shook hands with them all—young and old, black and white, large and small, friends and a few foes." Rosalynn recalled that one visitor "pumped my hand so hard that one of my earrings flew across the room!"[19] Miss Lillian, Jimmy's mother, maintained her own "one-woman receiving line." An estimated twenty-five thousand people came to the mansion, and twelve thousand went through the receiving line. At dusk there were still lines of visitors down the long driveway, so the Carters put on their coats and went outside to greet them. Afterward, they changed clothes and headed to the four inaugural balls. Rosalynn wore a pale blue chiffon dress with a gold-beaded bodice and a matching coat of gold brocade. She would later wear the same dress to the inaugural balls in Washington, D.C., when Jimmy became president.[20]

Making the mansion a home was a challenge. Rosalynn moved in with her sewing machine, fully intending to continue her tradition of making clothes for her youngest child, Amy. Time for such domestic pursuits, however, was in short supply, and Rosalynn later conceded, "I put the sewing machine in a closet at the mansion. . . . I only had time to make her a few skirts."[21] Rosalynn also liked to cook but was rarely able to find the opportunity, at least at first. She later

reflected, "When Jimmy was governor, I used to go to cooking classes taught by Ursula Knaeusel, just to keep my hand in. We would cook all her recipes and then get to eat it. I found cooking classes very relaxing."[22] As she became more familiar with the rhythm of the mansion, she started sending the staff home on the weekends. She remembers that she had planned to cook the family meals, but the staff left so much food already prepared in the refrigerator that there was little need for her to do so. The staff did come back on Sundays to have a large dinner ready for the family after church.

Rosalynn enjoyed her role as Georgia's first lady, something she would not have anticipated just a few years earlier. She admitted in her book *First Lady from Plains* that at first politics frightened her, and when asked to step in as a surrogate for her husband, she would break out in hives or cry. Writing for the *New York Times*, Phil Gailey detailed her transformation: "By the time she moved into the Georgia Governor's Mansion, she was at ease making speeches and meeting celebrities. She was well on her way to earning her reputation as the '[Steel] Magnolia.' Nothing and no one intimidated her anymore."[23]

For a time, all the Carter children lived in the mansion with their parents. Amy, who was three years old when the family moved in, slept in the room designated as the first lady's bedroom, adjacent to the bedroom her parents shared on the second floor. Jack, who had recently completed his tour with the navy and was attending Georgia Tech, and Jeff, who had recently transferred to Georgia State University, both moved into the family quarters on the second floor as well. Chip, also studying at Georgia State, selected a pair of rooms in the basement that had direct access to the outside. Chip's basement space became the children's headquarters, recalled Rosalynn, who added, "They could turn up their music as loud as they wanted, without our ever hearing it. They could entertain their friends and come and go as they pleased without being involved with official activities or the tourists. After all, they were twenty-four, twenty-one, and nineteen, not children anymore."[24] But the boys also enjoyed the mansion's comforts. A few days after the Carters moved in, one of the housekeeping staff members asked who needed their shoes shined, to which Jack replied, "I could get used to this in a hurry."[25] Eventually the eldest boys married, and Jack and his wife, Judy, lived in the red barn. When they left, Chip and his wife, Caron, lived there for a year before moving to Plains to help with the family business.

Miss Lillian, Jimmy's mother, was also a fixture at the mansion. She gave tours, helped with public events, and visited often. As the author E. Stanly Godbold explained, "Lillian asked for favors, gave advice, served on committees, and became a beloved political asset."[26] She loved baseball games, and Jimmy often sent his aide Hamilton Jordan with his mother to use the governor's lifetime pass to see the Atlanta Braves. When a group of Chinese editors was visiting Atlanta, Lillian attended events with them and gave them a private tour of the mansion.

Jimmy rarely worked at the mansion and was often at the capitol by 7:15 a.m. On the weekends, when he did not go to the office, the family made time for one another. On Saturdays, the Carters often took Amy to the zoo or the library. They also visited state parks,

Jimmy and Amy Carter at an Atlanta Hawks game, c. 1970s.
Courtesy Kenan Research Center at the Atlanta History Center.

panned for gold in Dahlonega, fished, and attended Georgia Tech football games or Braves baseball games.[27] The boys were wild about Frisbee throwing; Jimmy recalled that he and his sons would often enjoy games of Frisbee on the mansion grounds. The tennis court also proved to be useful, both as a source of recreation for the Carters and as a bartering tool to gain access to a neighbor's swimming pool. The court, which dated to the Robert Maddox period, was in poor condition by the time the Carters arrived. The Carters had it rebuilt, and the son of their neighbor Anne Cox Chambers would come over to play. In exchange, the Chambers family let Amy use their swimming pool, where Jimmy taught her how to swim.[28] Chambers recalled: "My house is right across from the mansion. So my family, who played tennis went over there, and oh, it was quite an unusual scene: the policemen were stopping traffic and the governor would come down across with Amy on his shoulders in their bathing suits."[29] A swimming pool was added to the mansion grounds during the Busbee administration.

Despite the mansion's amenities, Rosalynn found "settling into a house that was so big and unfamiliar" to be frustrating. With so many people living in the mansion, it was hard to keep up with everyone, and it was often difficult to gather everyone together. Rosalynn remembered the trouble she had in getting everyone's attention: "On more than one occasion I found myself standing in the middle of the foyer, calling at the top of my voice to anyone who could hear me: 'Dinner is ready' or 'Come to the telephone.'"[30] In an effort to bring order to the chaos, Rosalynn created a sign-up sheet for meals and set dinnertime at seven o'clock. Anyone who was going to eat with the family showed up in the dining room at that time. The family devised a system for managing phone calls by installing bells throughout the house and assigning a number of rings for each family member—Jimmy, one; Rosalynn, two; Jack, three; and so on. Rosalynn also felt uneasy at having a uniformed state trooper escort her everywhere she went, so she asked her troopers to dress in plain clothes. That way, she could shop and travel without attracting attention.[31]

Amy had the run of the mansion. A giant closet on the second floor became a perfect play space, but oftentimes Amy would want to go to the kitchen or outside to play. Rosalynn remembered, "You couldn't get to the kitchen downstairs without going through the people who were touring the house four days a week. If Amy went outside to play, people were there, too. She soon learned to walk through them in her own little world, without seeing or paying any attention to them. She had to. She's still perfectly and totally happy in her own world wherever she is. I think she learned that from living in crowds all the time."[32] Rosalynn adjusted, too, declaring that after a couple of months she stopped worrying about having staff members and state troopers around all the time. Away from the public eye, she returned to casual dress for her and Amy and even felt comfortable enough to go downstairs for breakfast in her bathrobe.[33] Amy's parents worked hard to give her a normal childhood in spite of living in the fishbowl of the Governor's Mansion. One Halloween, Jimmy accompanied Amy trick-or-treating along West Paces Ferry Road.[34] Rosalynn "always tried to be there when Amy awakened, when she left for school, and when she came home." Rosalynn's involvement extended to events outside the mansion: "She took her [Amy] to birthday parties, choir rehearsals, dances with the Little General Cloggers, and performances for children at the Atlanta Memorial Arts Center."[35]

The staff members, all of whom were trusties from the prison, helped keep things running smoothly. Mary Fitzpatrick, who served as Amy's governess at the mansion, was especially beloved. Mary had been selected to participate in the state's trusty program. The program placed convicted felons into jobs at governmental facilities, including the Governor's Mansion. According to Colonel William Lowe, Georgia's deputy commissioner for Offender Administration, a job at the mansion "was considered a very selective and highly sought-after assignment." The selection process was rigorous: "The trusties were screened thoroughly before they went there. We did psychological tests on them."[36] Mary later recalled being driven to Atlanta in December 1970 for an interview with the Carters for the position of governess. "I was thrilled," she remembered, adding, "All my life I had wanted to meet a governor or a President. But I was nervous, too. I wondered how the Carter family would take to me."[37] At the interview, Mary remembered, "Mrs. Carter asked me how I would like to take care of Amy." Mary was thrilled with the opportunity to look after the three-year-old, noting, "[Amy] took to me right away. She liked me to sing 'Swing Low, Sweet Chariot' to her every night, and I would rub her back and lie down

with her. She would even cry at night because she hated to see me leave."[38] On her first day on the job, Mary later recalled, "Amy took me by the hand and showed me all over the mansion. She was very active and played a lot. Sometimes she would play herself to sleep."[39]

Each morning, Mary, along with the rest of the trusties, was transported from the prison to the mansion. Mary cared for Amy during the day. They would play, read, make cookies, and climb trees on the mansion grounds. Mary remembered their many good times together: "Amy would try to help cook. She would make little biscuits for her father. And sometimes she would crawl in the kitchen cabinets and hang upside down. We played a lot of hide-and-seek. It was hard to find Amy, because she could get in the smallest places. But when she couldn't find me, she would say, 'Please, Mary, answer,' and I would."[40] At the end of each workday, Mary was returned to the prison. Pat Ford-Roegner, director of the work-release center that Rosalynn later helped establish, explained, "She's a very, very warm person, and kids take to her very well."[41] Through her relationship with Mary, Rosalynn became concerned about the status of the inmates at the women's prison. She joined the Women's Prison Committee of the Commission on the Status of Women and helped build a work-release center for sixty-five female prisoners.[42] Mary became such a valued member of the household that when the Carters eventually left the Governor's Mansion for the White House, she was paroled so that she could join them there.

The Carters took their role as Georgia's first family seriously and worked hard to protect the Governor's Mansion furnishings and its art collection, which had been lovingly assembled by Henry Green and the Fine Arts Committee. "We were living in a museum," Rosalynn noted.[43] The Carters' bedroom was furnished with a nineteenth-century canopy bed, a needlework portrait of George Washington, and a gold leather wastebasket.[44] They made very few changes to the mansion, and Rosalynn called upon Jimmy's aunt Emily "Sissy" Dolvin to help assemble a corps of volunteer docents to help coordinate and deliver tours on Tuesday, Thursday, and Sunday. Under Lester Maddox, the state patrol officers had given the tours, but Rosalynn felt that having a trooper take visitors through the house "seemed a little intimidating," so she decided that volunteer docents would lead the tours.[45]

To learn more about the collection, Rosalynn "asked two members of the original Fine Arts Committee to teach the volunteer docents and me the history of these treasures."[46] The docents also fielded a range of questions on other topics, including "Are the windows bulletproof?" and "Where does the baby eat?"[47] Because the mansion was still fairly new, the ballroom looked unfinished, so Rosalynn asked the High Museum of Art to consider lending pieces to the mansion for the Southern Governors' Conference.[48] At that event, Robert Shaw conducted the Atlanta Symphony Orchestra, and the Carters gave each governor's wife a gold nugget pendant from North Georgia.[49] On the morning of the event, as Rosalynn started down the steps to oversee the installation of the paintings in the ballroom, "suddenly the sound of beautiful music filled the house." The orchestra was rehearsing for the evening performance. Rosalynn recalled: "I stopped, poised in my steps, with the strangest feeling of wonder, as though I were in a dream. First, an exquisite collection of paintings on permanent loan to the Governor's Mansion. Now, the sound of a symphony filled the house. It was all so beautiful that it was breathtaking. The 'fantasy' lasted through the entire evening, and I couldn't help remembering the panic I'd felt at the governors-elect conference at the prospect of holding such grand entertainments myself."[50]

Rosalynn demonstrated her respect for the mansion and its collection when she canceled an invitation for Henry Kissinger and his wife to spend the night at the mansion because his security team would have insisted on "drilling 23 holes into the mansion's parquet floors to install special phone lines."[51] Rather than subjecting the mansion to such rough treatment, the Carters made arrangements for the Kissingers to stay in a hotel. Reflecting later on the fine collection of furnishings and artifacts in the mansion, Rosalynn noted that the White House antiques collection was "a post-graduate course for me, because we had a major collection of antiques in the Governor's Mansion in Atlanta."[52] Everyone in the family seemed to have a great appreciation for the mansion's collection. When Jeff's girlfriend (and now wife), Annette, wrote her thesis on interior design at the University of Georgia, Jimmy, who was a photography buff, agreed to take photographs of the Chinese porcelain collection at the mansion to illustrate the thesis.[53]

The Carters embraced their role as the state's hosts, and Rosalynn hired a housekeeper and Madeline MacBean,

who worked as social and press secretary. The housekeeper stayed only a short time because of sickness in the family and was never replaced. By then, Madeline had become an important addition to daily operations, helping establish some rules and regulations to streamline management of the household. Rosalynn and Madeline helped train the trusty prisoners to cook, and they tested dozens of recipes on the family to perfect them before serving them to guests. Rosalynn recalled that she and Madeline also "trained the prisoners to wait on tables, serving from the left and taking away from the right, lifting a water glass to fill it rather than reaching across."[54] In some cases, the trusties learned their lessons too well. They had been taught to trim the crusts off the bread for tea sandwiches, and when they were asked to prepare submarine sandwiches for a press event, they cut the crust off the French bread, much to Rosalynn's dismay.[55]

Among the famous guests who spent the night was the American pianist Van Cliburn. The Carters had barely settled into the mansion in January 1971 when Cliburn came to town to perform at the invitation of the Atlanta Music Club. The Carters invited him to stay at the mansion, and Rosalynn recalled, "He called in the afternoon before his performance to tell me how pleased he was to be coming to the Governor's Mansion." Upon arriving at the mansion after the concert, Cliburn was "whisked upstairs to the guest suite," where he was served a "big steak, at his request." The Carters had organized a formal reception at the mansion, and after finishing his meal, Cliburn came downstairs to mingle with the guests. "He was charming to everyone," recalled Rosalynn.[56] The evangelist Billy Graham also spent the night at the mansion and stayed up until three in the morning, eating cereal while discussing religion with Jimmy and the boys.[57]

The mansion became an important destination for Democratic candidates during the 1972 presidential campaign. Jimmy remembered: "Atlanta was a center for communication in the Southeast. All the candidates wanted to visit, so I invited them to stay with us in the mansion. I used the presidential suite to entertain almost every single Democrat running for president—Ted Kennedy, George McGovern, Ed Muskie, and Hubert Humphrey. I would sit there with them until long after midnight talking about federal programs, and I realized as governor I knew as much as they did about transportation, foreign affairs, education, and social welfare."[58]

Humphrey let Amy give him lemonade and brownies. Senator Muskie is remembered for requesting the most unusual nightcap—whiskey mixed with milk.[59] Ethel Kennedy visited for the Special Olympics, and Margaret Mead came to the mansion to discuss an issue important to Rosalynn, mental health. Musicians were frequent guests, including Bob Dylan, Otis Redding, and Gregg Allman, who broke a chair in the main dining room.[60]

The Carters held dozens of events for a range of groups, and Rosalynn established three rules for entertaining: she would not schedule events that she could not attend, she would not serve hard liquor, and she insisted that all the entertainment be auditioned beforehand. She often tried to have large functions on successive days in order to allow the menus to be coordinated and the flowers reused.[61] The Carters grew close to the German consul general, Roland Gottlieb, and his wife, Ruth, who became an informal consultant to the mansion for international events.[62] Before one such event, Ruth noticed a wrinkle in a tablecloth, grabbed an iron, and ironed the cloth directly on the table. Later, when the dinner was over, it became obvious that the iron had melted the pad under the tablecloth to the table. Fortunately, a good friend of the Carters' who was spending the night was able to repair the table the next day.[63] They hosted the Georgia Press Association, the Georgia Board of Regents, the Savannah Symphony, and the Democratic Charter Commission. The Carters even hosted Jimmy's thirtieth Plains High School class reunion at the mansion, as well as family reunions.[64]

Rosalynn recalled one of her "worst blunders" from her time in the Governor's Mansion with humor and humility. On the eve of a NASCAR race in Atlanta, Jimmy invited the drivers to the mansion for an informal dinner. A self-described avid NASCAR fan, Jimmy had previously driven the pace car and said the prayer for the drivers before the race.[65] Upon meeting A. J. Foyt and Richard Petty, he told them, "You two have been my heroes for more than ten years. This is the greatest honor I have had since I got into politics."

The Carters with visitors at the mansion, 1972. *Courtesy Georgia Archives, Small Print Collection, spc22-073.*

Rosalynn and Jimmy Carter with
state senator William Armstrong Smith
and his wife, Priscilla, c. 1971.
Courtesy Richard B. Russell Library
for Political Research and Studies,
University of Georgia.

Thrilled as the governor was to meet the drivers, the
drivers were equally impressed to be invited to the
Governor's Mansion. One driver commented, "[I] sat
there in the elaborate dining room and reflected how
far stock-car racing [had] progressed. A few years ago
you'd never have convinced the NASCAR old guard that
drivers would eat in the Governor's Mansion for two
hours."[66] But the event did not go as planned. The
evening's entertainment had not been vetted. When
the performance began, the Carters were horrified.
"Everybody was having a great time until the entertainer started singing—not very good light opera!"
recalled Rosalynn. "Our guests, who were expecting
country and western music, sat there with their mouths
open, but he went on and on. . . . It was terrible." The
performer had looked "very good on paper," Rosalynn
recalled later, but she and Madeline had learned a

valuable lesson—always audition performers before an
event.[67]

Christmas for the Carters was a time of celebration, and they continued the tradition of lighting a
large Christmas tree on the front lawn. For their first
Christmas season at the mansion, the Carters hosted
the Atlanta Boys Choir for the tree lighting and had
Santa hand out gifts to the children who attended
the event.[68] While the Carters made the mansion
their home, they did return to Plains for Christmas
Day and Thanksgiving to celebrate with friends and
family.

Participating in all these events made demands on
the first lady's wardrobe, but with her signature style,
Rosalynn came up with a clever solution. She explained,
"All of this entertaining required a huge wardrobe, and
the women in our family worked out a highly successful

arrangement for long dresses. It seemed very wasteful for everyone to have to buy so many new ones for special occasions. Jack and Chip both married while we were in the mansion, so there was Jack's wife, Judy; her mother, Edna Langford, who was at the mansion often and helped me with entertaining; Chip's wife, Caron; Jeff's girlfriend, Annette; and me. We all wore size 6 or 8; so we pooled our clothes. We had one large closet on the second floor that we called the 'gown room,' filled with an impressive collection of cocktail dresses, long gowns, evening wraps, shoes, and bags."[69]

Throughout his time in the mansion, Jimmy worked hard to bring the motion picture industry to Georgia. By the spring of 1973, *Escape from Andersonville, Conrack, Deliverance,* and *Dead Gangsters Have No Friends* had all been filmed in Georgia. By the spring of 1974, the state had commitments for fifteen additional movies and television series, including *First Blood, The Friday Job, Bessie Smith,* and *Poor Plain Jane.* Jimmy's aunt was cast in *Cockfighter,* and the first family attended the premiere in Roswell on July 30, 1974.[70] Jimmy recalled that at the showing of *Deliverance* at the Fox Theater on August 11, 1972, the author James Dickey—whose novel was the basis for the film—showed up in less-than-great shape. "He wore a Mexican hat with tassels, and was drunk," said Carter, adding, "When they got to the banjo scene, he was halfway awake. He played the role of the sheriff in the movie, and by the time he was on screen, he was awake."[71]

Since the Carters were from a farming background, it should come as no surprise that they loved the mansion grounds, with its hardwood trees, azaleas, crepe myrtle, and jasmine. The male trusties did most of the work on the grounds, but occasionally the Carters got their hands dirty. Rosalynn felt that it was important to have fresh flowers in the mansion every day, but there was no budget for such a luxury. So she made sure that there was always something growing in the greenhouse or on the grounds that she could cut and bring into the house. She took responsibility for creating the arrangements herself. She had taken a flower-arranging class in Plains, and in Atlanta she "bought books on flower arranging, studied the pictures, and had the flowers I needed for the arrangements planted in the beds."[72] She also created her own rock garden outside the garage doors and planted pansies, tulips, crocuses, and begonias. Sometimes when she was working there in her jeans, tourists would walk right

by without recognizing her.[73] A rose grower from California in town for a horticultural convention asked for a private tour of the mansion. After touring the mansion grounds, he sent Rosalynn 120 rosebushes for the grounds. She recalled, "It was one of the most wonderful things that happened to me, and when we moved to the White House, the few roses in the Rose Garden were disappointing in comparison."[74] So many tourists asked the Carters about peanut "trees" that Jimmy planted a border of peanuts around the rose garden and directed people to them so they could see that peanuts grew under the ground. Each year the family picked and roasted the peanuts as a special treat.

The most difficult part of being first lady for Rosalynn was the security. "I couldn't leave the house, even to walk in the yard, without someone following me," she noted. "But I didn't want to be constantly watched. I wanted to buy a blonde wig and go shopping incognito. I wanted to push a grocery cart up and down the aisles without everybody looking at every item I put in it. It used to be so much fun to go with Amy and put her in the basket and let her pick out the cereal and cookies. No more." So one day Jimmy suggested that she take the car and go for a ride alone. And she did, driving to Calhoun, Georgia, to visit her friend Edna Langford. They had a wonderful day discussing their children.[75] Starting with this brief getaway, Rosalynn began to find ways to adjust to the constraints of security in her life in the Governor's Mansion.

During their time in the mansion, the Carters began to look to the national stage, as Rosalynn later noted: "In 1971, when we went to the Governor's Mansion, I thought we would be going home to Plains in 1975 because the governor of Georgia could not succeed himself. But we weren't. Since early 1972, Jimmy had been quietly planning to run for president. His success as governor had brought him national recognition."[76] As Jimmy's term progressed and he began planning a run for the White House, he invited close advisers for informal gatherings. After he left the governor's office, he waged a two-year campaign for president and was elected in 1976. His successor at the mansion, George Busbee, allowed the president-elect continued access to the mansion. Recalling this interesting turn of events, Jimmy explained, "Governor Busbee was my floor leader, and we were like brothers. When he was elected governor, he let me use the mansion to interview possible members of the cabinet."[77]

WE AMERICANS ARE A GREAT AND DIVERSE PEOPLE. WE TAKE ~~FULL~~ *full* *wide-ranging*
ADVANTAGE OF OUR RIGHT TO DEVELOP ~~DIFFERENT~~ INTERESTS AND
RESPONSIBILITIES. FOR INSTANCE, I AM A FARMER, AN ENGINEER, *a businessman,*
A PLANNER, A SCIENTIST, A GOVERNOR AND A CHRISTIAN. EACH OF
YOU IS AN INDIVIDUAL AND DIFFERENT FROM ALL *the* OTHERS.

*old-
final
master
J.C.*

YET WE AMERICANS HAVE SHARED ONE THING IN COMMON: A
BELIEF IN THE GREATNESS OF OUR COUNTRY.

WE HAVE DARED TO DREAM GREAT DREAMS FOR OUR NATION. WE
HAVE TAKEN *quite* QUITE LITERALLY THE PROMISES OF DECENCY, EQUALITY
AND FREEDOM -- OF AN HONEST *and* RESPONSIBLE GOVERNMENT.

WHAT HAS *now* BECOME OF THESE GREAT DREAMS?

*12:00 NOON
1 Dec 1974*

-- THAT ALL AMERICANS STAND EQUAL BEFORE THE LAW;

-- THAT WE ENJOY A RIGHT TO PURSUE HEALTH, HAPPINESS
AND PROSPERITY IN PRIVACY AND SAFETY;

-- THAT GOVERNMENT ~~SHOULD~~ BE CONTROLLED BY ITS CITIZENS
AND NOT THE OTHER WAY AROUND;

-- THAT THIS COUNTRY ~~SHOULD~~ SET A STANDARD WITHIN THE
COMMUNITY OF NATIONS OF COURAGE, COMPASSION, INTEGRITY, AND
DEDICATION TO BASIC HUMAN RIGHTS AND FREEDOMS.

First draft of Jimmy Carter's speech announcing his candidacy for U.S. president, December 1, 1974. *Courtesy Georgia Archives, RG 1-1-45.*

Jimmy Carter with Holly Chute, Eva Andrews, and other staff members in the mansion's kitchen, c. 1981. *Courtesy Holly Chute.*

President-elect Carter and his family at the
World Congress Center on election night,
1976. *Courtesy Kenan Research Center at the
Atlanta History Center.*

Jimmy became the thirty-ninth president of the
United States and Rosalynn the youngest first lady since
Jacqueline Kennedy. When asked how moving into the
White House compared to moving into the Governor's
Mansion, Rosalynn explained: "It was incredible because
I had to do nothing about the entertaining or the operations of the White House. Someone else did all of that.
I did have sessions with my social secretary about all
events to review and help make decisions. But to leave
the Governor's Mansion, where I helped do everything,
and go to the White House was just amazing." Jimmy
echoed her sentiment, but referring to the superb fine
arts collection at the mansion, he added, "Well, it
was kind of a step down for us to move to the White
House. The collection at the Governor's Mansion was
simply that good."[78] So the Carters, with seven-year-old
Amy, moved to Washington. Their time at the Georgia
Governor's Mansion had prepared them well.

George and Mary Beth Busbee with Sam during the campaign, 1974. *Courtesy Jan Busbee Curtis.*

CHAPTER SIX

Southern Hospitality with an International Flair

THE BUSBEES

The Busbees became the third family to move into the Governor's Mansion, and they lived there for eight years, from 1975 to 1983. In their 1986 book, *Guess Who's Coming to Dinner: Entertaining at the Governor's Mansion; Menus, Recipes, and Anecdotes*, First Lady Mary Beth Busbee and her daughter, Jan Busbee Curtis, wrote that living in the mansion was "like living in a fishbowl," but with some advantages: "No fish have ever been so privileged."[1] The Busbees' youngest son, Jeff, who was fourteen when his father was elected, was wowed by the "expansive grounds" upon his first visit to the mansion and inquired whether he "would have to cut all that grass" himself, a chore that he had at the family home in Albany.[2] Jan recalled:

> My parents had lived in Albany for 25 years, where my father was an attorney. He was also a state representative for 18 years before becoming governor. Our family was excited to move into the mansion. With four children between the ages of 22 and 14, it was a busy time for my parents. My mother wisely hired a mansion manager, Mary Page Dwozan, a former banquet manager at Doublegate Country Club, who made the transition much easier for my family. All that my parents brought to the mansion were their clothes, Daddy's old recliner, my 14-year-old brother Jeff, and our 13-year-old black Labrador mix, Sam.[3]

A native of Dooly County in South Georgia, George Dekle Busbee was first elected governor of Georgia in 1974 on the slogan "a workhorse, not a showhorse." A constitutional amendment in 1977 allowed a governor to serve two consecutive four-year terms, and George Busbee was the first Georgia governor to do so. Before his eight years in the Governor's Mansion, he served in the state legislature and was chairman of the House Appropriations Committee under Speaker Tom Murphy. During Governor Carl Sanders's tenure, Busbee was floor leader before becoming majority leader for eight years.

According to Charles Bullock, a professor of political science at the University of Georgia, "He was the man who went a long way to define the governor as the chief international sales agent for the state. Before him, we did not think of ourselves as being involved in international commerce. Now we expect it."[4] Busbee was the first Georgia governor to cultivate foreign investment in Georgia aggressively, and he went to great lengths to relate to people from other countries in their languages,

An election-night telephone call, 1974.
Courtesy Jan Busbee Curtis.

although not always successfully. He often told an anecdote about trying to address a Japanese governor in his native language and calling him a "flat-breasted woman."[5] Despite this snafu, Busbee's international efforts were largely successful, and the number of international companies in Georgia increased dramatically, from 150 at the beginning of his term to 680 in 1982.[6]

Born in 1927, George Busbee attended the Georgia Military College and Abraham Baldwin Agricultural College before enlisting in the navy. Upon completion of his service, he finished his undergraduate degree at the University of Georgia in 1949 and earned a law degree in 1952. He met his future wife, Mary Beth Talbot, a native of Ruston, Louisiana, while at UGA. In 1949, they were married. Four years later, in 1952, the family moved to Albany, Georgia, where George established a law practice. The couple had four children, Beth, Jan, George Jr., and Jeff. Busbee's political career began in 1956 when he won a seat in the Georgia House of Representatives.[7]

Governor Busbee was a playful and energetic man who loved fishing, tennis, flying, and, especially, photography. He brought his darkroom equipment with him to the mansion, set up a space behind the greenhouse, and developed his own pictures. Closets throughout the mansion were filled with old cameras, and he took hundreds of

pictures while in office. Jeff recalled, "He was a real early riser, and he would go out to that darkroom, but would always drive. It was only half a block, but he loved having a chance to get behind the wheel of a car."[8] Governor Busbee became close friends with Ansel Adams, whom he met in October 1977 when the photographer was in town to do a lecture at the High Museum of Art. Adams, who was then seventy-five years old, visited the mansion often, and the two of them would work in the darkroom.

The move from Albany to Atlanta with four children was an adventure for the Busbee family. Jan, who was twenty at the time, was given the task of transporting Sam, the family dog, from Albany to Atlanta. Not accustomed to driving on the interstate or in Atlanta traffic, Jan found herself in the wrong lane as she approached the I-75/I-85 split on the north side of the city. She swerved across several lanes of traffic, a move that tossed Sam across the car and into the dashboard. Having been given a tranquilizer for the trip, Sam, unscathed, did not even notice the maneuver. Sam was so sedated, Jan recalled, that when she arrived at the mansion, two state troopers had to carry him into the house.[9]

George Busbee Jr. (known as Buz) recalled the sharp contrasts of life at the mansion.

> At 19, I found myself living at the Governor's Mansion and working at a gas station during the week, and driving to Albany on weekends to see Tammy (now my wife). These contrasting experiences are what I remember most while living there. One minute I am in blue jean overalls pumping gas for $2 an hour; the next I was running home to get cleaned up and go to a dinner or reception in the ballroom with Prince Charles or attend the party after the premier of *Sharky's Machine* with the likes of Burt Reynolds, Jim Nabors, and Jerry Reed.[10]

The Busbees worked hard to make the Governor's Mansion feel like home. Mary Beth explained, "We had a nice understanding with our staff here from the beginning that although this is a public building, it is our home and there are certain areas like the upstairs that are off-limits to people except when they have a reason to be there." But living in the mansion was not "like living in any other home." As Ron Martz of the *Atlanta Journal-Constitution* explained, "There was the round-the-clock security

Busbee campaign button, 1974. *Courtesy Richard B. Russell Library for Political Research and Studies, University of Georgia.*

George Busbee in the darkroom at the mansion, 1977. *Courtesy Kenan Research Center at the Atlanta History Center.*

furnished by the Georgia State Patrol. There were the public tours of the mansion. There were the gardeners. And the butlers. And the maids. And the cooks." Mary Beth lamented that when she tried to cook a meal for her husband, she "could never find a pot small enough to cook something for just two persons." Mary Beth missed cooking for her family and added that she was looking forward to getting back into the kitchen, although she warned her husband that after their return to civilian life, "You're really going to be experimented on for a few months."[11]

A staff of eight, including two butlers, two executive porters, and four maids under the supervision of Mary Dwozan maintained the mansion during the Busbees' residency. As the *Atlanta Journal* reporter Sharon Bailey noted in 1982, "Keeping the dust off the furniture, the light bulbs changed, the doorknobs polished and fresh linens on the beds in such a showplace—which spans three floors and has 30 rooms (plus 11 full bathrooms)—might cause a quake or quiver among some. But the mansion staff takes it all in stride." Southern hospitality and great care for the mansion's collection were key features of the Busbees' tenure. Every guest was treated as if he or she was an important visitor, according to Dwozan, "whether it's King Hussein of Jordan or an American Cancer Society volunteer from Macon."

Bottles of chilled Perrier were placed in each guest's room, because the staff were aware that a "change in drinking water—even to the sanitized tap water of an American city—can upset the system of a foreigner."[12] The state china with its gold-leaf edging was always hand washed, and plates were stored between paper doilies. Although the staff observed formal protocol, they also were versatile and able to help with multiple duties. Over the course of one afternoon, Jeffrey Buppert, one of the butlers, ushered a visitor into the mansion through the front door and later shed his gold-and-black butler's jacket to help the mansion's chef, Holly Chute (then Wulfing), prepare dinner, spearing chunks of beef tenderloin and wrapping them in pastry rounds to make beef Wellington.[13]

During the Busbees' eight years at the mansion, there were "children and grandchildren spilling in and out."[14] Only Jeff, who decamped in the basement bedroom, resided in the mansion full-time for most of his father's term in office. Transitioning to the mansion and a new school in Atlanta at midyear was quite an adjustment for the teenager. Before he was sixteen and could drive, the State Troopers took him to school. Embarrassed, he would often ask them to drop him a few blocks away so he could arrive unnoticed. When asked by his classmates where he lived, Jeff replied, "West Paces Ferry Road."

The Busbee family—Jan, Mary Beth, Beth, Buz, George, and Jeff—at the mansion, ca. 1976.
Courtesy Jan Busbee Curtis.

One student queried, "Near the Governor's Mansion?" Embarrassed to reveal how near, Jeff merely answered yes. Over time, Jeff found that it was hard to hide who he was, though, and he began eventually to make friends who regularly came to the mansion to play basketball and just hang out. On one occasion, Jeff put one of his friends in the dumbwaiter in the basement and tried to send her upstairs to the kitchen. Unfortunately, she got stuck between floors.[15]

Jan was a student at Georgia State University for the first few months of her father's time in office. She lived in the Governor's Mansion in the aide's bedroom adjacent to the presidential suite and worked part-time at a jewelry store in the mall. She soon transferred to the University of Georgia. She described her experience this way: "I felt like I had the best of both worlds. I was able to enjoy a relatively normal college life, but I also enjoyed the privilege of living in the Governor's Mansion and coming home to meet interesting guests from all over the world." Upon graduation, Jan and one of her friends, Wendy, moved back to the mansion. Jan was dating her future husband, Carlton Curtis, at the time, and he would come to the gate to pick her up. Being the oldest, Beth never lived at the mansion, and Buz lived there briefly before returning to college. Both Beth and Jan got married there.[16]

Beth Busbee Wiggins Kindt, who lived in Valdosta during most of her father's tenure as governor, had the Busbees' only grandchildren at the time. Her family often visited the mansion, and her twins and later triplets were a source of great joy and anxiety. The twin boys, Patrick and Brian, born on May 29, 1979, were not allowed to play on the main floor of the mansion near the priceless antiques but were instead sequestered in the basement, "where they could ride their Big Wheels with reckless . . . abandon."[17] George and Mary Beth were fondly known as Papou and YiaYia to the grandchildren. Mary Beth and Beth often strolled the boys around the mansion grounds. Because the mansion was open to the public for tours, Beth remembered that tourists often peeked in the windows when she was feeding the twins. In the morning, the boys would wake up and run into their grandparents' bedroom to snuggle and watch cartoons before breakfast. Each afternoon, they would sit on the front steps of the mansion and wait for the governor to arrive home from work via helicopter. Papou would sometimes let them sit in the cockpit and put on the pilot's headphones. After they

Chef Holly Chute with George Busbee, ca. 1980. *Courtesy Holly Chute.*

came inside, the twins would wrap themselves around his legs while he tried to change out of his work clothes. Afterward, he would juggle for them, let them join him for an informal tennis game, or sit in an empty box while they crawled all over him. One night when guests were arriving for a reception, Beth remembered seeing the twins peering out of the presidential suite windows and blowing kisses to the arriving guests.

When Beth learned that she was having triplets in 1982, her parents agreed to host the twins at the mansion for two separate weeks. After Stuart, Ashley, and Brooke were born on May 8, 1982, all seven members of Beth's family visited the mansion. On the last day of their stay, Beth recalled, the twins and the triplets had their picture taken on the curved staircase with U.S. senator Sam Nunn, who was visiting the governor.[18]

The Busbees used the Georgia Governor's Mansion very much like the U.S. president uses Camp David. As Mary Beth explained, "The governor's mansion is an extension of the governor's office, a place where he can meet in a home-like atmosphere with business leaders, legislators, and constituents. We also used the mansion as a place to receive and lodge distinguished visitors of Georgia."[19] Dinners and special events at the mansion included a wide range of guests, including Queen Beatrix of the Netherlands, Prince Charles of England, King Hussein of Jordan, and China's vice premier Deng Xiaoping, as well as the actors Burt Reynolds and Jerry

George and the twins in the ballroom, ca. 1981.
Courtesy Beth Busbee Kindt.

The Busbees' twin grandchildren at the front door, ca. 1981.
Courtesy Beth Busbee Kindt.

The twins in the helicopter, ca. 1981. *Courtesy Beth Busbee Kindt.*

Reed. Mary Beth noted, "I am sure we converted a few non-Southerners to the virtues of grits. One visitor from far away was so taken with them he asked, 'What tree do grits come from?' I suppressed a grin and replied, 'A corn tree.'"[20]

George Busbee's aide Cecil Phillips recalled:

I was at the mansion at least two or three times a week for private meetings. They might be over breakfast, lunch, or dinner. The mansion was their home, but it was also a place to help do business and promote interests throughout the state. They used the mansion as a venue; they had people over all the time. Some events were formal, but just as often they had informal parties or gatherings that were used to help people get to know each other. We had staff parties in the ballroom. They never acted like they were living in a museum. It was their home, a place where they entertained and worked.[21]

Governor Busbee started the tradition of Red and Green Carpet Tours to attract industry and finance to the state. Scheduled around the time of the Masters Golf Tournament, the opening and closing events were held at the mansion.[22] George occasionally had surprise visits. One night, Governor Jerry Brown of California arrived at 11:30 p.m. to chat with the governor and did not leave until 2:00 a.m. Ovid R. Davis, a senior vice president at the Coca-Cola Company, arrived a week early for a benefit breakfast. The governor, who was still in his pajamas, was surprised to see Davis, but he invited him into the library. George recalled, "[We] sat around and talked for a while until we finally discovered something was wrong. Finally, I said to him: 'As long as you're here, let's go in and eat.' So we did."[23]

In 1975, the Department of Industry and Trade worked hard to promote Georgia as a site for filmmaking. On July 18, the department asked George and Mary Beth to hold a small dinner party for Burt Reynolds, who was scouting locations for his film *Gator*. "At the appointed time," Mary Beth noted, "Burt and his producer arrived . . . Burt said we were missing one member of his party, and asked the cook to put dinner on hold. About that time, in walked Barbi Benton, the entertainer and former Playboy bunny. I could tell by the look on Burt's face that she was *not* the missing guest. She was in Atlanta for an engagement at Six Flags, and was crashing our party." The group finally gave up on

Sam Nunn with the Busbee grandchildren, 1982. *Courtesy Beth Busbee Kindt.*

the last guest and began eating dinner. As they began the main course, they heard a commotion in the foyer that made its way to the dining room: "The double doors flew open and in strode Burt's good friend and movie sidekick Jerry Reed, holding a big sack of Krystal hamburgers. Throwing his leg over the back of a chair, he said, 'Don't worry about me, folks, I brought my own supper.'" It was "an informal evening," Mary Beth recalled, adding, "I learned at times there is nothing one can do but roll with the punches."[24]

During a later visit, Mary Beth recalled that Reynolds and two other guests were "dumped onto the 19th century French Aubusson carpet" when the couch they were sitting on collapsed. The legs on the valuable, 1815 antique simply snapped under the weight. According to the *Atlanta Journal* reporter Sharon Bailey, Reynolds jokingly threatened to sue the governor. "We had a good time with it," said Sharon Greene, personal secretary to the first lady.[25]

On June 24, 1975, Secretary of State Kissinger was scheduled to come to breakfast with Peter White,

president of the Southern Center for International Studies; Dean Rusk, the former secretary of state; and Rusk's wife. Mary Beth recalled:

> Shortly after their arrival, I slipped out of the room to check on the status of breakfast. As I passed by the elevator, off stepped three young ladies who were supposed to be in class at that moment—at The University of Georgia seventy miles away. Our youngest daughter and her roommates had shown up, unannounced and uninvited. . . . They had gotten up at 5 a.m. for the drive from Athens "just to see Secretary Kissinger come through the mansion gates." They were upstairs with their faces pressed against the windows when Dr. Kissinger arrived. They had gotten all dressed up to get a peek at our guest, so I took them in and introduced them. Dr. Kissinger was delighted by the girls' unexpected appearance.[26]

Upon learning that the girls had skipped class in order to see him, Kissinger "wrote and signed an excuse for each one," though they did not get used: "Needless to say, those excuses wound up in the girls' scrapbooks instead of on their professors' desks."[27]

Breakfast with Henry Kissinger, 1975. *Courtesy Jan Busbee Curtis.*

One memorable visit in October 1976 involved Minister President Hans Filbinger, who served as a governor of the state of Baden-Wurttemberg, West Germany. The weather was cold, and Minister Filbinger and his wife had a separate thermostat in the presidential suite. Each morning at breakfast when asked how they slept, the couple replied that they needed more blankets. Unsure why they were so cold, Mrs. Busbee recalled: "After they left, we checked the thermostat in the presidential suite for a possible malfunction and discovered why they needed so many blankets. Our hale and hearty German friends had turned off the heat in their room and slept with all their windows open. It must have been toasty under all those blankets, but the getting in and out had to be a little brisk."[28]

In December 1976, the Governor's Mansion became a different kind of headquarters. Before the presidential election of 1976, Jimmy Carter used the mansion, at Busbee's invitation, to interview possible vice presidential candidates.[29] After the election, Carter recalled: "I went to Atlanta and borrowed from Governor George Busbee an office and a couple of rooms in the governor's mansion. From that familiar setting I conducted my final interviews with those I was considering for Cabinet posts."[30] Mary Beth Busbee wrote of this time: "President-elect Carter made no announcements to the media during the Cabinet selection process. This, of course, fed the curiosity of reporters and television news crews, who stood in a pack at the mansion gates trying to catch a glimpse of the final contenders as they drove through. The crush of media people made it almost impossible for anyone to enter or leave the mansion grounds. Knowing the president-elect faced years of eating fancy gourmet meals, we fed him simple Southern meals during his visit."[31]

According to Mary Beth, although all their guests at the mansion were interesting, the most exciting "by a healthy margin" was His Royal Highness Prince Charles, Prince of Wales. Prince Charles's visit to Georgia in October 1977 was the "first ever made to the Southeast by British royalty," recalled Mary Beth. The prince stayed at the mansion for two days and nights. The Busbees extended to Prince Charles their usual southern hospitality, and Mary Beth noted, "Our guest of honor was not intimidated by the array of 'strange' foods on the buffet. He served himself generously—until he came to fried okra. He warily put two pieces of okra on his plate. As he walked back to his place at the

dining table, he popped a piece into his mouth, whirled around, and served himself some more."[32]

Jan Busbee Curtis recalled why the newspapers showed particular interest in the prince's visit:

The Prince was still unmarried, so all his travel in the U.S. was covered by the British tabloids, always speculating that there might be a Princess Grace moment where he would fall in love with an American woman. On the first evening, my parents hosted a small dinner at the mansion for Prince Charles and our immediate family. My oldest sister was married, but I was not, and the tabloids had already started to speculate. My father, anticipating the potential awkwardness, asked me to invite my boyfriend, Carlton Curtis, to the dinner. Carlton showed up and was nervous. He knocked on the front door of the mansion and when my father opened it, he said, "Governor, I'm the pauper. Where is the prince?" My Dad loved that story and told it for years. Carlton and I have been married now more than 35 years and still laugh about that moment.[33]

George and Mary Beth Busbee with Prince Charles, 1977. *Courtesy Jan Busbee Curtis.*

That same year, the Busbees hosted His Majesty King Hussein, King of Jordan, who had been in Washington meeting with President Jimmy Carter. Throughout the visit, Mary Beth recalled, "King Hussein was accompanied by the commander-in-chief of the Jordan Armed Forces, who served as his personal bodyguard." No other guest was as "security conscious" as King Hussein, noted Mary Beth, adding that the king's "bodyguard selected fruit for him from the family fruit bowl in the kitchen, instead of from the fruit bowl we had placed in the presidential suite . . . apparently as a precaution against poisoning."[34]

Joan Mondale, wife of Vice President Walter Mondale, was witness to the destruction of one of the mansion's precious antiques during her visit in May 1978. In Atlanta to help promote the arts, she spent the night of May 2 at the mansion. While Mary Beth was showing her around the presidential suite, a gust of wind came through the open window, slammed the door shut, and knocked a nineteenth-century vase off a table. It crashed to the marble floor into pieces. Without missing a beat, Mondale ran to her cosmetic bag, found two cosmetic brushes, and, along with Mary Beth, got on her hands and knees to sweep up every shard of porcelain. The vase was later restored.[35]

The annual dinner for legislators and their spouses at the Governor's Mansion was a special treat, and the 1975 dinner was particularly memorable. As the first lady later recounted:

> Feeling quite confident now with the menu selection for the evening, I watched contentedly as our guests began to eat their baked Alaska. Suddenly I noticed something strange. On some faces a look of pure pleasure—on others a look of confusion and a certain pucker of the lips. I tasted my dessert and realized, to my complete horror, that some of the baked Alaska had been made with salt instead of sugar . . . George went up to the microphone and said, "You are not being poisoned. I want you to at least have a chance to pass my legislative programs. If this had been intentional, I would have seen to it that only our beloved Speaker of the House, Tom Murphy, got a dessert made with salt."[36]

The mansion staff, while "capable of creating the most formal of dinners," was "also adept at putting on delicious, yet informal buffets," noted Mary Beth. One such event was the annual party for the Washington-based aides to Georgia's senators and representatives. They were organized as casual affairs with "a relaxed atmosphere in which various state department officials could put a face with a name for the congressional aides with whom they usually dealt by long-distance telephone." One year Mary Beth decided to make the event a "nostalgia party which had all of the elements of the rock-and-rolling fifties, right down to the jukebox." According to Mary Beth, the governor "balked when we suggested that he dress like 'The Fonz.' George didn't object to the character—he just didn't know who 'The Fonz' was." Jeff gave his father a "briefing" on *Happy Days* and Fonzie, and the governor finally agreed to dress the part. He donned a white T-shirt and a leather jacket with "The Gov" emblazoned across the chest. Writing about the event in 1986, Mary Beth noted, "Who had the best time of all? You guessed it—'The Fonz.'"[37]

Buz recalled another occasion notable for its lack of formality: "When someone is in your home all the time like the mansion staff and the security detail with the state patrol, you get to know them on a personal level."[38] Many of the mansion staff members who served the meals and helped take care of the mansion were state prisoners, and Buz remembered an impromptu party that took place after one of the big dinners at the mansion. "Everyone was gone and the staff was cleaning up. Tammy [his girlfriend at the time] and I grabbed some cocktails and a radio and busted the rug while they were cleaning up. Pretty soon, no one was cleaning and they were showing us how to really dance! The mansion manager and troopers (who were waiting for them to finish so they could take them back to prison) probably didn't appreciate it but they let us have 'our' party."[39]

Buz recounted an event involving a golf cart that got him in trouble with his father. Buz and his friends "were racing around the grounds and went under a low-hanging limb on a magnolia that was over the sidewalk." The results were predictable:

> We went flying down the sidewalk and hit the limb, which tore the hard plastic roof completely off the golf cart. Being a carefree and stupid teenager, I parked the golf cart in the garage and propped the roof back up on the cart so it would appear fine. Daddy was a photographer and had a darkroom behind the greenhouse. The next morning he jumped into the golf cart to go to the darkroom, put it in reverse, hit the gas, and the roof collapsed on his head. That is probably when I decided to move back to Albany.[40]

One of the most frightening things to happen at the Governor's Mansion occurred just three months into the family's residency. On the morning of March 24, 1975, a tornado ripped through Buckhead, killing three people and injuring dozens of others. Although no one was injured at the Governor's Mansion, the tornado tore a path through the property, hitting the front of the building and uprooting fifty trees. The cost of the damage to the mansion exceeded half a million dollars.[41] Mary Beth, who was home at the time, recalled the event:

> George and I and our younger son, Jeff, were home when the tornado came through in the early hours of the morning. . . . Within seconds, scores of beautiful hundred-year-old oak trees were reduced to splinters. Others were totally uprooted. The huge columns on the front side of the mansion were ripped off and deposited throughout the surrounding area. The roof was heavily damaged. Debris littered the sculptured gardens. Jan heard the news on her car radio minutes before a state trooper pulled her over to tell her we were OK. As soon as telephone communications were restored, we called the rest of our family to let them know we were unhurt.[42]

Jeff had returned early that morning from a spring break trip and arrived around three in the morning with a friend. They left their Jeep in the front driveway and came into the house to go to sleep. Several hours later, Sam, the family dog, began pacing frantically in the basement bedroom where Jeff and his friend slept. The next thing he knew, he heard a sound like a freight train and saw debris flying around. One of the columns fell and covered the small basement window. After the tornado hit, the family went out to survey the damage, and the Jeep was surrounded by downed trees, pieces of the roof and columns, but it was unharmed. Jeff recalled that his father was the first person outside and took his camera to document the damage. The troopers on duty saw the tornado come up the driveway of the mansion and did not have time to warn the first family. Later, Jeff heard that one of the troopers that night began to confess all his sins to one of the prisoners who worked in the guardhouse. Unharmed, both men were found holding onto the toilet.[43] Governor Busbee later commented, "It only lasted about two minutes, but a world of damage was done in that two minutes."[44]

Back of the mansion after the tornado, 1975. *Courtesy Georgia Governor's Mansion.*

Governor's mansion after the 1975 tornado. *Courtesy Georgia Governor's Mansion.*

Mansion grounds after the tornado. *Courtesy Georgia Governor's Mansion.*

Seven of the columns that surrounded the mansion were knocked down. Replacement columns were ordered from the company in Ohio that had made the original columns less than a decade earlier. Georgia Building Authority director Steve Polk explained, "They cost $1,200 apiece when the mansion was built (in 1967), but I have no idea what they will cost today." Commenting on the planned repairs to the grounds, Polk noted, "When we get through, it will be prettier than ever."[45]

Beth, who was in South Georgia, was expecting her mother to join her at a bridal shower when she heard the news. As she explained, "Once I found out that no one was hurt, then it hit me that this might destroy our plans to have the wedding on the mansion grounds. But the mansion staff and the grounds crew worked like crazy to get things back in order so we could have the wedding there."[46] The wedding was held on June 7 without incident.

The mansion, more than anything else, was a home for the Busbees. Holidays were especially important. Jan remembered, "Our family was big, close, and gregarious. My mother was the ultimate hostess and she loved having the extended Busbee clan for Thanksgiving dinner at the mansion. Our father's two brothers and two sisters and their children joined us each year. It gave our parents great pleasure to gather everyone together on this one day. The mansion staff used our family recipes to prepare the same meal that my mother had prepared for twenty-five years."[47] The first year that the family was in the mansion, things did not go as planned. With forty people expected for dinner, Pearline, the cook, walked out after a scheduling disagreement with the mansion manager, Mary Dwozan. While most of the meal had been prepared, there was still work to be done. Mary Beth recalled:

I've made a lot of dressing in my time, but never for forty people. Mary and I stood in the kitchen in total dismay, wondering how to tackle such a large amount of dressing. In walked my then twenty-year-old son, Buz. He marched up to the sink and began to "scrub up," as if for surgery. Soon Buz was presiding over the most enormous mixing bowl any of us had ever seen. He crumbled cornbread and biscuits into the bowl as though he really knew what he was doing (which, of course, he didn't). As Buz mixed, Mary and I poured broth. Buz was literally up to his elbows in dressing. Together the three of us finished the dressing and got

it into the oven before the rest of the family even knew about the mini-crisis in the kitchen.[48]

Christmas at the mansion was a much more subdued affair, with just the immediate family. Over the eight years that the Busbees lived in the mansion, their family grew from six to thirteen through marriages and the addition of the twins and triplets.

The swimming pool was an important addition to the mansion, though its planning and construction were orchestrated without Governor Busbee's knowledge. While the governor was traveling, Steve Polk of the Georgia Building Authority ordered work to begin on the pool. Polk "decided Busbee's absence was an opportune time to start [the] long-planned—and long put off—swimming pool." Knowing that the governor would think it too extravagant, Polk said, "By the time he got back, I wanted that hole to be so deep that we couldn't back out."[49] Cecil Phillips, who oversaw Busbee's international outreach, remembered, "Busbee did not want to be perceived as someone who was frivolous. And a swimming pool would not have played well in the public when people were looking for jobs."[50] By the time the governor returned from his trip, "the hole was just too deep," according to the *Atlanta Constitution*.[51] Mary Beth, who regularly swam at the YMCA in Albany, probably used the pool the most. George played tennis, but loved to swim with the grandchildren. All the children remember him cannonballing in the pool with the twins.[52]

After visiting Japan on a trade mission, the governor invited the press corps to the mansion for a reception. Phillips recounted what happened next:

Rick Allen, the political columnist for the Atlanta paper, got thrown in the pool. Now Rick and Bill Shipp, also a political commentator for the *Atlanta Journal-Constitution,* frequently needled Busbee. The governor did not like his middle name—Dekle—so when Shipp wanted to get his goat, he printed "Governor G. Dekle Busbee" in the papers. Rick Allen must have written something recently that irritated the governor, so when Governor Busbee ambled past him by the pool, he tapped Allen with his arm and the reporter went into the water. There is a photograph that captured the moment showing a drink is coming out of his hand and his sport coat flew open.[53]

Busbee's sense of humor was on full display that day.

The twins enjoying the swimming pool, ca. 1982. *Courtesy Beth Busbee Kindt.*

The mansion's chef, Holly Chute, recalled that upon returning from trade missions to Japan, Governor Busbee always wanted a good southern meal. His favorite was fried chicken and black-eyed peas. After one trip, Holly decided to play a joke on him: "I made some fake sushi, with the seaweed and rice and a large piece of raw scrod carved into the shape of a rose. The governor, always one to play along, said, 'You don't think I can eat this?' He popped that scrod in his mouth and immediately spit it out and took a big swig of his scotch."[54]

George and Mary Beth loved their time in the mansion, but acknowledged the lack of privacy. Jeff remembered, "I recall Daddy on a Saturday morning getting into his car and taking off to a local sporting goods store without the ever-present security. They would jump in the car and follow him."[55] To help maintain as normal a family life as possible, Mary Beth allowed the staff to go home on the weekends, and the family would then cook meals together. That was one small step toward keeping everyone grounded. Other incidents had the same effect. Tourists regularly walked around the mansion's porch during visiting hours, and one day a tourist came to the window and began taking pictures. Mary Beth Busbee paused and smiled politely for the camera, only to be shooed away. The photographer wanted a picture of the cook making biscuits.[56]

Toward the end of his time in office, on one Saturday in January 1983, George walked into a Duluth grocery store alone, dressed in his soiled work clothes. When he walked to the counter, a group of teenage girls recognized him and said, "Oh, governor, you're going to be one of us before long."[57] Upon leaving office, with "an enviable record of progress and stability," some of his close friends bought him a Mercedes sedan.[58] Being chauffeured for eight years had left George's driving skills a little rusty. He got into the driver's seat at the Capital City Club and promptly turned the wrong way onto a one-way street.[59]

In an effort to help make the transition easier on the incoming governor, Joe Frank Harris, the Busbees moved from the mansion before Christmas, allowing the Harrises to enjoy the holiday in their new home.[60] George and Mary Beth moved to a four-bedroom house on seven acres in Gwinnett County with a view of the Chattahoochee River. He became a partner in the law firm King & Spalding. Reflecting on his long career, Busbee said, "I'd like to be remembered for two things. One that I worked hard. I tried. I wasn't the smartest man that's been in this chair, but I tried as hard. And certainly I'd like to be remembered as having as much integrity as anybody that's ever sat in this chair, and that I would have no scandal or blemish in my administration."[61] George died in July 2004 at the age of seventy-six, and Mary Beth passed away in March 2012 at the age of eighty-five.

Harris family Christmas card portrait, 1983. *Courtesy Elizabeth and Joe Frank Harris.*

CHAPTER SEVEN

Not in Our Wildest Dreams

THE HARRISES

Joe Frank Harris was the second Georgia governor to enjoy two terms in office, following George Busbee. Once called "a Democrat with the soul of a Republican businessman," he moved into the mansion in 1983, as a forty-seven-year-old executive of a concrete company in Cartersville. Born in Bartow County, Joe Frank graduated from the University of Georgia in March 1958 with a bachelor's degree in business administration. He joined the Air National Guard at age seventeen, served six months of active duty in the army, and finished his military service in the army reserves before returning to Cartersville. With his brother, Fred, he joined his father's family business, Harris Cement Products, Inc. Joe Frank met Elizabeth Carlock, his future wife, in 1960 at Faith United Methodist Church in Cartersville, where Elizabeth's father was the pastor. They were married a year later on June 25, 1961, shortly after Elizabeth graduated with a degree in science from LaGrange College. Joe Frank recalled that Elizabeth's "father gave her away and then walked around the altar to perform the ceremony."[1] The Harrises' son, Joe, was born in March 1964. One month later, at the behest of his friends, Joe Frank decided to run for state representative. He was elected to the Georgia House of Representatives in November 1964 and went on to serve nine consecutive terms before running for governor in 1982. Joe Frank, who never lost an election, defeated Republican Robert H. Bell to become Georgia's seventy-eighth governor.

The Harrises elected to host their inauguration outdoors on the capitol steps on January 11, 1983, and Joe Frank put Elizabeth in charge of "praying for sunshine." The Georgia National Guard fired a nineteen-gun salute that was so loud that "sound waves reverberating between the Capitol and Atlanta City Hall shattered windows and scattered pigeons."[2] Before the ceremony, the Harrises hosted a prayer service at Trinity United Methodist Church. Afterward, the family had a small, private luncheon, and Joe Frank went to the governor's office to begin the Harris administration.[3] That evening the Governor's Ball was held at the Atlanta Civic Center.

The Harrises moved into the mansion a week before the swearing-in ceremony and were fortunate that Governor George Busbee and his wife, Mary Beth, agreed to orient them to their new life. "All we needed were our clothes, and we just moved right in," Joe Frank reflected later, adding, "It's a beautiful home, and we felt very

Elizabeth and Joe Frank Harris on their wedding day, June 25, 1961. *Elizabeth and Joe Frank Harris.*

we won. Young Joe remembered as a child coming on a tour group and putting his nose on the kitchen window to see the chefs. Only when I walked through the door of the Governor's Mansion did I little realize how much our lives were about to change. It was such an awesome adventure that opened the world to us, not only the state of Georgia. We knew that campaigns can go either way, and one of our friends warned us to be as prepared to lose as to win. Well, we took that to heart, and we were so prepared to lose that we didn't even talk about winning. The campaign is so costly and so tiring. You have little time to focus ahead.[7]

Elizabeth recalled one of the biggest surprises about life in the mansion: "We packed up our clothes in Cartersville and sent them to the mansion. When we arrived and went upstairs, our suitcases were all unpacked and clothes put away in drawers and closets. That was a shock. I realized I had lost all of my privacy right then and there. Maybe I would have thrown away some old underwear or a tattered nightgown. I did not expect my clothes to be on display."[8]

Living in the mansion was a very public experience, as Joe Frank explained: "There's a hidden agenda involved in the operations of the Mansion that the public doesn't really know about. In fact, it's almost like operating a hotel. It's such a public place, and even the private residence on the top floor is not really private. You constantly have staff moving through. The custodial people are all state prisoners. You're protected by security twenty-four hours a day but have prisoners working and moving freely throughout your home. This was an adjustment, but it works well. You understand very quickly what's required and how to deal with those things."[9]

The Harrises made the mansion their home and did not spend a single night in their Cartersville home during Joe Frank's tenure as governor. Joe Frank explained, "Of course, distance was not really a factor, being only forty-one miles from Atlanta, but the demands were so great I just didn't feel I could take the time off."[10] Elizabeth, like her predecessors, took the lead in running the house. She had to oversee the schedule, special events, and the hiring and firing of staff members, all bound by the fiscal restraints set by the General Assembly. She explained the need to be very attentive to the

fortunate that the state of Georgia has that kind of facility. It's a real tool for economic development and for entertaining, especially foreign dignitaries."[4] Going into his first term, Joe Frank noted, "I knew the schedule was going to be tremendously intense and that my family was going to be deeply affected by it."[5] Prepared as the family was for their new role, there were still some surprises. During the governor's first week on the job, his car was stolen while he was downtown speaking to a group of attorneys. The vehicle, its battery missing, was eventually recovered nearby.[6]

Mary Beth Busbee agreed to give Elizabeth a tour, and the new first lady was grateful for any advice. As they walked through the public and private quarters, Elizabeth began preparing for life in the family's new home. Many years later, Elizabeth recalled:

> Never, never in our wildest dreams did we ever dream we would live at the mansion. As the campaign was winding down, we never even had a discussion about where we would live if

Harris campaign button, 1982.
Courtesy Elizabeth and Joe Frank Harris.

Inaugural Program

January 11, 1983—Washington Street Entrance—The State Capitol

PRE-INAUGURAL MUSIC .... *Cartersville High School Band*

11:30 A.M.

POSTINGS OF COLORS *(stand)* .... *Georgia National Guard*

THE NATIONAL ANTHEM *(stand)* .... THE REVEREND ROBERT J. BEAVERS

JOINT SESSION .... *called to order by* THE HONORABLE THOMAS B. MURPHY, *Speaker, House of Representatives*

INVOCATION *(stand)* .... THE REVEREND ERNEST D. CARLOCK

RECOGNITION OF STATE OFFICIALS AND DISTINGUISHED GUESTS .... THE HONORABLE THOMAS B. MURPHY, *Speaker, House of Representatives*

PRESENTATION .... *of* THE HONORABLE GEORGE D. BUSBEE, *Governor*

DELIVERY OF THE GREAT SEAL OF GEORGIA TO GOVERNOR .... THE HONORABLE MAX CLELAND, *Secretary of State*

12:00 NOON

ADMINISTRATION OF OATH OF OFFICE TO GOVERNOR .... THE HONORABLE GEORGE T. SMITH, *Associate Justice*
Supreme Court of Georgia

HONORS - 19 GUN SALUTE *(stand)* .... *Cartersville High School Band*

DELIVERY OF GREAT SEAL OF GEORGIA TO SECRETARY OF STATE .... THE HONORABLE JOE FRANK HARRIS, *Governor*

INAUGURAL ADDRESS .... THE HONORABLE JOE FRANK HARRIS, *Governor*

ADMINISTRATION OF OATH OF OFFICE TO LIEUTENANT GOVERNOR .... THE HONORABLE EDWARD H. JOHNSON, *Judge*
State Court of Fulton County

REMARKS .... THE HONORABLE ZELL B. MILLER, *Lieutenant Governor*

RETIRING OF COLORS *(stand)* .... *Georgia National Guard*

BENEDICTION *(stand)* .... THE REVEREND JIMMY ROGERS

DISSOLUTION OF JOINT SESSION .... THE HONORABLE ZELL B. MILLER, *Lieutenant Governor*

POST-INAUGURAL MUSIC .... *Cass Comprehensive High School Band*

1:00 P.M. to 4:00 P.M.

TOURS .... *The State Capitol and Executive Mansion*

9:00 P.M. to 12:00 P.M.

CELEBRATION GALA AND INAUGURAL BALL .... *The Atlanta Civic Center, Atlanta, Georgia*

Honorary Escorts
Campaign County Coordinators
The Old Guard of The Gate City Guard and The Gate City Guard

Inaugural program,
January 11, 1983.
Courtesy Bartow
History Museum.

Inauguration night,
January 11, 1983.
Courtesy Elizabeth and
Joe Frank Harris.

budget: "We recorded every meal we ate as a family. We had to cover all of those costs. The state paid for state events, but we had to cover family meals. It was a bookkeeping nightmare. Watergate was still fresh in people's minds, and we wanted to be very careful."[11]

Each week, Holly Chute, the mansion's chef, worked with Elizabeth to plan the family dinners. Holly was a classically trained chef, but Elizabeth proudly declares that she taught Holly how to make a good rump roast. The Harrises liked simple fare, and getting used to having a chef prepare meals for them took a little bit of practice. Elizabeth explained:

> I would plan the menus a week ahead. Joe Frank was a meat-and-potatoes guy. But I will never forget when, before the first meal, Holly asked me what he liked. Well, chocolate is one of his favorites. So she made a triple chocolate cake that was so rich that you could hardly eat more than one bite. Joe Frank joked with her that she needed to tone down the chocolate. He tried to be healthy, and he stayed the same weight while we were in office. I can't say the same. I got kind of fluffy. You just eat so much that it's hard to stay fit.[12]

Before major events for heads of state or special guests, Elizabeth and the staff would plan menus and let Joe Frank review them. The week before, she would ask the kitchen staff to cook the entire meal so they could test the recipes. Those events, which often involved mansion staff members as tasters, were fondly remembered. To try to remain healthy in the face of all the rich food, the Harrises put exercise equipment on the bottom floor of the mansion.

Scott Peacock, who followed Holly Chute as chef, recalled sitting in the kitchen and planning the night's menu for the first couple soon after he arrived. Elizabeth mentioned that she wanted "something nice and light for dessert." Peacock offered, "How about angel food cake, with fresh fruit and lemon curd or some sorbet and freshly baked cookies?" to which Elizabeth responded, "No, let's have something light and delicious. Something really good, you know, like Jell-O." Peacock reflected, "I was new at the mansion and didn't know the first lady very well yet, but I was certain she must be joking. After all, I was a chef! Surely she wasn't asking me—the one who made for her elaborate desserts, often crowned with golden clouds of spun sugar—to demean myself in such a 'housewifey' way. But she wasn't joking. In fact, she was quite serious. That night, I 'prepared' my first ever Jell-O."[13]

The mansion had some secrets that the first family came to know and appreciate. As Elizabeth explained, "There was the buzzer under the carpet in the family dining room so you could notify the staff when you needed attention. Our guests always wondered why, when we needed something, it just miraculously appeared. How did it all work, they pondered? When we finished, the butlers arrived at the perfect time and cleared the plates. Dessert and coffee seemed to appear just when we wanted it." Joe Frank Jr. added, "We had more fun with that buzzer. It was like magic, and Dad loved using it on guests."[14]

The Harrises also learned a lesson that many first families had discovered before them—there is no such thing as an offhand comment. During a trip to Ireland, Elizabeth was sitting with the chief executive of the House of Waterford, and she commented on some of the crystal pieces, noting that the Governor's Mansion did not have any iced-tea glasses that matched their current pattern. She later recalled what happened about three months later: "These huge boxes from Waterford [came] to the State of Georgia, and to my surprise there were forty-eight glasses, just as I had mentioned. I just made a passing comment, and that was enough." Another time, she mentioned to Steve Polk of the Georgia Building Authority that the greenhouse should be a working greenhouse that could cultivate plants around the mansion's grounds. And so that happened, as she recalled: "We left for a trip, and when we returned on Sunday the greenhouse was empty and ready to be transformed. You had to be careful because everyone wanted to accommodate you."[15]

On the rare occasion when they did not have a special event or overnight guests, the Harrises made the most of their time at the mansion. Elizabeth occasionally cooked, Joe Frank nearby happily working as her assistant. She played tennis and sometimes invited friends from an Atlanta Lawn Tennis Association team from Cartersville to play at the mansion. Joe Jr. also played regularly. On one occasion, he had a friend from the University of Georgia join him, with his black Labrador retriever in tow. The dog was roaming around the mansion grounds and surprised the first lady. Elizabeth remembered, "I was outside searching for native plants in the woods. I was bending over one plant and all of the sudden this large bark came from behind me. It was so loud that it scared me to death. He had snuck up behind me, and I took a tumble head over heels."[16] The

Place setting with the new Waterford crystal, July 1987. *Courtesy Christopher Oquendo.*

mansion was a place for all kinds of recreation. Joe Jr. recalled, "I learned to scuba dive in the pool, and former Governor George Busbee came back and took the class that Senator Peter Banks taught. I also played a lot of basketball, but would sometimes look up and see tour groups peering down. You really were living in a fishbowl."[17]

The mansion's collections were something that all the first families had admired, and Elizabeth played a significant role in adding to the book collection. On their first night in their new home, the first couple toured the house after dinner. In the late 1960s, the Fine Arts Committee had purchased books related to Georgia history for the library, but the family sitting room was filled with random titles that had been purchased by the yard just to fill the shelves. Elizabeth decided to help build the mansion's collection by adding books by Georgia authors. She wrote to some authors directly and also asked her friend the journalist Celestine Sibley to write a column about the idea. Her efforts paid off, and books came pouring in from the public. Elizabeth's idea helped the collection acquire many first editions and autographed copies, including a treasured copy of *Cold Sassy Tree*. Its author, Olive Ann Burns, gave Elizabeth a draft of the manuscript for review in advance of its 1984 publication. Other authors who contributed signed copies of their works included Eugenia Price, Athos Menaboni, Terry Kay, and Stuart Woods. The Georgia Public Library Service helped catalogue the collection, which includes a first edition

of Margaret Mitchell's *Gone with the Wind*, Erskine Caldwell's limited-edition autobiography *With All My Might*, and a 1797 book titled *The Natural History of the Rarer Lepidopterous Insects of Georgia*. Lamar Veatch, head of the state's library system, explained, "These are treasures owned by the state. This is really good for Georgia history and good for the state of Georgia."[18]

As governor, Joe Frank worked closely with the international community, especially Japan, to bring businesses to Georgia. In 1986, during his first term as governor, Crown Prince Akihito was invited to stay at the mansion, but an illness prevented him from coming. Later that year, Joe Frank and Elizabeth were able to visit the prince in Japan. The crown prince became emperor toward the end of the Harrises' tenure, and he visited the mansion during Zell Miller's time there. The Harrises' favorite guest was Billy Graham, who came to the mansion for an event for the Democratic National Convention. Elizabeth recounts the story of how he came to Georgia: "Joe Frank and I were talking about the event, and we began to discuss who should do the blessing. Joe Frank said maybe we could get Billy Graham. To which I replied, 'Sure, maybe we could have the Pope do the benediction.' Well, Billy Graham did come, but we never got the Pope."[19] Joe Jr. talked about the impact that the Graham visit had on him: "This was one of the highlights of my time in the mansion. I asked him so many questions, including, 'What do you do when you run out of ideas of things to preach

Harris family Thanksgiving gathering, 1990. *Courtesy Elizabeth and Joe Frank Harris.*

Billy Graham giving Bibles to the first couple, 1987. *Courtesy Elizabeth and Joe Frank Harris.*

Steve Polk at the mansion during Christmas, c. 1983. *Courtesy Elizabeth and Joe Frank Harris.*

about?' To which he replied, 'I go ask my wife.'"[20] Other guests included Erskine Caldwell, Princess Anne, the International Olympic Committee, state governors, and national officeholders.

Like so many first families before them, the Harrises celebrated Christmas in grand style, with a formal tree lighting that was open to the public. The event included choral groups and readings from the Bible. The mansion was then opened for visitors so that they could see the elegant decorations. One year, a young girl from a Brownie Scout troop marched up to Joe Frank and asked, "If you're as rich as they say you are, how rich are you?" Joe Frank tried to explain to her that the house "really belongs to you and all the people of Georgia." The girl seemed puzzled, Joe Frank recalled, and he was relieved when her troop leader said, "Don't worry, Governor, I'll explain it to her." Later, as the scout troop prepared to leave, the little girl shook Joe Frank's hand and said, "Governor, you take care of my house now, you hear?"[21]

Early in their tenure in the mansion, Elizabeth mentioned to Steve Polk that she thought a live nativity scene would be a nice addition to the Christmas celebration. Overnight, he gathered donkeys, goats, and other animals and built a crèche with a manger. The plan worked until the goats ate the clothes off the mannequins.[22] On Christmas Day, the Harrises returned to Cartersville and allowed the staff to celebrate with their families. For Thanksgiving, though, the mansion was the site of a family reunion. Both families gathered for a feast, and Joe Jr. would always host a touch football game on the lawn with his friends from the University of Georgia, much to the delight of those driving along West Paces Ferry Road.[23]

Elizabeth Harris was well known for her love of gardens, which she credited to living in ten different Georgia towns as the daughter of a Methodist minister. She loved the outdoors and believed that "the grounds of the Governor's Mansion should display something for natives to be proud of and give visiting dignitaries an impression of Georgia horticulture and plants."[24] A number of people and organizations supported her efforts, including Jim Gibbs and Steve Murray with Gibbs Landscape Company, Pete Pike of Pike Nurseries, Bill Barrick of Callaway Gardens, the Garden Clubs of Georgia, the Rhododendron Society, Rose Society, and other individuals who donated time and resources to the care of the grounds.[25] Each year, she gave her husband a tree that was to be planted on the mansion grounds. Joe

The Elizabeth Carlock Harris rose garden, 2014. *Courtesy Christopher Oquendo.*

Frank recalled, "The word went out and donations of trees came in, and she planted many kinds of trees. . . . One year the peach crop was so great, she recruited every available staff person, troopers included, to peel peaches for the freezer. These were enjoyed at many an elegant dinner."[26] Elizabeth advised the staff on tending the vegetable garden and was a particular authority on tomatoes. A rich blend of beans, squash, okra, strawberries, and raspberries often graced the mansion's dinner table. After walking the grounds, she sometimes left notes for the grounds crew to trim a hedge, cut back some honeysuckle, or clear a walkway. Later in the Harris administration, a ramp was added to improve access for mobility-impaired visitors.

Staff members created a rose garden in Elizabeth's honor in 1983, and they surprised her with a plaque that read, "This garden is dedicated to the glory of God in honor of Elizabeth Carlock Harris—1983."[27] The staff often found her working in the garden in the evenings, which became a source of relaxation for her after a long day. She would take faded blooms, dry them in the mansion's boiler room, and make them into potpourri sachets, which she distributed during their travels to Europe and Japan.[28] She also gave those sachets to special guests or to the mansion volunteers as hostess gifts. Every Monday, Elizabeth sent fresh roses to the capitol

Elizabeth Harris in the mansion's rose garden, 1983.
Courtesy Elizabeth and Joe Frank Harris.

via the state troopers. Elizabeth created a small, wild retreat in the woods that had "tall trees, cool shade, and the sound of real spring water cascading over a rock wall."[29] Those gardens remain a part of the mansion grounds.

The Harrises' son, Joe, proposed to his girlfriend, Brooke Gurley, on the mansion grounds. Unbeknownst to her, weeks earlier he had asked her father for permission after the two of them had taken her to the Atlanta airport for a trip she was taking

Joe Frank Harris Jr. and Brooke Gurley after the proposal at the mansion, 1989.
Courtesy Joe Frank and Brooke Harris.

to Boston. On November 18, 1988, a cold fall evening, Joe persuaded Brooke to tour the grounds on a moonlit walk after an event. She had forgotten her coat, so he borrowed his mother's white cashmere coat for the stroll, and they walked down the spiral staircase and out the front door. Brooke recalled the beautiful full moon and their conversation regarding their first blind date during the walk. He detailed his plans: "I had in mind that we would walk around the driveway, toward the tennis courts, and end up at the gazebo. I got down on my knees and I proposed to her by the swing. Then I presented the ring, and I pulled out the flashlight that I had hidden in the leaves earlier that day. We went in to tell my parents, and I wanted to get a picture to capture the moment. So we walked back to the gazebo with my parents to take pictures."[30] On the walk back, Brooke remembered, "I stopped at every light that lined the driveway to admire the ring. It was so exciting."[31] After Joe Jr. graduated from the University of Georgia Law School and joined the Atlanta firm of Kilpatrick & Cody, he and Brooke married at Oak Grove United Methodist Church in Decatur. Both the rehearsal dinner and the reception (for four hundred guests) were held at the mansion.

Like all the families that came before them, the Harrises enjoyed their time in the mansion, but they did not like giving up their private lives. Joe Frank once complained to a reporter that being governor "made it hard to go shopping at Rich's."[32] Elizabeth especially missed private time with her husband, and she let him know it:

Joe Frank and I didn't have much time together. We cherished meal times. After living here for a while, I finally one day got really frustrated. I said, "This is not working. I married you but not the state of Georgia. You're sweet to let me live here, but we need some time together." So each day, he would give me fifteen minutes in the afternoon, and we walked the grounds. Unless there was an event, that was our time together. He would always try to make it in before dinner so we could cherish it.[33]

Elizabeth used the first lady's bathroom as a sort of retreat and prayer center. She explained:

I had Post-it notes all around the mirror. They were prayer requests. I had many names on there—friends, family, staff, and even people that made me mad. Bill Shipp from the *Atlanta Journal-Constitution* was on there because he wrote such unpleasant articles about Joe Frank. Every time I saw him, I said, "Bill, I'm having

Elizabeth at the first lady's mirror where she posted prayer requests, 2014. *Courtesy Jennifer Dickey.*

to love you because I'm praying for you." I had those requests going all around that mirror over the sink. I kept it pretty full because prayer is powerful.[34]

Joe Frank was not above a few practical jokes, and he played one on Elizabeth after she purchased kudzu baskets as gifts for the Southern Governors' Conference at St. Simons Island. Joe Frank reminded her that kudzu was not an especially popular plant, but Elizabeth was determined to give a gift that reflected plants that were well known in Georgia. When Elizabeth left the mansion to run an errand, Joe Frank went to work "decorating" the place. He went into the yard and cut a large quantity of kudzu. Elizabeth recalled that when she returned home, "[There was] a kudzu vine wrapped around the downstairs railing. When I got into the elevator, there was another vine. That vine led to the bedroom, where kudzu covered the bed and touched down to the basket. Joe Frank had gone out and cut all this kudzu and strung it throughout the mansion. He said, 'I told you that if you left it alone it would continue to grow.'"[35]

Leaving the mansion after eight years was not an easy task. Elizabeth recalled, "I can't say I was ready to go, because it had all gone so fast. We all had this sudden realization that eight years were gone. I would have liked to have sat in the Brumby rockers or the gazebo more. At the very end, it felt like you were dropped out of a helicopter. We had no support staff, nobody to pick up my laundry, nobody to shop for me, nobody to cook my meals. It was a shock."[36] To ensure a smooth transition, the Harrises moved out before the next inauguration to allow Zell and Shirley Miller time to adjust to their new home. As Joe Frank explained, "Time was winding down, and we had lost our lease on the high-priced 'public housing' where we had lived for eight years. We had enjoyed living in the beautiful Governor's Mansion."[37] Joe Frank left a gift for Zell Miller on his desk that read: "To Zell Bryan Miller, 79th Governor of Georgia, Inaugural Day, January 14, 1991. May God grant you the courage, patience, and wisdom to meet the challenges you

Lieutenant Governor Zell Miller with Governor Harris, 1986. *Courtesy Kenan Research Center at the Atlanta History Center.*

face in the days ahead, and may prayer be your source of strength."[38]

The Harrises attended Miller's inauguration at Alexander Memorial Coliseum at Georgia Tech. After the ceremony, a senator from Augusta saw Joe Frank and later remarked, "You know, I saw you standing outside Alexander Memorial coliseum after the inauguration and you looked sad. I'm not sure that there wasn't a tear in your eye." To which Joe Frank responded, "Well, Senator, I probably was sad, and there may have been a tear in my eye. But it wasn't because I was leaving the governor's office. It was because I wasn't sure if I had a ride home!"[39] The Harrises did get a ride home. Lieutenant Jim Dixon, who had served as head of the Harrises' security detail, arranged for Captain Jerry Wheeler to drive them back to Cartersville. Joe Frank recalled, "He let us out at the door where he had picked us up over eight years earlier when we left for the Governor's Mansion in Atlanta."[40]

Formal portrait of Zell and Shirley, 1990. *Courtesy Richard B. Russell Library for Political Research and Studies, University of Georgia.*

CHAPTER EIGHT

From the Mountains to the Mansion

THE MILLERS

Zell and Shirley Miller were better acquainted with the Georgia Governor's Mansion than any other first family that had occupied it. After his 1966 election as governor, Lester Maddox asked Zell to serve as his executive secretary. Governor Maddox had never held public office, and he needed an adviser who knew the political landscape of the state senate and house, something that Zell knew well, having served as a state senator from 1961 to 1965 while teaching at Young Harris College. Zell accepted Maddox's job offer and embraced his new role with enthusiasm. He and Shirley became fixtures at the mansion long before Zell occupied the governor's chair.[1]

A native of Young Harris, Georgia, Zell Bryan Miller was born in 1932. Seventeen days after Zell's birth, his father, Stephen Grady Miller, a former state senator and professor at Young Harris Junior College, passed away. The family had been living at the college, and the death of Grady Miller meant that they could no longer reside in on-campus housing. So Zell's mother, Birdie Bryan Miller, purchased a small plot of land and then dragged rocks from nearby Brasstown Creek to build a house for herself and her two children.[2] The rock house, as it is known, came to symbolize the persistence, determination, and independence of Birdie, who would serve for twenty-five years on the Young Harris City Council and two terms as mayor. She raised her two children alone during the Depression in the rock house.[3] Zell graduated from Young Harris Junior College in 1951 and enlisted in the Marine Corps in 1953. Following three years in the U.S. Marine Corps, he was granted an honorable discharge. He always said that his success in life was shaped by his mother and by his time in the Marine Corps. He completed a BA (1957) and an MA (1958) in history at the University of Georgia, where the historian E. Merton Coulter served as his mentor. Zell had met Shirley Carver, from Rail Cove, North Carolina, while at Young Harris, and they married in 1954. Their two sons, Murphy and Matthew, were born in 1955 and 1956.

Following in his mother's footsteps, Zell was elected mayor of Young Harris in 1959. At age twenty-six, he was the youngest person to ever hold the job. He recalled that when he was sworn in, "They gave me the books of the lists of everybody that had been fined over the years in it, they gave me a Smith and Wesson .38 Special,

George and Mary Beth Busbee with Shirley and Zell Miller at the mansion, May 7, 1977. *Courtesy Richard B. Russell Library for Political Research and Studies, University of Georgia.*

and they gave me a blackjack."[4] Earlier that year, he had taken a teaching position at Young Harris Junior College. Zell's first foray into state politics came in April 1960, when he successfully ran against Kiser Dean, a political boss in Towns County, for the Georgia Senate. Miller's grassroots campaign, which involved knocking on the door of every known Democrat in the county, helped him win the election by 151 votes.[5] He represented the fortieth district for one term (1961–63) and, following redistricting, the fiftieth district for a term (1963–65).

Miller served as Governor Maddox's executive secretary from 1968 to 1971. Governor Carter named him executive director of the Democratic Party in Georgia in 1971. Three years later, Zell was elected lieutenant governor, a post he held for sixteen years, longer than anyone else in the state. In 1990 he defeated Republican

Zell Miller
GOVERNOR
Georgia Is His Cause.

Johnny Isakson to become Georgia's seventy-ninth governor.

Zell made an appearance on the national stage when he was asked by presidential nominee Bill Clinton to give one of the three keynote speeches at the 1992 Democratic National Convention. During his speech, the audience held up signs that read, "Give'm Hell, Zell." The next night, the crowd roared when fellow Georgian and former president Jimmy Carter asked, "What do you think of my governor, Zell Miller?" Zell was reelected governor in 1994 in a tight race against Republican Guy Millner.

Miller left office in 1999, and Zell and Shirley moved back to the rock house in Young Harris. Thinking that he had retired from politics, Zell began teaching at Young Harris College, Emory University, and the University of Georgia. Following the death of U.S. senator Paul Coverdell in 2000, Governor Roy Barnes asked Zell to fill the seat. Zell went on to serve in the U.S. Senate until 2005, when he finally retired from politics for good and returned home to the rock house once again. For eight years, though, between 1991 and 1999, Zell and Shirley Miller called the mansion at 391 West Paces Ferry Road home.[6]

The Millers loved the mansion and knew a lot about it. When interviewed about how it looked at its opening in the late 1960s, Zell described the downstairs ballroom as a "concrete slab" where an indoor swimming pool appeared in the original plans. Lester Maddox "nixed the idea" of the pool, however, because he believed it to be "too showy."[7] During the Maddox administration, the unadorned ballroom was used mainly for legislative events. When Zell was working as Maddox's executive secretary, Shirley worked at a bank nearby and often assisted First Lady Virginia Maddox with special events. Shirley remembered, "I was working at the other end of the street at C&S Bank at Peachtree and Pharr Roads in Buckhead. At the end of the workday, I would go to the mansion to be an extra pair of hands for special events. I would change clothes at the bank and then drive to the mansion to do whatever my chore was. I had a demanding job and young children, but I helped out a lot."[8] The Millers became fixtures around the mansion during later administrations. During the Busbee and

Miller campaign button, 1990. *Courtesy Richard B. Russell Library for Political Research and Studies, University of Georgia.*

Harris administrations, Zell served as lieutenant governor, so the Millers knew the mansion quite well. They also had many close friends in the neighborhood, including Addie Loudermilk, J. B. and Dottie Fuqua, Anne Cox Chambers, Carl and Betty Sanders, and J. Mack and Nita Robinson, among others.[9]

When the Millers moved into the mansion in 1991, they opened the doors to the whole state. Shirley remembered that she was given a box of keys during her first week. She did not seem to need them, because the mansion was rarely closed. The mansion's manager, Caroline Ballard Leake, recalled, "Governor Miller felt strongly that it was the people's house and it would be open to everyone. The first year they were in office, they held more than 500 events at the mansion. We did breakfast, lunch, dinner, and even cocktails. It was all hands on deck, so I remember reading cookbooks and planning menus and going from one event to the next."[10]

On the Sunday before the inauguration, many friends from Young Harris came down to see the mansion on a day that was both thrilling and tiring. Shirley understood the difference between being a first family in a state where the governor's mansion was in a major city and being one in a state where it was in a much smaller town. As she explained: "What goes on in the Governor's Mansion depends on whether the capital is a city. If it is, then the mansion is a busy place. Florida is a good example. Tallahassee is not a very busy city. Many of their events were in Orlando, Miami, or Tampa. Columbia, South Carolina, was much more like us. They were busy all the time."[11] And so were the Millers.

Shirley took on her new role with energy and enthusiasm, but the transition from bank executive to first lady was not easy. For thirty years, while her husband had "been riding the merry-go-round of politics," Shirley had pursued her own career as a banker and businesswoman. She worked as a bank clerk and then a loan officer, owned a number of dress shops, and finally served as founder and president of the Mountain Bank in Hiawassee, Georgia. While Zell was running for lieutenant governor, Shirley recalled, "I was the only Miller with a job."[12] With Zell's victory in the gubernatorial race, however, Shirley had to put her career on hold, although she worked "almost to the moment Zell was sworn in." She and her assistant, Beverly Messer, had to train the people who were replacing them at the bank. Beverly had worked with Shirley at the Mountain Bank for many years, and she agreed to serve as Shirley's assistant when Shirley moved into her new role as first lady.[13]

Carl and Betty Sanders with the Millers, 1990s.
Courtesy Richard B. Russell Library for Political Research and Studies, University of Georgia.

Speaking to the *Atlanta Constitution* reporter Alan Patureau, Shirley commented, "I feel very strange; I'm programmed to get up early and go to work. You can't imagine how sad I am. I miss my customers. I love banking . . . I figured out a long time ago that Zell would always be a running politician—and if I wanted to be happy, I'd better find something enjoyable to do."[14] But on January 14, 1991, she started a new job without a salary or a clear job description—that of Georgia's first lady.[15]

The Millers opened the mansion for public tours on the days that had been established by their predecessors. Caroline Ballard Leake, who served as the mansion manager, recalled that her mother and Shirley Miller recruited nearly a thousand people to become docents. Amy Huckaby, who followed Caroline in that role, remembered, "Some volunteer docents came only one time, and other groups had a regular schedule. The wife of the mayor of Acworth had a group of volunteers that she brought. We had one group of school bus drivers

Christmas decorations, 1990s. *Courtesy Richard B. Russell Library for Political Research and Studies, University of Georgia.*

from south of the city. They would drive their route in the morning, come to the mansion and give tours, have lunch, and then drive their route in the afternoon. A woman whose husband was an executive for Delta had a group of volunteers that she drew from. This was a very talented group."[16]

The mansion truly became the Millers' home, and they used it as both a private residence and a public facility. When asked which room was her favorite, the first lady vacillated between the kitchen and the family dining room. Governor Miller loved the library, and on the family's first night in the mansion, he crept downstairs to see whether the large collection of books by Georgia authors included his published works. It did.[17] They both made good use of the swing in the gazebo, where they would often take work or materials to read when they really wanted to concentrate. Shirley explained that her favorite times involved bringing staff members together to meet and eat as they prepared for upcoming functions. They brought their event folders and planned invitations, menus, seating charts, and other details in these informal sessions. As a busy executive, Shirley had become used to using computers in her daily work. The space designated as the first lady's office was on the second floor, and because the mansion was made of concrete, installation of the infrastructure would have been difficult and costly. Instead of rewiring the building, she moved her office to the ballroom level and shared the space with her assistant, Beverly Messer.[18]

The family moved into the mansion with photo albums, books, the governor's signed baseball collection, and one round oak table that Shirley said "goes everywhere with us."[19] In the study, Zell had stacks of CDs, and Shirley noted that the governor's musical taste ranged from Mozart to Randy Travis.[20] The Millers made almost no changes to the family living quarters on the third floor but did leave one lasting legacy—the Carter Bedroom. Early in their first term, she and Zell attended Governor's School in Kentucky. There she learned that in states where a former governor went on to become president, a room was usually named after him in his home state's governor's mansion. Upon Shirley's return from Governor's School, she and Beverly saw to it that the furniture the Carters had used in the master bedroom was moved into what had been the first lady's office, at the front of the mansion, and then dedicated the room as the Carter Bedroom.[21]

Waylon Jennings at the mansion, September 25, 1996. *Courtesy Richard B. Russell Library for Political Research and Studies, University of Georgia.*

Perhaps no Georgia governor loved music more than Zell Miller, and the Governor's Mansion hosted more musicians during his tenure than during that of any other governor. Describing his inauguration in January 1991, the reporter Jeanne Cummings of the *Atlanta Journal-Constitution* wrote, "Take the classical strings of the Atlanta Symphony, add a note from a U.S. Marine Corps band and pour on a lot of country and you've got Gov.-elect Zell Miller's inauguration."[22] The celebration included the musicians George Jones, Bill Anderson, Joe South, Bertie Higgins, and Alan Jackson, who all agreed to perform without charge. Following tradition, the Millers opened the Governor's Mansion to the public on the weekend before the inauguration. It was a cold day, and members of the enormous crowd queued up outside for hours. One gentleman crossed the threshold and said to the newly elected governor, "I have been waiting for two hours to get in this place," to which Zell replied, "That's nothing, I have been waiting for 20 years to get in!"[23] Zell shared his love of music with all the citizens of Georgia. He led a program to distribute classical music to all newborns in the state after learning about studies showing that exposure to music stimulates neurological development.[24]

In 1985, Georgia State University's Government Documentation Project began an effort to gather and publish oral histories of the state's living governors.

Six years later, on January 25, 1991, to celebrate their work, Governor Zell Miller hosted seven former governors, who came together to receive bound copies of the interviews. Jeanne Cummings noted that the size of the binders reflected the personalities of each governor—"Former President Jimmy Carter's was the thinnest; Lester Maddox's was the largest."[25] The gathering included Herman Talmadge, Jimmy Carter, Lester Maddox, Carl Sanders, Joe Frank Harris, Ernest Vandiver, and George Busbee. The men teased each other as they autographed one another's copies. Lester Maddox, who lost the Democratic nomination for governor to George Busbee in 1974, commented that he told Busbee, "If it had been 10 years ago, I wouldn't have signed his book. He told me, if it'd been 10 years ago, I wouldn't have let you sign it."[26]

On the rare evening that the Millers did not have a special event at the mansion, Zell and Shirley sat down to dinner with a small portable television sitting on a chair at the end of the mahogany table in the small family dining room. They often ate a simple dinner of pork chops and talked about the day. Sometimes they would go out to Houston's, Piccadilly Cafeteria, or the Colonnade and come home to watch a movie. On the weekends, they would try to go to a matinee.[27] When the first lady wanted a bowl of cereal in the middle of the night, she would put on a bathrobe and slippers and walk downstairs to the main kitchen.[28] Sometimes Zell would sneak out without the state troopers to the grocery store, Oxford Books, or the Varsity for a quick bite.[29]

The staff managed the mansion, and each morning inmates from the state prison system arrived at 7:30 a.m. to do housework and tend the grounds. When the Millers moved into the mansion, there were two chefs and two porters, but they trimmed back the staff dramatically as part of the budget cuts in 1991. The state budget was about $8 billion, and there was a huge shortfall because of the recession. The governor cut five thousand jobs and nearly two hundred programs in his first term. To show that the Governor's Mansion was not immune to the cutbacks, Shirley recalled that Zell declared, "Nobody is going to cut as much as we are in the operation of this house." The governor reduced the staff in the mansion from about thirty people down to single digits, Shirley recalled.[30] Among the casualties were the two full-time chefs. But the Millers did not mind making their own breakfast. Zell would often scramble eggs, and Shirley loved making waffles.

The Millers had four grandchildren, ages fifteen to two and half, when Governor Miller took office. The spare bedroom had extra cribs, and there were children's books throughout the house. Describing the role of first lady to the reporter Charles Walston in 1994, Shirley explained, "In my mind, being a governor's wife is maybe like being a preacher's wife and living in a parsonage. The congregation is just bigger." Walston noted that Zell and Shirley's forty-year marriage had "taken them from a house made of rocks in the North Georgia mountains to the white-columned mansion on West Paces Ferry Road" and that Shirley had "given up much more than her privacy." "There is plenty to do," commented Shirley, noting that she had tried to make the mansion "more accessible to the taxpayers who own it." The Millers allowed the mansion to be used for "charity fund-raising events," and it was open for tours three mornings a week. Shirley liked to be there to talk to the groups that came through, especially groups of students, and to answer their questions. The most frequently asked question, she reported, was "Where is Zell?"[31]

Under the Millers the mansion became a cross between Camp David and the White House. Governor Miller held staff and strategy meetings there when he wanted to escape interruptions that were so common at his office in the capitol. Keith Mason, Miller's former chief of staff, recalled, "In the summer of 1991, we were going through severe budget cuts. We invited legislative leaders to the mansion for meetings for weeks to work on a productive strategy. We could have a five-hour meeting out there and really hammer through an agenda. The mansion was a great event space, but it also functioned as an executive retreat."[32] Staff members recalled the mansion meetings fondly, mainly because of the good food. As Mason quipped, "If we wanted to influence a particular legislator, we served them the mansion's spareribs. That usually worked."[33] Significant decisions in the Miller administration—major appointments, initiatives, priorities—were discussed at the mansion. "The mansion was a good place to meet without interruption and gave home-field advantage," recalled Zell.[34] The decision to appoint Thurbert Baker attorney general in 1997 was made there, and Zell made his decision to run for reelection at the mansion. It was a place where the governor and his team could really think.

Early in the Millers' first term, Hollywood came to Atlanta when the mansion became a movie set for

Miller family, ca. 1997. *Courtesy Shirley and Zell Miller.*

the 1992 miniseries *Grass Roots*. Corbin Bernsen, well known at the time for his role on the popular television show *L.A. Law*, played a Georgia attorney defending a white man accused of raping and killing an African American woman. It was a sequel to the 1983 miniseries *Chiefs*, both based on novels written by Stuart Woods. In the *Grass Roots* production, Zell and Shirley Miller had a two-minute scene as a wealthy political contributor and his wife. After watching Zell perform his lines, Bernsen cracked, "Hey, this guy's good." Miller was supportive of the whole production, saying, "We just want to cooperate with the film industry. If they'd wanted me to stand on my head at the mansion, I would have."[35] Leake recalled, "We worked all night long on that production. We did one scene that was a costume ball with women in hoop skirts. That was a lot of fun."[36]

The Millers tried to open the doors to the mansion to Georgians and actively sought to host events that helped institutions throughout the state. Shirley explained, "These organizations would expect financial contributions from the state. But the state has no money to give them, so we are trying to support them in this way." In his first year in office, Zell echoed the point: "This is the people of Georgia's house, bought and paid for by them. We only have a four-year lease. . . . We have had over 10,000 people through here in the last eight months. And after this budget thing is settled, I plan to do even more—like an evening focused on the late Georgia poet Byron Herbert Reece. . . . or

Zell Miller with Santa, 1992. *Courtesy Richard B. Russell Library for Political Research and Studies, University of Georgia.*

a reception for Georgia's two living Baseball Hall of Famers, Johnny Mize and Hank Aaron."[37] In September 1991, the mansion hosted a fund-raiser for the Fernbank Natural Science Museum, throwing "open the doors for festivities sponsored by organizations that contribute to Georgia's cultural and economic wealth."[38] Throughout the spring of 1992, the Millers hosted cultural dinners to raise money for the Georgia Council for the Arts to fund fellowships for Georgia artists. The author Alfred Uhry, the violinist Robert McDuffie, the author Ferrol Sams, the artist and illustrator Benny Andrews, and the painter Mattie Lou O'Kelley were all honored at these events.[39] In March 1992, Governor Miller and the Members Guild of the Atlanta Historical Society held a lunch for Henry D. Green, who had served as chair of the Fine Arts Committee for the mansion. Governors Busbee, Carter, Harris, Maddox, and Sanders were on hand to honor him.[40]

The Millers hosted a wide range of guests at the mansion, including members of royalty. In June 1994, Emperor Akihito and Empress Michiko of Japan visited with the Millers at the mansion when they came to Atlanta to meet with former president Jimmy Carter and to honor the legacy of Dr. Martin Luther King Jr. Keith Mason recalled that Bill Clinton was one of the most frequent and popular guests. Clinton visited the mansion in September 1991 when he was in town to give a speech for the Democratic Party. "He had been contemplating a run for the presidency," recalled Mason.

> We had a breakfast for him with Bruce Lindsay, Dick Riley, and others that we thought he should meet. When I arrived that morning, the governor told me that Clinton was very interested in having James Carville become his campaign manager. Carville had helped Zell with some of his past campaigns as early as 1980, and Zell asked me to find James before we sat down to eat. James was a consultant in Washington, D.C., and he was running a campaign for Harris Wofford in Pennsylvania. Well, this is before cell phones or e-mail, but I managed to find him on that Sunday morning at his girlfriend Mary Matalin's house. I got Carville on the phone with Zell, who then introduced him to Clinton. They made their first connection in the library at the Georgia Governor's Mansion.[41]

Zell later married James and Mary in New Orleans at a wedding ceremony that featured George Stephanopoulos and Rush Limbaugh on opposite sides of the aisle, literally and figuratively.[42]

The Millers with the Emperor Akihito and Empress Michiko, June 1994. *Courtesy Richard B. Russell Library for Political Research and Studies, University of Georgia.*

The Millers greeting Bill Clinton and Al Gore, March 30, 1995. *Courtesy Richard B. Russell Library for Political Research and Studies, University of Georgia.*

When Clinton was still governor of Arkansas, he and Zell occasionally went out to dinner. They both loved a local Atlanta chain, Houston's, as Zell recalled: "One time we went when he was president; it practically caused a riot. He loved talking to people and did not want to leave." On an earlier trip, "a trooper told me that Clinton insisted that they go to McDonald's, this after eating a whole meal, and get two Big Macs. Clinton ate them both before they drove the two miles back to the mansion."[43]

During one of Clinton's early visits as president, he brought an entire entourage, including a navy chef laden with pots and pans and all the ingredients needed to prepare the president's meals. Before the first meal, President Clinton walked through the kitchen, saw what the mansion's cook, Eva Andrews, had on the stove, and declared, "I'll eat what Eva's cooking." Clinton enjoyed Eva's cooking so much that he never again brought his own cook when he visited the Georgia Governor's Mansion.[44]

A presidential visit to the mansion always meant tight security. The Secret Service brought bulletproof glass and communications equipment that had to be installed on the second floor and the roof of the mansion. Before any event, everyone had to leave the house to allow the bomb-sniffing dogs to do a full security sweep.[45] When President Clinton and Vice President Gore were in town for an economic summit at Emory University in 1995, the Millers hosted the participants at the mansion. Ovid Davis, a longtime lobbyist for Coca-Cola, was invited to the event, and he arrived at the front gate with a loaded pistol in his trunk. Davis had forgotten about the pistol, but the troopers on duty reacted swiftly. They called chief of staff Steve Wrigley and reported, "Ovid's at the gate, and he's got a loaded gun." Wrigley told the troopers to "unload the gun, lock it in the trunk, and send Ovid on in."[46]

For Zell, the most memorable event at the mansion tapped into his great love of baseball. Miller had coached the Young Harris team when he was a history professor there. Over the years, he had become friends with Hank Aaron and Mickey Mantle. In 1994, he invited both to the mansion to help raise funds for a new baseball field for Young Harris College. With an overflow crowd in the mansion ballroom, the two men talked about

Zell Miller with Hank Aaron and Mickey Mantle, October 1994. *Courtesy Richard B. Russell Library for Political Research and Studies, University of Georgia.*

Zell Miller with Atlanta Braves players, 1991. *Courtesy Richard B. Russell Library for Political Research and Studies, University of Georgia.*

Shirley Miller, Beverly Messer, and Caroline Ballard Leake at the Lacey Champion carpet factory, 1990s. *Courtesy Shirley and Zell Miller.*

their careers and other ballplayers of bygone days. Zell remembered, "The audience loved it. It was my favorite event. You could write on a slip of paper a question, and they really tried to answer them all."[47]

All the events and tours of the mansion took a toll on the furnishings, especially the Aubusson rug (which had dry rot) in the drawing room. After nearly every event, Caroline Ballard Leake and Shirley Miller could be found on their knees, stitching the rug back together. J. B. Fuqua, who had been a great friend of the mansion and had been instrumental in getting it built, and his wife, Dorothy, stepped in quietly to have the rug duplicated by Lacey Champion.[48] Shirley Miller recalled:

J. B. Fuqua called me one day, and the rug became the topic of conversation because the Olympics were coming. His wife, Dottie, had seen what bad shape the rug was in, and he said, "I'll pay for it as long as we can have the work done in the U.S., not in Europe." We knew that in North Carolina, Lacey Champion had duplicated some period rugs for the governor's mansion there and had worked in other states. So Caroline went up to see her. They took the pattern off, got the wool, and had dozens

of women working from numbers and measurements on strips of paper. We cut it close, but the rug was there for the 1996 Olympic Games. When it was finished, I called Mr. Fuqua to come see it. He arrived, glanced at the rug for a minute, said, "Looks good to me," and then continued his conversation with Zell. I never knew what it cost, but it was a tidy sum.[49]

The Governor's Mansion became a hub of activity before and during the Olympics and the Special Olympics in 1996. The former mansion manager Caroline Ballard Leake, who had left to head the Georgia Council for the Arts, came back to the mansion to help the first family coordinate all the special events. She remembered, "We did a lot of planning with ACOG [Atlanta Committee for the Olympic Games] and the IOC [International Olympic Committee]. There were so many international visitors. We had tents on either side of the mansion, and we rocked that place for three months."[50] Shirley recounted, "The planning and preparation for the Olympics was very, very time consuming because we had responsibility for . . . doing everything right. We worked on that for two years."[51] Because of

Shirley Miller and
Elizabeth Harris with the
Executive Fine Arts Committee,
December 1990, a month after
Zell Miller was elected. *Courtesy
Richard B. Russell Library for
Political Research and Studies,
University of Georgia.*

security concerns during the Olympics, no large trucks were allowed in or out of the Buckhead neighborhood, where the mansion is located. This meant no food deliveries or trash pickup for several weeks. So the Millers had refrigerated trucks full of food parked behind the tennis courts, and as they were emptied, the staff used them to store trash.

There were dozens of events at the mansion, including a lunch for President Clinton, his family, members of his cabinet, and other dignitaries.[52] On the day of the opening ceremony, all the guests left the mansion after lunch, and the Millers did not expect to see them again until that evening at the Opening Ceremonies. Much to Shirley's surprise, members of the Clinton entourage returned to the mansion later that afternoon to take a shower and have dinner. The mansion staff was unprepared for this unexpected turn of events, and there was not enough food in the building for everyone. Shirley quickly called the Georgia Building Authority and asked whether it had any food that it could spare at Lakewood, where the security team was being fed. The answer was yes, so Shirley and the staff quickly "put up tables and got out warming dishes" in preparation for the arrival of the food. That afternoon, Clinton's cabinet secretaries "ate what the security folks ate before going to the

opening ceremonies," recalled Shirley.[53] The unexpected arrival of the cabinet secretaries, all of whom wanted to take showers, also stretched the limits of the mansion's linen supplies, so Shirley called over to the troopers' barracks and said, "'I need to borrow every dry towel you have.' And so in just a few minutes, I saw this laundry cart coming across the driveway with towels."[54]

In addition to being the executive residence, the mansion was also the boss's house—a place for the governor to entertain friends and coworkers. The Millers regularly hosted casual events for the staff at the mansion at which they could swim or play tennis or Ping-Pong. Zell, who was quite a good Ping-Pong player, routinely beat all comers. Chief of staff Steve Wrigley remembered that at one staff event, "We had just hired a young man right out of college who happened to be very good at Ping-Pong. The governor was quite competitive, so we decided to have a tournament. Well, this young gun did not know that you don't go out in your first week and beat the governor. But he did. I joked with him later that he should go clean out his desk."[55]

Perhaps the favorite guests of the Millers at the mansion were the high school students that the governor and his wife hosted each spring. Zell, whose parents met while teaching at Young Harris College, and who had taught there himself after completing his degrees at the University of Georgia, had a deep appreciation for students who worked hard to succeed. He wanted to do something to honor them, and in the spring of 1991, he and Shirley decided to invite the top graduate from every public and private high school in Georgia to attend a special "Valedictorian's Day" reception at the mansion. In that first year, they did not know better than to invite every valedictorian in the whole state to come on the same day. Groups of students lined up at 10:00 a.m. outside the mansion gates for an event that did not begin until 2:00 p.m. As they greeted each student and asked where they were going to college, the Millers and their staff members were dismayed to learn that most were leaving the state.

Zell had been discussing the possibility of using a lottery to fund education, and the valedictorian event gave him the ammunition he needed to promote the lottery as a source of funding to help keep Georgia's best and brightest students in the state. That idea became the HOPE Scholarship program (the acronym stands for Helping Outstanding Pupils' Education), the most generous scholarship in the nation. It was paid for by the state lottery, as approved by a constitutional amendment in 1992. Miller directed most of the money to

scholarships for students who maintained a B average. The remaining funds went to prekindergarten programs. When asked how he came up with the idea, Miller said he was inspired by observing the curiosity of his own young grandchildren and realized that the current school system was not adequately challenging them.

Toward the end of his second term, around Christmas in 1997, the Millers were surprised by two new additions to their family. Their longtime friend A. D. Frazier, who had been the chief operating officer of the Olympics, called Steve Wrigley to reveal that he was going to surprise the Millers with two six-week-old yellow Labrador puppies. Wrigley recounts the story:

> Keith Sorrells was the head of Miller's State Trooper unit, and we were afraid that Governor Miller would get mad. He did not like surprises. When Frazier brought them to the podium, Zell was not pleased. There is a photograph of both him and Shirley holding one dog each, and he has this sourpuss look on his face. Well, it only took them a day to fall in love with those dogs. Frazier had named them Pierre and Thomas after the Lieutenant Governor Pierre Howard and the Speaker of the House Tom Murphy. But Miller changed those names to Gus and Woodrow, after his favorite characters in Lonesome Dove. Those dogs lived to be 13 years old, and he talks about them in his final State of the State speech.[56]

A. D. Frazier giving the Millers two Labrador puppies, 1997. *Courtesy Shirley and Zell Miller.*

Zell on the porch of the stone house in Young Harris, ca. 2000. *Courtesy Shirley and Zell Miller.*

Zell fondly remembered that one of his favorite things to do was to walk the mansion grounds with the dogs.[57]

In 1998, the Millers began making plans to leave the mansion at the end of the governor's second term. It was an emotional departure. "We have tried to open this house to a lot of people," Shirley told the reporter Colin Campbell, and indeed they had, from heads of state to high school students.[58] At an event honoring his twenty-five years in politics, Shirley unveiled a portrait of Zell painted by Thomas Nash, a portrait artist from Roswell. The portrait showed the governor wearing a blue suit with his Marines pin on his lapel and standing next to the rock house that his mother had built more than sixty-five years earlier in Young Harris. Joking about the governor's rusty driving skills, his press secretary, Rick Dent, warned the attendees "not to get in his way because he hasn't driven in quite a while."[59] Reflecting on his political career, Zell paraphrased a quote from one of his favorite fictional characters, Gus McCrae, from Larry McMurtry's *Lonesome Dove*: "Quite a party, my friends. Quite a party."[60]

Zell and Shirley moved back to the rock house, and he began teaching again. The governor explained: "I'm doing exactly what I planned to do all along. No melancholy. No nostalgia. I've always known I was going back home."[61] With years of politics behind him, Zell returned to his great love—the classroom. He taught at Emory University, the University of Georgia, and Young Harris College. Miller described a leadership class as focused on "a combination of philosophy, literature, history, practical everyday living and Marine Corps boot camp."[62] One reporter summed up Miller's legacy: "The governor has always been a true son of the South, with all the quirks and contradictions that phrase implies. His speech and mannerism reveal him as a product of an old Georgia that is quickly disappearing, yet in his foresight he has ushered the people of his native state to the brink of a new millennium well prepared for whatever the future might bring."[63]

A few months after he left office, the journalist Colin Campbell recounted that he had run into Zell at Emory University and thought that the former governor looked younger. According to Campbell, Zell was adjusting well to life after the governor's mansion, claiming that he "had never been happier" and that he and Shirley were enjoying being back in the North Georgia mountains. "It was magical as well to sleep in the same room I'd slept in as a child," Zell added.[64]

After appearing on the ballot twenty-two times, Miller seemed finally ready to leave politics. But his retirement was short-lived. In 2000, Governor Roy Barnes appointed Miller to fill the U.S. Senate seat of Republican Paul Coverdell, who had passed away that July. In November, Zell ran for a special election and won, allowing him to complete the four remaining years of Coverdell's term.[65] So Zell packed his cowboy boots, and he and Shirley moved to Washington, D.C., to start the next chapter in their lives.

Barnes family, 2002. *Courtesy Marie and Roy Barnes.*

Come On In

THE BARNESES

Roy and Marie Barnes moved into the Governor's Mansion in January 1999. According to the journalist Dick Pettys, the Barneses were "more fun loving" and "less spit-and-polish" than their predecessors.[1] This laid-back style was a hallmark of their tenure at the mansion, and it manifested itself in myriad ways—through practical jokes, down-home hospitality, and holiday decorations that became the stuff of legend.

Roy Barnes met his future wife, Marie Dobbs, in January 1969 on a blind date arranged by their roommates. Marie was born in Cobb County and graduated from Marietta High School before completing her associate's degree at Kennesaw Junior College. They married eighteen months later, in August 1970, after she graduated from the University of Georgia and Roy completed his first year of law school there. Describing his marriage, Governor Barnes explained: "If there has ever been a marriage where you become one, it's us. We think so much alike and are so very close, you know, she's just a part of me, and I'm a part of her. It's been a true blessing."[2] As Roy completed law school, Marie taught school for two years in Madison County. They then moved to his hometown of Mableton, where she did volunteer work and he practiced law. During the two years when Roy served in the Cobb County district attorney's office, he and Marie started a family. Roy ventured into politics in 1974 when he was elected to the Georgia Senate.[3]

Marie was twenty-six years old when she and her husband attended their first legislative function at the Governor's Mansion. Reflecting on that visit, Marie recalled, "My biggest impression was the state seal in the floor, and now I have one in my house."[4] A young mother and wife of the youngest state senator at that time, Marie never imagined that one day her family would live in such a public house. Roy served eight terms in the state senate before making an unsuccessful run for the governor's office in 1990 against Zell Miller and Andrew Young. Three years later, he was elected to the Georgia House from the thirty-third district. In November 1998, Barnes defeated businessman Guy Millner in the gubernatorial election, and he and Marie moved into the Governor's Mansion on West Paces Ferry Road in January of the following year.[5]

Proud parents at daughter Allison's wedding.
Courtesy Lois Salter.

The transition from private citizen to governor can sometimes be jarring. As Roy explained, "You don't know if you are going to be elected. Then, this first Tuesday in November comes around and you do. It just happens overnight. You're really thrown into this new role."[6] Marie recalled, "We were at the hotel on election night when we found out we had won. Roy had met with Jerry Regan about his security detail, and we went to bed. The next morning, I got up and threw on a casual dress to go get ice for my Diet Coke. I opened the door, and two big state troopers snapped to attention. They asked me what I needed, and I said I was going to get ice. They said, 'No ma'am, we'll get it for you.' And so it began."[7]

First Lady Shirley Miller helped Marie make the transition by inviting her to participate in a Christmas event, along with former first lady Betty Vandiver, in December 1998. Marie recalled:

> Shirley was gracious to invite me to go with her on a couple of events and to kind of get my feet wet. I remember the first one was the Mayor's Motorcade where the mayors across the state gather toys and gifts for patients at

Milledgeville—or at the mental hospitals across the state. . . . That was my first little speech or time to say anything. And so, I thanked them for letting me come and I wished them a Merry Christmas from Mrs. Vandiver from Christmas past, Mrs. Miller from Christmas present, and Mrs. Barnes from Christmas future.[8]

Such public events meant the end of the relatively low-profile life that Marie had led, but in the final month before she moved into the mansion, she did manage to retain a bit of her anonymity. While Christmas shopping at K-Mart in December 1998, she recalled, the cashier looked at her credit card and asked whether she was related to Roy Barnes who owned a pest control company in Cobb County. The soon-to-be first lady smiled and politely said no.[9]

The first night in the mansion was not quite what the Barneses expected. The Millers had moved out before the inauguration, and Marie and Roy, who were in Mableton, decided one afternoon to move into the mansion without any fanfare. They recalled:

> We just decided to go on down to the mansion. We didn't know who to call. We just showed up. The staff did not know we were coming and did not know to stay. Roy was working in the transition office. Nobody was at the mansion. I looked in the refrigerator and didn't see anything to eat. We did not know the mansion well enough to know about the pantry downstairs. So Roy said, "Let's call Ray [Roy's brother] and his wife, Jackie, to see if they want to come down for dinner." I thought that would be fun. So Roy called, and said, "On the way, stop at Kentucky Fried Chicken and pick up a bucket of chicken." Well, when Jackie walked in, she said: "You've been in public housing one night, and we're already having to feed you."[10]

Marie remembered that Roy was not often to be found at home: "We were there for six weeks before the staff saw Roy." Because he left the mansion around seven each morning and often returned after eight in the evening, they thought he was a "phantom governor." Then when they finally saw him, he was always dressed professionally. Holly Chute, the chef, joked, "We didn't see him for the longest time, then when we did he was always in a tie. Does he sleep in one?"[11]

Roy used the mansion very much like many of his predecessors. He explained, "My office at the capitol was a zoo; there were just so many people coming and going. It was hard to get any work done. The mansion was great for when you had something important to

Roy Barnes, painted by
Carol Baxter Kirby, 2003.
*Courtesy Richard B. Russell Library
for Political Research and Studies,
University of Georgia.*

Meeting with the Canadian ambassador on the family floor, 2001. *Courtesy Marie and Roy Barnes.*

do and you wanted a quiet place. For small meetings, it was the better choice."[12] He often had private meetings in the library on the main floor of the mansion and regularly worked in his office on the upper floor. His mornings followed the same routine: "The troopers put the newspapers on the elevator for me early in the morning so I could read them. Then I went through e-mails that had come in overnight and read any faxes that had arrived. I would shower, get dressed, and leave the mansion by seven, especially when the legislature was in session."[13]

As Georgia's new first lady, Marie Barnes worked hard to move her family into the Governor's Mansion without much fanfare. She was determined to preserve the family traditions that had developed over the past twenty-eight years and to maintain a sense of stability. The mansion became "home base" for the Barnes family. Although the three Barnes children were all adults by the time their father was elected governor—Harlan, twenty-five, worked at a consulting firm; Allison, twenty-two, was in her second year of law school at the University of Georgia; and Alyssa, eighteen, was a sophomore at Samford University in Birmingham—the girls often came to stay at the mansion. Harlan lived there for two years during Roy's tenure as governor.

Commenting on the prospect of moving into such a large home, the new first lady joked, "You could probably put my house in the basement!"[14] The mansion was not only much larger than her family home, but also fully furnished. "I brought my dog and her chair," said Marie, "but she wouldn't stay in it." Marie also brought her toolbox and her sewing machine, both of which proved useful, as well as some family photos, a filing cabinet, a treadmill, a few paintings, a lingerie chest, and a few additional chairs for the family living quarters.[15] The Barneses made minimal changes to the family living quarters on the third floor, painting their bedroom and rehanging curtains that had been used during the Busbees' residency.[16]

Marie Barnes came to the mansion with a clear perspective on her role. Early in their tenure, the Barneses attended the National Governors Association's Governor's School in Delaware. While the governors attended sessions focused on becoming effective chief executives, the spouses attended separate sessions about how to succeed in the role of first lady. The first ladies were assigned a mentor, and Marie was given Rhea Chiles, wife of Florida governor Lawton Chiles. During one of the sessions, Marie recalled, First Lady Janet Huckabee, wife of Arkansas governor Mike Huckabee,

Marie Barnes greeting schoolchildren, 2001. *Courtesy Marie and Roy Barnes.*

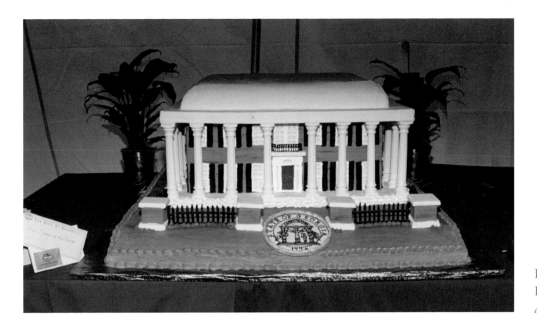

Inauguration cake made by Kroger, 1999. *Courtesy Marie and Roy Barnes.*

passed on her wisdom to the group: "Don't think that you're special, and don't take yourself too seriously. You just had the good sense to marry a man who became governor. There isn't a shelf life for a former first lady. So keep that in perspective."[17]

Like many first families before them, the Barneses opened the mansion for public tours—in their case, starting on January 11, 1999, the weekend before Roy's inauguration as Georgia's eightieth governor. They had been living in their new home for less than two weeks and were still unsettled, but on that bleak and wintry day, they opened the doors to the people of Georgia. People came in droves, even though the event was scheduled at the same time as an NFL playoff game between the Atlanta Falcons and the San Francisco 49ers at the Georgia Dome. Dr. Larry Clements, who made the decision to forgo the football game in order to visit the mansion, commented, "We actually had tickets to the Falcons game. We can go to a later game any time. I assume they'll continue winning."[18]

For the event, the grocery chain Kroger donated a two-hundred-pound cake in the shape of the mansion, carrying forward a tradition that the company had begun with the Harris administration. The six-foot-tall cake, which took three chefs five days to make, used 216 eggs, 108 pounds of flour, and 132 cups of milk.[19] Visitors snacked on the cake and peach punch, excited to see their new governor at his West Paces Ferry Road residence. Wanda Baxter of Boone, North Carolina, came for a visit, remarking, "We just had to see Roy and Marie. He was my attorney 20 years ago."[20]

The Barneses embraced their new roles and new home. Reflecting on some of the niceties of living in the mansion, Marie mentioned that her son Harlan especially liked the "magic laundry basket." The family put their dirty clothes in the basket each evening, and seemingly like magic, the clothes came back clean the next day. This was, of course, not really magic, but rather the result of hard work by the trusties who helped maintain the mansion. Marie's favorite room was the wrapping-paper room—a large closet on the third floor that Elizabeth Harris, wife of Governor Joe Frank Harris, had converted into a space for wrapping the many gifts that a first lady was obliged to bestow upon guests and visitors. Marie commented that after "living with Roy Barnes for 44 years, nothing surprises me," but the wrapping-paper room had come as a surprise. So beloved was this feature of the mansion that Marie had one included in the new home that she and Roy had built after he left office.[21]

The Barneses brought with them a family pet. Their tricolored, mixed-breed beagle, known as C.C. (short for Champion of Champions), was fifteen years old when Marie and Roy moved into the mansion, and she was not in the best of health. C.C. had been given the run of the Barneses' house and yard at their Mableton home, going in and out at will. At the mansion, such freedom was impossible. Although Marie brought with her the chair in which C.C. slept, the dog would not stay in it. Marie recalled, "I went to great lengths to keep her from messing up the carpets and sofa. I would never let her go downstairs. When we moved in here,

Marie Barnes and C.C.
(Champion of Champions),
ca. 2000. *Courtesy Marie and
Roy Barnes.*

Allison Barnes's wedding, October 2001. *Courtesy Marie and Roy Barnes.*

I took that hallway by my office and set up an adjustable pen. I put heavy duty plastic on the floor with old towels and puppy pads on top. Her bed was on there."[22]

This arrangement worked fine until the night of Harlan's wedding. When Marie and Roy arrived home around 2:00 a.m., C.C. had fallen out of the bed and was stuck on her back. She had soiled herself. Still wearing her wedding finery, Marie scooped up C.C. and took her to the bathtub, where she began bathing the dog. "Roy is unzipping my dress so I could clean her up," said Marie. C.C. died soon after and was buried in the side yard of the Governor's Mansion.[23]

Occasionally, a first family found that the mansion was not outfitted to suit its needs. Roy and Marie quickly learned that they did not have enough linens and towels to accommodate overnight stays by their children and their children's friends. With her signature can-do attitude, Marie took control of the situation:

I went to Linens & Things or Bed, Bath and Beyond with the state trooper and bought washable stuff that I could keep on the beds that would look nice. If we had state guests, the staff would put the regular linens back on the beds. I couldn't let my children or their friends sleep under a bedspread that cost $450 a yard. I bought more casual sheets and stuff for the beds. We did things a little differently. Roy signed an executive order that the governor and his staff couldn't take any gifts from lobbyists. The textile industry wanted to do all the towels and sheets for the mansion. But I said, "I can't take it. If I can't buy it with my own money, it cannot go in the mansion." I took those things with me when I left, but I had bought them with my money.[24]

Keeping the family's budget separate from the state budget was also a challenge. Marie remembered:

> When we were moving in, the head of the Georgia Building Authority came to give me a credit card with my name on it. They said, this weekend you might need to buy something, and you won't have time to do a purchase order. I said, listen, I am not going to end up on the front page of the *Atlanta Journal-Constitution* for using state funds. If we can't afford to live here, I won't buy it. The Building Authority asked what kind of shampoo or toothpaste I liked, and I made it clear that I would pay for all of those personal items. My daughter Allison got married while we were living here, and we paid for everything: the staff labor, the tent, the flowers, and the food. That was our expense and should not come out of state funds.[25]

Christmas was an especially important time for the Barnes family. Marie had always filled the house and yard of their family home with Christmas decorations, but she brought only a few Christmas things to the mansion. Her initial plans for the family's first Christmas in the mansion were modest—she would make her famous sausage balls and decorate the mansion with three trees, including one upstairs.[26] But as Christmas approached, Marie missed her decorations from home, so she called her handyman and asked him "to pack up [the] family decorations and bring them down to the mansion." "We had a live tree in every room," she recalled, "and I invited four friends to come help me decorate. We worked all day, breaking only for lunch. I put all the lights on the tree, and we brought in all of my moving figures and placed them throughout the mansion. We also put up papier-mâché angels."[27]

During her second Christmas in the mansion, Marie used her decorations to convince her husband to support an initiative that would help the children of

Decorations featuring pieces from the mansion's collection, 2000. *Courtesy Marie and Roy Barnes.*

Georgia. Among the decorations on the third floor of the mansion were a series of cartoon characters, including Scooby-Doo in a Santa suit, that moved and played Christmas music. As Governor Barnes labored in his upstairs office to trim $50 million from the state budget, Marie mentioned to him that he should consider including $2.5 million in the budget to provide equipment for hospitals across the state to conduct hearing screenings on newborns. During her time as first lady, Marie had dedicated herself to the health of children, birth to age three, and the hearing screening of newborns was a cause that was near and dear to Marie. A friend of her daughter, Alyssa, was hearing impaired, but she had not been diagnosed until she was three years old. Roy responded, "I don't have 2.5 million. I'm trying to cut 50 million." As Marie left the room, she turned on Scooby-Doo, who sang "Jingle Bell Rock" in an endless loop. After about fifteen minutes, Governor Barnes, using his pet name for his wife, shouted, "Mayree, come turn that thing off." Marie poked her head in his office and asked, "Do you have my 2.5 million dollars?" He said, "I'll find it. Just turn that thing off." So, Scooby-Doo helped bring newborn hearing screening to Georgia.[28]

The Barneses also helped children in a much less public way. Each year at Christmas, they invited thirty to forty disadvantaged children, sometimes from the Carrie Steele-Pitts Home, to a private family party at

Hanukkah display, 2000. *Courtesy Marie and Roy Barnes.*

Kwanzaa display, 2000. *Courtesy Marie and Roy Barnes.*

Scooby-Doo and Sylvester the Cat Christmas decorations, 2000. *Courtesy Marie and Roy Barnes.*

the mansion. The party had a different theme each year, and the children were given clothes, a gift card, and a toy. After learning that children in foster care had no luggage and had to carry their belongings in trash bags, Marie embarked on a mission. She found a duffel bag and backpack combination at Kohl's in Mableton that would make a perfect gift for the children, and she negotiated with the store manager to sell about fifty of them to her for five dollars each. She stored them in the basement of the mansion, and the next Christmas at the mansion, the children were given their new bags, along with other gifts, by Santa Claus from Phipps Plaza.[29]

When they were not hosting state functions or entertaining out-of-town guests at the mansion, the Barnes family enjoyed informal dinners. Marie hoped that living in the mansion would help get her husband to eat more healthfully. She joked, "If it's fried, he'll eat it."[30] Because Roy often worked late, Marie allowed executive chef Holly Chute and the kitchen staff to prepare a meal and leave it on the stove so that they could go home to their families. Roy and Marie's favorite local restaurant

was the original Longhorn on Peachtree Road, but dining out was not always easy or relaxing. The security detail would have to drive the first couple to and from the restaurant, and oftentimes other guests would recognize them while they were trying to eat.[31]

On weekends, Marie took over in the kitchen. She confessed, "I'm a messy cook. My mother would not let me in the kitchen. Holly did everything she could to keep me out of the mansion's kitchen. She hated to come in after a weekend. I think I had used every pan we owned and always left a big mess. I cooked these big family meals and would often feed the troopers who had to stay on duty."[32] But try as each family did to make the mansion feel like home, it was no ordinary house. Soon after they moved in, Marie decided to go downstairs to the kitchen to get a piece of Holly's red velvet cake as a midnight snack. Her late-night foray tripped an alarm, and she suddenly found herself in the kitchen facing one of the Georgia State Patrol security guards with his gun drawn. She quickly learned that after-hours trips into the kitchen warranted a call to security.[33]

The Barnes family with Canadian Mounties at the mansion, 2001. *Courtesy Marie and Roy Barnes.*

Governor and Mrs. Roy E. Barnes
Request the honor of your presence
at a
Reception and Dinner
Celebrating the
University System of Georgia
Corporate and Foundation Supporters
of the University System of Georgia
and a
Special Salute to Chancellor Stephen R. Portch
on
Tuesday, September 11, 2001
6:30 p.m.

Governor's Mansion
391 West Paces Ferry Road
Atlanta, Georgia

RSVP by August 31   Black Tie
404-656-2202

Invitation to the University System of Georgia Dinner,
September 11, 2001. *Courtesy Marie and Roy Barnes.*

Event cancelled due to WTC bombing.

Event cancellation because of the
September 11, 2001, terrorist attacks.
Courtesy Marie and Roy Barnes.

An avid tennis player, Marie had been part of the Atlanta Lawn and Tennis Association (ALTA) A-5 intermediate-level championship team in May 1998. Known as the "Slice Queen" for the spin she put on the ball, five-foot-eight-inch Marie was an intimidating player who often rushed the net.[34] She probably used the mansion's tennis court more than any other resident. If one of her ALTA games was canceled, she would often schedule a makeup match at the mansion. On one occasion, after a match on a particularly hot day, Marie and her tennis partners cooled off in the fountain at the base of the terraced garden. For her birthday one year, Roy gave her tennis balls with "Georgia Governor's Mansion" printed on them. She and Roy used some of the funds left over from the inauguration to improve the tennis courts at the mansion.[35]

Like their predecessors, Marie and Roy recognized the value of the mansion as a platform for promoting Georgia. "We brought in people we hoped would do business with the state," said Marie, adding, "The Governor's Mansion is a wonderful place to sell the state of Georgia." Marie "loved hosting events at the mansion," and among those events were the red carpet and green carpet events. Red carpet functions were held in partnership with the Georgia Chamber of Commerce to promote economic development, and the green carpet events attracted the financial industry and businesses.[36]

Another favorite event was the valedictorian reception, a tradition begun by Roy's predecessor, Zell Miller. "I enjoyed having the valedictorians from all across the state come in one day," said Marie. "We would set up a big tent, and we would have speakers and refreshments. It made for an eight-hour day for us, but I enjoyed using the Governor's Mansion to show off the state because it is a state treasure." Reflecting on the effort involved during the 1960s to bring the mansion to fruition, Marie noted, "I think it's just wonderful that the state has [the mansion], and we can thank the Sanderses for that because they were so instrumental in getting it built."[37]

Among Marie's personal possessions that she brought to the mansion was her toolbox, which she put to good use on more than one occasion. One night during a reception, she discovered a leaking toilet in one of the main-floor restrooms. "Water was just pouring out of the top of the toilet," she recalled, so she grabbed her toolbox and turned off the water to stop the leak until a plumber could come and make the necessary repairs. On another occasion, Marie very nearly resorted to making an electrical upgrade in the presidential suite herself after the maintenance staff informed her that they could not install an outlet in the closet to accommodate a small refrigerator. The maintenance workers were reluctant to drill through the plaster walls to run the conduit. When Marie suggested that the maintenance men replace the light switch with a switch and plug that could provide an outlet for the refrigerator, she received a blank stare. "Finally, I explained it well enough that they got it. It goes in the existing light-switch box. I had them in my house; I had a sewing machine plugged into one in one of the kids' bedrooms. I knew they made them, but I thought I was going to have to do it myself with my toolbox," she recalled.[38]

She also took her hammer and tools with her to help do a First Ladies Build event for Habitat for Humanity. While working on site, she recalled: "I'm out there working with my hammer, and someone said: 'You're not supposed to do that.' To which I replied: 'I've been working with my hands all my life, and know what I'm doing.'"[39] Marie's sewing machine also proved useful. Her daughter once stayed in one of the mansion's bedrooms that had a bed skirt that was too long for the bed. The mansion's staff had implemented a temporary fix by pinning up the skirt to keep it off the floor. When Marie and Roy's daughter climbed out of the bed one night, she was temporarily entangled in the bed skirt when the pins got caught in her clothes. Marie pulled the skirt off the bed and used her sewing machine to shorten it so that it would not be a hazard to the next guest.[40]

The Barneses had a number of notable guests, including Prince Philip, the Duke of Edinburgh. The prince was a special guest of the governor for a Boys and Girls Club dinner, and Roy invited him to spend the night in the presidential suite at the mansion. Marie was eager to make a good impression on such a notable guest,

and when she realized that there were no nice towels, at least not a full set "fit for a king (or prince)," she dashed out to buy some. As she and Roy stepped out front to wait for the prince, she discovered that the wind had blown debris onto the front porch. The staff members who normally tended to such chores had left for the day, so Marie sent her son to fetch a broom and had him quickly sweep the porch. Prince Philip and his entourage, including a personal assistant and valet, stayed in the bedrooms across the front of the house on the third floor, including the presidential suite, and the two adjacent bedrooms.[41]

Roy and Marie had received protocol training in how to interact with royalty. Among the rules was the prohibition against touching a member of the royal family. The prince was scheduled to leave after breakfast the next morning, but the governor, who had an early event that day, would not be there for breakfast. So as the governor and first lady were bidding good night to the prince, Roy placed his hand on Prince Philip's shoulder and said "Prince, I'm not going to be with you in the morning because I have an early speech." Marie was momentarily aghast at this breach of protocol, but Prince Philip never flinched. He gracefully thanked the governor for his hospitality and bid the first couple good night. After the prince retired to his room, Marie pointed out Roy's gaffe, to which the governor responded, "We beat these folks twice, so I don't think there's going to be a lot of bowing and curtsying here."[42]

Breakfast the next morning brought a fashion revelation. Marie noted that the prince used a large diaper pin to hold his tie in place. "I guess that's why it stays in place when he puts his hands behind his back like he does. He's got his coat buttoned and his tie stays in place," she remarked, adding, "Roy's tie goes from one end to another along with his rumpled hair."[43]

The Barneses also entertained Crown Prince Philippe of Belgium and the vice president of the United States. Preparations for Al Gore's visit included a thorough advance inspection by the Secret Service, whose agents, Marie recalled, had no sense of humor. When they asked Marie whether they could bring in the bomb-sniffing dog to inspect the presidential suite, she said in jest, "You better be glad that my dog C.C. just had surgery or she would take on your dog." The agents, according to Marie, "did not think that was funny." When the agents expressed some qualms about whether it was appropriate to bring the vice president of the United

Marie and Roy Barnes with Prince Andrew, 2002. *Courtesy Marie and Roy Barnes.*

States up the spiral staircase, Marie joked, "If he wants to put a ladder outside the balcony and let him come through the window, that would be ok, too." The agents did not think that was funny either.[44]

Both Marie and Roy have a great sense of humor, and living in the governor's mansion did not dampen their enthusiasm for playing practical jokes. On one occasion, Marie squeezed herself into the dumbwaiter that connects the main kitchen on the second floor with the ballroom kitchen on the first floor. The sous-chef was more than a little surprised to open the dumbwaiter door and find the first lady. On another occasion, a state trooper rigged up a cooler in the trunk of the governor's car with a rubber snake. The plan was to scare the governor's driver by having him open the cooler to find the snake. The governor had been informed of the plan, but it slipped his mind. As he approached his car and saw the cooler in the open trunk, he said to the troopers, "Do you have something cold in here?" and pulled open the cooler before the troopers could stop him. The governor jumped back, frightened, before bursting out in laughter. He was so amused that he asked the troopers to leave the cooler in the car so that he could play the joke on his lieutenant governor, Mark Taylor, and

on one of the other troopers, who was so startled that he nearly drew his gun to kill the rubber snake. "We got so much mileage out of that snake," recalled Marie.[45]

Roy and Marie Barnes left the mansion an important legacy—an hour-long documentary titled *The House That Georgia Built*. While visiting the White House, Marie learned about Hillary Clinton's effort to make a video about the White House for distribution to schools. Inspired by this effort and aware that there were nine living Georgia governors, Marie and her staff began working with local television station wsb to produce an hour-long documentary that featured interviews with the surviving governors and first ladies. Governor Maddox's wife, Virginia, was no longer living; Governor Talmadge had suffered a stroke; and Governor Miller was recovering from surgery. But the remaining first couples, from the Vandivers to the Barneses, were able to participate. Marie Barnes recalled: "All of the other governors and their wives came, even President and Mrs. Carter. We sat around the dining room table with television news anchors John Pruitt and Monica Kauffman and talked about how the current mansion was built. Carl Sanders told about how he and Betty traveled around looking for an existing house to serve as the mansion and about Lester Maddox being the first to live in the new Executive Center. Then they interviewed each governor and first lady about personal stories."[46] The production team later visited Zell and Shirley Miller at their home, so their voices were also included.

Though Roy and Marie loved their time at the mansion and were disappointed when Roy lost his reelection bid in 2002, they were also ready to return to their civilian lives. Roy explained, "The Governor's Mansion is a beautiful place, but as Joe Frank Harris once said, it's like living in the lobby of a hotel. There are people coming and going all the time. The big fence is not to keep people out, but to keep the governor in. It's a beautiful place, a great honor, but it's not home."[47] They certainly missed the staff and the friendships they had made, but were prepared for the transition. Marie elaborated, "I'm not good at having people do things for me. It was a relief to get my life back. After we got our old house renovated, we were happy." Although she was sad to leave the mansion, Marie had no regrets about her time there. "The only thing I wish from the first lady's perspective was that there was a six-year, one-time term. That would give you time to get things done, and the first lady would know when she's going home."[48]

As Marie and Roy readjusted to their regular lives, both of them found that one of the greatest challenges was to relearn to drive. For security purposes, the governor and his wife are not permitted to drive themselves, and a trooper is assigned to drive them at all times. As a result, many of the first families were out of practice when they again got behind the wheel of a car. Marie

nearly wrecked her car the first time she left the mansion. She kept her Mustang while she lived at the mansion, and would often ask the state trooper to drive it when she went to play tennis. She did not drive herself, and was rarely alone. The lack of privacy is a recurring theme in stories from all the first families, and it becomes noticeable in many ways. As Marie quipped, "There's nothing like going to have a mammogram with a six-foot-five-inch state trooper standing behind you. He wasn't in the room with me, but he knew what I was doing."[49] Being able to return to a regular life was a relief and a privilege.

On the last Sunday in the mansion, they gathered friends and family for a farewell. During the event, the governor choked up: "Let me tell you how much I appreciate you [for] sticking with me through the good and the bad." When asked what he looked forward to, he mentioned learning to use the laptop that he had recently received for Christmas.[50] Upon leaving office, Governor Barnes returned to the practice of law. He volunteered for the Atlanta Legal Aid Society, Inc., for a while, and then established the Barnes Law Group with his daughter Allison Barnes Salter, his son-in-law John Salter, and his longtime law partner Charles Tanksley. The family returned to their newly renovated home, where they lived before building a new home in Marietta. They also bought a seventy-acre farm in Powder Springs. Visitors to the Barneses' Marietta home notice immediately a legacy of their time at the mansion—the great seal of the State of Georgia that graces their entryway, reminding them of their service to the state and its people.

Mary and Sonny Perdue, 2006. *Courtesy Richard B. Russell Library for Political Research and Studies, University of Georgia.*

CHAPTER TEN

Down-Home Style

THE PERDUES

In January 2003, George Ervin "Sonny" Perdue became the first Republican governor elected in the state of Georgia since Rufus Bullock in 1868.[1] A native of Perry, Georgia, Sonny Perdue earned his degree in veterinary medicine from the University of Georgia, where he also played football. While in school, he volunteered to serve in the air force, from which he was discharged as a captain in 1974. Sonny practiced briefly as a veterinarian before embarking on business ventures in agriculture and transportation. His political career began in the 1980s when he won a seat on the Houston County Planning and Zoning Board. In 1990, he successfully ran for the Georgia Senate, where he served for eleven years, eventually becoming majority leader and president pro tempore before resigning to run for governor.

A native of New Orleans who grew up in Atlanta, Mary Ruff also attended the University of Georgia, where she studied dance and graduated with a degree in speech pathology. When she was eighteen years old, she met Sonny on a blind date, a concert by the Fifth Dimension. "I thought he was handsome," she recalled, "but there was something besides physical attractiveness that was intriguing. He was mature for his age and had strong faith."[2] Sonny and Mary dated for four years and married in September 1972.

Sonny Perdue was elected governor in November 2002, and the Perdues moved from their home in Bonaire, a small town near Warner Robins, to the Governor's Mansion in January 2003. Moving to the mansion was quite an experience, recalled Mary. Although she had grown up in Atlanta and had attended high school there, the city had changed considerably since she had last lived there. "We had lived in our hometown since the mid-1970s, and in our home since mid-1980s," she recalled, adding, "We were excited and nervous, had that unbelievable feeling." At their home in Bonaire, the family was known for their brunches, for which Mary cooked biscuits, country ham, sausage casseroles, quiche, pancakes, and grits. As Sonja Lewis reported in the *Atlanta Journal-Constitution*, "Her husband would tell stories, and she wouldn't sit down and eat until she was sure everyone else had a full plate and glasses."[3] They were about to inherit a 24,000-square-foot, thirty-room mansion with a sixteen-member staff, including two chefs. But Mary was accustomed to playing hostess. Her friend Lanie Nash ventured, "[I can see] Mary serving the servants. Or trying to. She's going to say, 'Let me fix the tea. Let me help you with those biscuits. Let me do the dusting.'"[4]

Planning the first Republican inauguration in more than a century required some attention. As Alec Poitevint, cochairman of the Perdue inaugural committee, explained, "We've been waiting 130 years for this. There's been a lot of us excited about it and always wanting to do an inauguration. So we're gonna make sure we do this right." On Monday, January 13, several hundred people gathered for a prayer service at the Church of the Apostles, where Truett Cathy, founder of Chick-fil-A, and Mark Richt, UGA's football coach, spoke, and Sonny and Mary's son, Jim Perdue, gave the sermon.[5]

The inauguration was held at Philips Arena, breaking with the tradition of holding it on the capitol steps. Performances at the inaugural ball on Monday evening included "The Battle Hymn of the Republic" by the Perdues' hometown church choir and "Georgia on My Mind" by Ray Charles. The event attracted ten thousand guests who paid fifty dollars a ticket. The Atlanta Symphony Orchestra performed for a dance featuring

Open house at the mansion, 2003.
Courtesy Mary and Sonny Perdue.

Sonny and Mary. Expressing the kind of anticipation that most first ladies felt at the beginning of their terms, Mary reported that although she did not "know everything that was involved" in being the first lady, she was "excited," adding, "But I'm not nervous."[6] The Perdues brought with them a few furnishings from their home in Bonaire to go in the family quarters on the second floor—Sonny's recliner and Mary's chair and ottoman. They also brought family pictures, which were distributed throughout the family quarters, along with scripture references, to help make the mansion feel like home.[7] Mary had long enjoyed playing the piano, and soon after they moved in, Sonny bought her a baby grand piano that was placed in their bedroom. Jen Bennecke, her assistant, remembered: "She really missed playing and especially loved hymns. This helped her relieve stress."[8]

When the Perdues moved into the mansion in January 2003, their youngest son, Dan, a mechanical engineering student at Georgia Tech, moved in with them. Pondering the change in his family's life, Dan projected that his mother's life was likely to be the one most altered. "She's always been the one that liked to take care of the family," he said, adding, "Now she'll have a definite set of duties. She'll do a great job, because she's such an advocate for children, but it's a definite change."[9] The Perdues' three older children, Leigh, Lara, and Jim, "were all amazed, but not completely surprised" when their father was elected governor, according to Lara, who added, "Every day, he's in the newspaper somewhere. It took some getting used to. I am somewhat protective of him and want people to understand who he is and what he stands for. There's almost this feeling like you have to explain . . . like you're a warrior carrying the message." Leigh, a speech therapist who was married and had three-year-old twin daughters, Mary Kate and Sunni, noted that one day her daughters would study Georgia history, which will include their grandfather. When asked about her father's new job, she said: "It's exciting, and these are memories that we'll have for a lifetime."[10] She also noted, "I think it's going to be a journey for all of us, a journey into the unknown. And at the end of the four years, going to the Governor's Mansion won't be a big deal. Which will be odd."[11] Jim Perdue, a seminary student in North Carolina, had to get used to "Sonny" chants at an SEC championship game at the Georgia Dome in December

Mary Perdue greeting guests at a foster-family appreciation event, 2006. *Courtesy Richard B. Russell Library for Political Research and Studies, University of Georgia.*

2002.[12] It was quite a spectacle: "People were running down the bleacher aisles, leaning over the railing and thrusting their programs forward—asking Perdue for autographs."[13]

The Perdues' love of children was well known. Before becoming governor, Sonny and Mary cared for eight foster babies over a two-year period through Covenant Care in Macon while the children were waiting to be placed with adoptive parents. Mary made child welfare the centerpiece of her work as first lady. While living in the governor's mansion, the Perdues had their hands full with their own expanding family. When they moved in, they had two grandchildren. By the time they moved out, they had twelve. The children and grandchildren were regular visitors to the mansion, and as Mary explained, in the minds of the grandchildren, "it was their house, a place they came to visit." She and Sonny welcomed them with open arms: "We tried to make them comfortable. You have to live here, and if you have family, you have to find a way to make them comfortable."[14] The Perdues loved having the grandchildren visit, and as the reporter Mia Taylor noted, "It's not unusual to see the governor-elect, whom his granddaughters call 'Big Buddy,' down on the living room floor on his hands and knees, giving them rides on his back, or his wife sitting, one girl on each side of her, reading quietly to them to settle them down at day's end."[15] Mary remembered

that the first things they unloaded from the moving truck at the mansion were the twins' tricycles. Like so many governors' grandchildren before them, Mary Kate and Sunni learned to ride their tricycles in the mansion ballroom.

The Perdues made healthy eating a priority, so mansion chef Holly Chute dispensed with much of the traditional southern fare that had been favorites of previous residents. Holly often packed the governor his favorite lunch—a shrimp chopped salad or watermelon and coleslaw marinated in vinegar and Sweet'n Low. As a result, the governor lost thirty pounds while in office. Holly noted, "He would be so busy and who knows when he would have time to eat, so I would pack the cooler and he would have it with him."[16] Sonny's assistant, Joyce White, recalled that the governor ate all kinds of fruit and especially loved watermelon, something that he was happy to eat every day, along with peach- or orange-flavored water.[17] For dinner, Holly served such dishes as grilled fish in citrus vinaigrette, snap peas, tomatoes, squash, and okra.[18] Since the family typically didn't like to be waited on by the staff, they ate in the kitchen instead of the family dining room. Sonny had few demands, but always wanted to have raisin bran and Honey Graham Oh's cereal on hand. An early riser, he would start each day with a bowl of cereal at the mansion around 5:45 a.m., after which he would head down to the Georgia State University Recreation Center for a game of racquetball before arriving at his office in the capitol by 7:15 a.m.[19] On weekends, Sonny liked to cook something more substantial for breakfast. One weekend morning, he came down to the kitchen and began looking for some bacon. In an effort to support the healthy diet that the Perdues advocated, Holly had chosen to replace the traditional pork bacon with turkey bacon. The governor was less than thrilled. As Mary's executive assistant, Jen Bennecke, recounted, Sonny left Holly a note inquiring, "Where on the turkey do you find the bacon?"[20]

The Perdues ate most of their meals at home, because, as Mary recalled, "It's very difficult for the governor and his wife to go to a restaurant. People want to speak to you. If we wanted private time together, we would have to stay in. Sonny and I often sat in the kitchen when it was just the two of us. Most nights, Holly would fix our dinner and leave it. I didn't feel it was necessary to have the staff stay to serve us dinner."[21] Sometimes Mary cooked, making soup in the winter or her son's favorite meal of country-fried steak, mashed potatoes, and zipper peas.[22] In the evenings, they retired to the family sitting room upstairs, and Mary worked on crossword puzzles or Sudoku. Sonny watched sports on television. As she explained, "Just sitting together was enough. We had so little private time together."[23]

The Perdues' brindle boxer, Ivy, was a much-loved member of the family. She became a fixture at the mansion, often napping under the table in the family dining room during public tours. After Ivy had to be put down near the end of Sonny's second term, the Perdues adopted another boxer, Mercy. As Mary remembered, "This place was dog crazy. Everybody wanted to train her."[24]

By the time the Perdues moved into the mansion, the building was thirty-five years old. Very few changes had been made to it since its opening in 1968, and the place

Commanders' Lunch, 2006. *Courtesy Richard B. Russell Library for Political Research and Studies, University of Georgia.*

Governor Perdue delivering remarks at a Friends of the Mansion event, 2005. *Courtesy Richard B. Russell Library for Political Research and Studies, University of Georgia.*

was in desperate need of repair. Even before they moved in, Mary had a foreshadowing of what lay before her. She recalled:

> After Sonny was elected and before we moved in, we were at an event, and someone commented to me the last time they visited, they said it looked shabby. I was mortified. The mansion could not look shabby. When we finally moved in, I began to see what they were talking about. Draperies had been hung for too long, and they had dry rot. There were stains on the rugs. I thought we really needed to do something to take care of this museum-quality collection. If we failed to do so, it will be gone in a few generations. The way the state budget worked, there was nothing on a regular basis to take care of the collection. The Georgia Building Authority was in charge of the building, but the mansion's collection had no protection in the annual budget. I decided to create a non-profit organization called Friends of the Mansion to help protect the collections. We received some criticism in the press, but people were very generous and contributed funds so we could make long-overdue repairs."[25]

Friends of the Mansion was created in 2005 to support the preservation and restoration of the residence's collection of furnishings and art. Mary explained, "Any sitting governor who might go to the legislature and say, 'We need a new rug; we need a new drapery; we have furniture that needs to be repaired,' would be criticized if they tried to put something in the budget like that

annually."[26] Friends of the Mansion provided a way to raise money for the collection without having to worry about the politics of doing so. "The Perdues recognized that caring for the mansion's collection was going to be a challenge," recalled Jen Bennecke, who went on to explain:

> We coordinated with a reconstituted Executive Fine Arts Committee to renovate and restore the pieces in the collection. After 40 years there were things that needed conservation and repair. For example, nearly everything needed repair in the guest bedroom on the first floor. The rug was in such disrepair that you couldn't walk on it. The curtains had dry rot and holes in the back. The gilt on the frames had become so worn. The furniture had been broken; one chair was held together with duct tape. We had the rug reproduced. Because there was no way to repair original English gros point carpet from 1805, we had pillows made out of the remnants.[27]

Perhaps the most visible change during the Perdues' residency was the kitchen renovation. The kitchen had not been updated since its original construction. As Mary noted, "The 1968 kitchen was not beautiful, but strictly functional. Sonny used to joke that it looked like something from a Waffle House. There was an old electric stove, and a larger gas stove that was hard to operate."[28] Jen Bennecke added: "The kitchen wasn't even up to code. There was one working burner. Holly

Keeping Time at the Mansion

Among the furnishings at the Governor's Mansion are ten antique clocks—timepieces chosen by the Fine Arts Commission as part of the mansion's original collection of furnishings in 1967. Until 2006, most of those clocks did not work. That was the year that Atlanta Chapter 24 of the National Association of Watch and Clock Collectors began overseeing the antique timepieces in the mansion.

The club first became involved with maintaining clocks for the state government in 1998, when its members volunteered to work with the Department of Natural Resources to assess clocks at state-owned historic sites. The volunteers deemed fourteen clocks worthy of restoration and made the necessary repairs to get them working. Ever since, the club has stayed involved in maintaining historic clocks that belong to the state, including those at the capitol. After club members presented a restored clock to Governor Sonny Perdue in August 2005, he invited the club to assess the mansion's collection of antique timepieces. The members made their first visit to the mansion in 2006 and identified ten clocks that needed cleaning or restoration. Some of the clocks had been stored in the attic for some time. The collection includes wall and mantel clocks, including seven made in France, two banjo-style clocks, and a grandfather clock that marks time with Westminster chimes dating from 1920.

Mary Perdue with chapter members. *Courtesy Atlanta Chapter 24 of the National Association of Watch and Clock Collectors.*

George Waterhouse coordinates the Committee for the Restoration of Georgia Governor's Mansion Clocks with volunteers Brooks Coleman, Donna Kalinkiewicz, Christian Brown, Bernie and Carol Tekippe, Warren and Kathy Brook, Randy Grunwell, Richard Mangum, Kathi Edwards, Martha Smallwood, Pete Schreiner, Chris Martin, and Mike Mellard. The club members visit the mansion regularly to wind and clean the clocks. As Warren Brook explained in 2014 to H. M. Cauley of the *Atlanta Journal-Constitution*, "I know that for many people, a mechanical clock or watch holds no interest. . . . But there is virtually nothing you can buy today that will work in its same purpose in another 50 or 200 years. A clock can do that." Thanks to the members of Atlanta Chapter 24 of the National Association of Watch and Clock Collectors, the beautiful timepieces that are part of the collection at the Governor's Mansion are no longer just decorative—they once again keep time.

From the mansion clock collection. *Courtesy Christopher Oquendo.*

used to make 18,000 cookies to give to the public during the Christmas tours in that 1960 oven."[29] The eighteen-month project, funded by the Georgia Building Authority, displaced the kitchen staff but did not slow down the events calendar. Holly and her team moved to the serving kitchen in the basement and operated as best they could until the new kitchen was ready.

The Perdues faced a few natural disasters during their tenure. In September 2008, a small fire broke out at the mansion. The family was not home, and damage was limited to the framework of the front door. The cause was not determined, but it seemed to be related to waterproofing work that had been recently completed.[30] In 2008, a series of thunderstorms destroyed a number of trees on the property. The Perdues used the incident to draw attention to the importance of conservation, since the state had been suffering from a multiyear drought. As Governor Perdue explained when planting an Athena elm, "Fall planting of trees and shrubs is one of the practices we want to encourage in building a culture of conservation. By planting drought-resistant and disease-resistant trees, Georgians will be able to conserve our resources and keep our state beautiful."[31] The Perdues also added a rope swing

The mansion's kitchen before the renovation, c. 2007. *Courtesy Georgia Governor's Mansion.*

Mary Perdue in the mansion's renovated kitchen, 2014. *Courtesy Jennifer Dickey.*

Tree planting on the mansion grounds, 2008. *Courtesy Richard B. Russell Library for Political Research and Studies, University of Georgia.*

in the backyard and worked with the trusties to build a playground for children.

Every governor and first lady host notable guests, and the Perdues were no exception. In April 2008, they welcomed His Highness the Aga Khan to Georgia for a luncheon in honor of his fiftieth anniversary as imam. He was the forty-ninth spiritual leader of Ismaili Muslims and was the founder and chairman of the Aga Khan Development Network, a series of agencies working to empower communities in sub-Saharan Africa, Central and South Asia, and the Middle East.[32] The Aga Khan had already visited Texas, California, and Illinois, and made Georgia his final stop. During the Golden Jubilee year, he made official visits to thirty countries to promote cooperation and global partnerships. In May 2008, the Perdues hosted UN Secretary-General Ban Ki-moon at a state luncheon with 130 guests.[33] The first lady of Argentina, Senator Cristina Fernández de Kirchner, spent the night at the mansion. She arrived with a valet, an assistant, and several other staff members who attended to her many needs during her stay. But the mansion staff had to help when she requested such things as an obscure type of loose-leaf tea that was available only at the DeKalb Farmer's Market. According to Jen Bennecke, "She had so many specific demands, and our staff was working behind the scenes to help complete all these requests."[34] Mary recalled, "She assumed the mansion was a five-star hotel. I learned to be very careful to understand our guest's expectations before extending an invitation to stay overnight."[35]

Governor Perdue greeting the Canadian ambassador to the United States, Frank McKenna, 2005. *Courtesy Richard B. Russell Library for Political Research and Studies, University of Georgia.*

The Perdues also used the mansion to recognize the long hours of service and dedication of the staff. Sonny had a special event for his assistant, Joyce White, and her family near the end of his second term—something that meant a lot to Joyce and her daughters. As Joyce recalled:

> I had a very demanding job, and I missed a lot of my daughters' soccer games and events. . . . I think the governor was trying to tell me how much he appreciated that sacrifice. He invited our family to have dinner and spend the night, and [he] let the girls swim. They could bring a friend. That was very memorable for us. We had one of Holly's meals, played tennis, swam, and rode the Gator [a utility vehicle] around the lawn. It felt like being with best friends. We are close to the Perdues, but that night was really special. You're in the trenches every day; you never know where the shots are fired from, so you become a very close team.[36]

Many of the events that the Perdues hosted focused on children and teenagers. On May 25, 2004, the Perdues invited members of Diana DeGarmo's family to join friends and neighbors at the mansion to watch the live broadcast of *American Idol*. DeGarmo, a sixteen-year-old singer from Snellville, was one of seventy thousand people who auditioned for the show, and she rose to become one of the two finalists in the third season. Sonny "abandoned all pretense of neutrality" and signed a proclamation declaring Tuesday "Dial for Diana DeGarmo Day." He invited DeGarmo's friends and family members to join them at the mansion and

urged Georgians to watch the show and call in and vote for DeGarmo by telephone. In spite of the governor's efforts, DeGarmo came in second to Fantasia Barrino. But the governor's pride in having a citizen of Georgia in the finals was evident.[37]

In May 2006, the Perdues hosted an unusual gathering, the first of its kind—a prom after-party for 240 teenagers that lasted until four in the morning. As the *Atlanta Journal-Constitution* reported, "In the ballroom, a space where state lawmakers dine and captains of industry hear pitches on the virtues of Georgia, Gwinnett County teenagers lounged in shorts and jeans, T-shirts and camisoles."[38] Sonny and Mary invited students from Brookwood High School in suburban Snellville to the mansion to enjoy a safe and alcohol-free party after their prom. They played Ms. Pac-Man; ate hash browns, waffles, hamburgers, and eggs from the Waffle House; and danced with the fifty-nine-year-old governor. The school was chosen because it had "extensive programs that promote responsible decision making, particularly around the time of spring break, prom and graduation."[39] Jonathan Post, a senior, said: "It's cool to come to his house, and the fact that I don't drink [makes this] the best after-party." The students enjoyed basketball in the parking lot, karaoke on the patio, and games on the lawn. Sonny wore a black polo shirt, khaki pants, a Waffle House visor, and a glow-in-the-dark necklace. He danced with the students and "jammed on the air guitar."[40] The festivities lasted long into the morning,

Mary and Sonny Perdue at a mansion-hosted *American Idol* party, 2004. *Courtesy Mary and Sonny Perdue.*

Playing foosball at the mansion's prom after-party, 2006. *Courtesy Richard B. Russell Library for Political Research and Studies, University of Georgia.*

when five buses picked up the teenagers, all of whom were given a T-shirt and towel as parting gifts. Maggie McDaris, a junior who danced with the governor, said that she and the governor "are BFF now, because we did the Cha-Cha Slide together." She planned to stay in touch: "I'll hit him up on his cell."[41] The event was sponsored by the Georgia Sheriff's Association and was intended to keep students off the roads and safe on what is traditionally a very dangerous night for teenagers.[42]

In June 2007, the Perdues invited seventy families to the Governor's Mansion to celebrate Foster Family Appreciation Night. This issue was very close to the Perdues' hearts, since they had long served as foster parents. As Mary explained, "Sonny and I are thrilled to celebrate with those who have found families and those who will find families in the future. We want to highlight the children who are the stars of Wednesday's Child and were courageous enough to be on television and focus on their need for a permanent family."[43] The dinner was part of Mary's "Kid's First" initiative, which focused on abused and neglected children. Later in the fall of that same year, the Perdues hosted players and families from the 2006 Columbus Northern and 2007 Warner Robins American Little League teams. They were the World Series Little League Champions.[44] In August 25, 2009, Mary Perdue hosted a Reading under the Stars event at the mansion for Georgia's prekindergarten students. She gathered the students in the mansion's gardens and read *Bedtime in the Jungle* by John Butler. One event, though, did not go as planned, as Joyce White remembered:

> We were having this big economic-development event in the mansion. They invited VIPs, and Bill Elliott, the NASCAR driver, was on the invitation list. The night came for the dinner, and the staff received guests at the door. Bill Elliott was scheduled to sit at the head table with the governor. This guy named Bill Elliott showed up, [and he] was clearly out of place. Whoever sent the invites pulled the address from Google or the phone and sent it to the wrong Bill Elliott, not the NASCAR driver. There were dignitaries in the room, so Governor Perdue just had to roll with it. The governor was always doing something with Atlanta Motor Speedway, so after the event he got a cardboard cutout of Bill Elliott and brought it back with him to show Joy Forth, the mansion manager, and others what he looked like. He walked around and introduced the cardboard Bill Elliott to everyone. Joy got a lot of ribbing about that. Bill Elliott (the cardboard one) spent time in a variety of offices because Governor Perdue moved him around.[45]

Governor Perdue with his grandchildren, Jack, Sunni, and Mary Kate, at the mansion's Easter Egg Hunt, 2005. *Courtesy Richard B. Russell Library for Political Research and Studies, University of Georgia.*

Like most of the governors' families before them, the Perdues celebrated the holidays with a public flair. Easter was always quite an event, with hundreds of children invited to the mansion for the annual Easter egg hunt. During their time in the mansion, the Perdues hosted foster kids, medically fragile children, and children of veterans. At their fifth annual egg hunt, held in April 2007, the Perdues opened up the event to the public. Around two hundred children showed up, and as Andrea Jones of the *Atlanta Journal-Constitution* reported, "The kids descended down the mansion's front lawn like a horde of ants, snatching up eggs before you could say 'Happy Easter.'" The "camera-wielding parents had to be quick" to get photographs of their children grabbing up the 1,400 eggs scattered across the lawn, noted Jones.[46] Participants were asked to bring donations for Families First, a nonprofit agency that helped foster and adopted children. The event took much advance planning by staff members, who dyed hundreds of eggs and baked hundreds of cupcakes and cookies for the guests.[47] During the event, the children bounced in a moonwalk, had their faces painted, had their photographs made with the Easter bunny, and decorated hard-boiled eggs. At the egg-decorating station, Jones observed a seven-year-old who "carefully lettered the word 'Jesus' with stickers (delighting his mom) and then picked up a marker, writing 'Green Bay' underneath," on a hardboiled egg, adding, "I love them both."[48]

Mary and Sonny Perdue with their family, 2011. *Courtesy Mary and Sonny Perdue.*

Christmas entertainment during open house at the mansion, 2009. *Courtesy Richard B. Russell Library for Political Research and Studies, University of Georgia.*

Christmas, another holiday that was always a production at the Governor's Mansion, found every first family's taste reflected in the mansion's holiday decorations. For their first Christmas there, Mary selected a style described by the reporter Alma Hill as "simple and elegant." Inspired by Colonial Williamsburg, Mary wanted "the decorations to enhance and not cover the beauty of the mansion." She blended greenery, pinecones, nuts, faux fruit, and berries with nineteen trees, nearly twenty thousand lights, and "enough swags, poinsettias and wreaths to stock a small nursery."[49] The Perdues also had a "wild game" tree that reflected Sonny's love of hunting. The twelve-foot Fraser fir was decorated with stuffed pheasant and quail borrowed from the Perdues' Bonaire home, along with "bird feather ornaments, silk ribbon and feather garlands," all of which were "intertwined among copper, gold and rust pine cones and balls." The tree was topped with pheasant tail feathers.[50] Like many first families before them, the Perdues created a Hanukkah display in the family dining room, and the Metro Atlanta Kwanzaa Association created a Kwanzaa display in the north end of the ballroom. Students decorated four trees that represented ways the holidays were celebrated in Scandinavia, Brazil, Poland, and Japan.[51]

For their second Christmas in the mansion, the Perdues invited schools from four regions of the state to decorate trees. Oglethorpe Point Elementary School, from coastal Georgia, sent 130 prekindergarten and kindergarten students and more than five hundred handmade ornaments to the mansion. Nine students traveled to Atlanta to help decorate the ten-foot tree. Among the ornaments made by the children were flip-flops made out of a manila folder, painted sand dollars, a cardboard snowman with a beach towel slung over his shoulder, and clear plastic ornaments with sand and tiny seashells inside.[52]

According to Mary Perdue, living in the Governor's Mansion was "a wonderful experience. It was an honor and a privilege. There is no place else like living in the governor's mansion, with the history and the families that have been here. It was a unique and special place to be." After eight years in the "people's house," however, the Perdues were ready to move back to their home in Bonaire. "We knew when it was time to go," said Mary, adding, "Sonny would tell you I moved out early emotionally. I loved our time here, but in the last few months I was ready to go home."[53] The Perdues turned their attention to the future and moved back to Bonaire. Shortly after leaving office, Sonny became the founding partner of Perdue Partners, an Atlanta-based economic-development firm specializing in global commodity trading and consulting services, and made way for Nathan and Sandra Deal, who would succeed him and Mary.

Sandra and Nathan Deal in the second-floor sitting room, 2014. *Courtesy Christopher Oquendo.*

CHAPTER ELEVEN

Georgia Grown

THE DEALS

Since it opened, the Georgia Governor's Mansion has been the "people's house," and nobody has taken the role as its hostess more seriously than Sandra Deal. Guests who walk through the front door are often surprised to see the first lady waiting to greet them. Ember Bishop, her assistant, explained, "She shakes everyone's hand, from the pre-K student to the member of the senior citizen's club. You are made to feel as if you are the most important person in the room. At Christmas, her hand is bruised because she greets so many people."[1] The warmth and hospitality that Sandra's presence exudes on public tour days reflects her approach to the mansion and its collection of fine antiques. She is, at heart, a storyteller who loves to share the mansion's history with visitors. Whether talking about the battleship silver from the USS *Georgia*, the needlepoint portrait of George Washington, or the chandelier that was recovered from the Progressive Club, she shares her infectious enthusiasm with visitors. Her interest in the mansion is not just part of her official duties; it is a personal passion that served as the genesis for this book. Sandra's stewardship of the mansion, supported by the governor, leaves a significant legacy for the state, one of her many contributions as first lady.

The Deals became in 2011 the eighth family to occupy the mansion on West Paces Ferry Road. Governor Nathan Deal was sworn in as Georgia's newest governor on January 10 of that year. He grew up on a farm in Sandersville, where his family raised livestock and grew hay and some grains. His father, Noah Jordan Deal, taught vocational agriculture at Sandersville High School, and young Nathan was active in 4-H and Future Farmers of America (FFA).[2] Nathan developed his competitive spirit while showing cows and pigs, and even won a gold medal at the National FFA Convention in livestock judging. His mother, Mary Mallard Deal, taught school for forty years, and his father taught for thirty years.

The daughter of schoolteachers George and Ida Lou Dunagan, Sandra Dunagan grew up in Gainesville, Georgia. She and Nathan met in 1962 while they were in college. Their first outing was a blind date, arranged by his former high school classmate and her college roommate, Bonnie Kessler Tanner. Sandra explained, "My college roommate invited me down for a weekend, and when I got there, he was my substitute for a trip to the beach."[3] They dated for four years while she finished

Sandra and Nathan on their wedding day, 1966.
Courtesy Sandra and Nathan Deal.

her undergraduate and master's degrees in education at the Women's College of Georgia (now Georgia College and State University) and he completed his undergraduate and law degrees from Mercer University. Sandra and Nathan were married on June 12, 1966, one week after his graduation from law school. Nathan completed judge advocate general school in Charlottesville, Virginia, and served two years in the U.S. Army as an instructor at the Military Police School at Augusta's Fort Gordon. Sandra taught school in Griffin, Macon, Augusta, and Gainesville. Their backgrounds in education fueled their interest in the history of the mansion.

After Nathan left active duty, with the rank of captain, the family settled in Sandra's hometown of Gainesville, where Nathan joined Senator Robert Andrews in his law practice. He became the first full-time assistant district attorney for the Northeastern Judicial Circuit in 1970 and later served as a juvenile court judge before becoming a partner in the firm later known as Greer, Sartain & Carey. Active in the Gainesville Jaycees, Nathan was influenced by the organization's creed, "Service to humanity is the best work of life." This sentiment would shape the couple's public and private lives for decades

to come. Nathan represented the forty-ninth district in the Georgia Senate (1981–93) and was chairman of the Senate Judiciary Committee and president pro tem. When Congressman Edward Jenkins retired, friends and colleagues encouraged Nathan to run for Congress. In 1992, he completed a successful campaign for the U.S. House of Representatives, took office in 1993, and eventually became chair of the Health Subcommittee of Energy and Commerce. He resigned his seat in March 2010 to run for governor. The Deals have four children (Jason, Mary Emily, Carrie, and Katie) and six grandchildren (Fallin, Rosemily, Noah, Dawson, Cordelia, and Ethan).

Like many politically active families in Georgia, the Deals were familiar with the Governor's Mansion before they became residents. Nathan regularly attended events and meetings there when he was in the state senate and later as a U.S. congressman, and Sandra attended several luncheons during the Harris administration. As a member of the Dogwood Garden Club in Gainesville, she once volunteered as a mansion docent.[4] Sandra also visited the mansion with foreign-exchange students during public tour days.[5]

After Nathan won the election in the fall of 2010, Mary Perdue, wife of Governor Sonny Perdue, invited Sandra to take a private tour of the mansion. In late December, as the scheduled move approached, Sandra requested a second visit, to photograph the rugs in the family living quarters to help her decide which recliners and lamps to bring from their Gainesville home.[6] She remembered some good advice from Elizabeth Harris, wife of former Governor Joe Frank Harris, that still makes her laugh: "She told me to do our underwear shopping before we moved in because that was the most embarrassing thing, to shop for something so personal with a state trooper. I took Nathan to the store and bought enough to last. He joked later, 'I don't know why you made me buy so much, they wash it every day, and I only wear the top two pairs.'"[7]

The Deals arrived at the mansion on Thursday, January 6, before Monday's inauguration. Preparing to relocate to the Governor's Mansion had required some thought, but as many first families had discovered, not much packing. The Deals brought clothes, some lamps, and two of the governor's leather recliners. Nathan admitted that he "didn't find any of the chairs upstairs very comfortable," so like governors before him, he brought his own.[8] To remind them of their roots, the Deals brought artwork painted by his mother in the

Deal family, Easter, 2012.
Courtesy Andrea Briscoe.

1930s and hand-painted china from her retirement years. The move itself was fairly quick and painless. As Sandra explained:

> It never occurred to us to enter through the front door. We were coming to work. The moving truck pulled up, and we unloaded our clothes, shoes, recliners, boxes of books, and pictures and came in through the carport. We put all of our belongings on the elevator. With little instruction, the men put the furniture in place, and we hung our clothes in the closet and unpacked the other items. The staff helped me put the books on the shelves in the Governor's office, which now held three small office desks for my assistant, Ember Bishop; Nathan; and me. I hung one of Nathan's mother's oil paintings on the wall in the bedroom, set out a few family pictures and keepsakes, and we were ready for a big crowd of family and friends to arrive. People kept asking if we were settled. It didn't take half a day before we were finished. We slept well that first night and awoke to the smell of coffee and bacon wafting up the stairwell. After only a few days, I learned to keep that door closed, otherwise the wonderful smells from the kitchen tempted us all day.[9]

The Deals' first meal in the mansion consisted of a few sandwiches that they had brought with them from Gainesville's In Between Deli. Then, Holly Chute took over and prepared pork tenderloin, sweet potatoes, and asparagus for their first official dinner.[10]

Their inaugural weekend was filled with activities. On Friday, in a ceremony at the capitol, the couple was presented with Cabbage Patch dolls made in their image, compliments of employees of Babyland Hospital in Cleveland, Georgia, to celebrate their new hospital. On Saturday, the Deals hosted a day of service, which reflected Sandra's "With a Servant's Heart" platform. Nathan went to the Atlanta Mission, and Sandra traveled to Gainesville to visit Good News at Noon (which serves the homeless) and the Good News Clinics (which offer health care to the homeless and low-income families). That evening, they hosted a volunteer-appreciation concert at the Buckhead Theater, where their daughter Katie and son-in-law, Chris, performed. On Sunday morning, the Deals attended services at Second Ponce de Leon Baptist Church before returning to welcome friends and family from all over Georgia to the mansion.

As the governor-elect prepared for his swearing-in ceremony, he kept an eye on the sky and was in constant contact with local meteorologists, who were tracking a winter storm that was forecast to hit Atlanta. Sandra explained, "Nathan had to leave the reception for a while to meet with Governor Perdue and be briefed on the weather predictions and state of emergency preparations."[11] Plans for an outdoor inauguration had to be scrapped. Late on Sunday afternoon, after entertaining guests all day, Nathan and Sandra stopped by the Wild Hog Supper at the Freight Depot, a tradition that has celebrated the opening of the legislative session since 1962, and then attended a dinner at Garrison's in Vinings hosted by Nathan's fraternity brothers. When they arrived at the restaurant, the sky was clear. When they came out, the storm was well under way, and almost two inches of snow was on the ground.[12] Nathan's friends ended up watching the inauguration on television in their hotel rooms. Two of the Deals' children and families stayed at the mansion with their parents, and two stayed at a hotel near the capitol to ensure that they could get to the inauguration safely. Governor-elect Deal urged friends and supporters to stay off the roads and watch the official swearing-in on Georgia Public Television.[13]

On Monday, the inaugural prayer service at Mount Paran Church of God was canceled. The state patrol ferried the Deals from the mansion to the capitol. The swearing-in ceremony, which had been planned for two o'clock on the steps of the capitol, had to be moved into the House chamber. The inauguration was a family affair. Mary Emily, Carrie, and Katie and their mother held the family Bible during the ceremony, and Jason, a superior court judge, swore in his father as Georgia's eighty-second governor. The inaugural ball at Philips Arena was canceled. Although the icy and snowy conditions caused many events to be called off, the Deals demonstrated their good cheer and resilience. A little

snow was not going to prevent them from embracing their new roles as governor and first lady.

Because the mansion was filled with irreplaceable treasures, Sandra immediately took measures to educate her family about the new residence. She took her role as caretaker seriously. When her grandchildren came for their first visit, Sandra said, "You need a formal tour of this house. It is not a place to play hide and seek. This is a museum. The things here are precious because we cannot replace them."[14] The Deals added some personal touches to the mansion that delight visitors. The "adopted" Cabbage Patch dolls are often on display, usually in the two chairs at either end of the large dining table in the state dining room or on the sofa in the state drawing room. Visitors often "do a double-take," according to Nathan, when they walk through and see the dolls. They also added to the front porch a pair of rocking chairs that say "governor" and "first lady." The chairs were made by Spurgeon Ambrose, one of Nathan's fraternity brothers who also happens to be a "very good craftsman," according to Nathan. When Ambrose came towing his huge grill for the Alpha Tau Omega fraternity cookout, he also brought the chairs.[15]

Making such a large, public house into a home took a little bit of work, but it also revealed some unexpected surprises. As Sandra explained, "We had three rooms assigned to us—the office, bedroom, and sitting room. I did not open any additional drawers for months. I was taught to be polite and not ramble around in somebody

Cabbage Patch dolls made in the Deals' likenesses, 2014. *Courtesy Jennifer Dickey.*

Nathan and Sandra Deal on the mansion's front porch, 2014. *Courtesy Christopher Oquendo.*

Sandra Deal and Ember Bishop, 2014.
Courtesy Andrea Briscoe.

else's home. I'm a curious person, but I'm also respectful. The house is really not mine. It belongs to the people of Georgia." Ember concurred, "We were here for a little while when I came in one morning and Mrs. Deal said, 'You have to see this view.' We walked into the aide's bedroom and looked out the window. We were so busy that we hadn't opened the blinds, and there was this amazing view of the formal, terraced gardens that we enjoyed for the first time."[16]

Many first families have commented about having to adjust to the constant presence of staff and security, but the Deals explained that it just required a little bit of planning. Sandra elaborated, "You have to be dressed when you leave your room because there are so many people present who help the mansion run smoothly—from housekeeping to the troopers. On weekends, Nathan will go down and make coffee and bring me a cup before we dress for breakfast."[17] They both had to adjust to having a security guard with them at all times. "I was accustomed to driving myself wherever I went," Nathan stated, noting that when he was serving in Congress, he drove himself to and from the Atlanta airport and sometimes took the Metro to his apartment in Washington, D.C. It took a little time to get used to asking another person to drive him whenever he wanted to go somewhere. Once when the Deals were at their Habersham County residence for the weekend, Nathan slipped off alone to go to a health food store. While shopping, he ran into a friend of Jim Andrews, one of the state troopers who worked for him. The friend reported back to Andrews that he had seen the governor out and about. "Jim knew about it before I got home," recalled Nathan, "and he let me know that if something bad had happened to me, he would have been in trouble. So the only thing that Sandra and I get to drive now is an atv on the farm."[18] Like most of the mansion staff members, the state troopers quickly became part of the family. David Herring, Tony Henry, Jim Andrews, Bobby Mathis, Darin Rice, Mike Coverson, Jimmy Sumner, Chris Wiggington, Braxton Cotton, and Eric Smith have served as the Deals' security detail.

Nathan and Sandra often rise early and eat breakfast in the kitchen to begin their day. During the week, chef Holly Chute and Simon, who has trained as a sous-chef, oversee preparation of their meals. On weekends when they are not at their cabin in Habersham County,

Jim Andrews, Nathan Deal, Sandra Deal, and David Herring, 2010. *Courtesy Andrea Briscoe.*

Georgia-grown products in
the mansion kitchen, 2014.
Courtesy Jennifer Dickey.

Stanley Simon and Sandra Deal with produce from the mansion's
organic garden, 2014. *Courtesy Christopher Oquendo.*

they go out for meals or eat leftovers. Sandra cooks at the cabin but rarely in the mansion kitchen. When the Deals first moved in, Holly continued the tradition begun with Sonny Perdue of packing the governor a lunch to take with him to the office. "I felt like since it was a custom, I had to go along with it," Nathan said. But Nathan did not relish the idea of eating a sandwich by himself in his office. "I am a social person around meals," he explained, adding, "I'd rather go with my staff across the street and eat at the cafeteria and chat informally. I gave the sandwiches away or had the cooler picked up at the end of the day and had the guys downstairs eating it." When Sandra learned that he was giving away his lunch, she put a halt to the custom. "She got tired of paying for it," Nathan explained, with Sandra adding, "I had to put a stop to that, because it was coming out of my budget."[19]

Not everything goes as planned in the mansion. One night, the Deals were jolted awake at 3:13 a.m. when the decorative top of a mirror made in 1775 fell off, making a terrible racket as it crashed to the floor. On another occasion, the governor was resting on the sofa one evening when the scuttle bucket next to the fireplace began to rattle. Earlier that evening, the Deals had hosted all the former governors and their wives for

dinner, and Elizabeth Harris teasingly said, "You know, there is a ghost in the house." The governor reflected on Elizabeth's "ghost" statement and chuckled to himself: "Maybe we made him mad."[20] In fact, a bird had flown down the chimney and was flapping around in the scuttle bucket. The bird eventually made its way downstairs, and the next morning it was chased outside by one of the trusties, but not before leaving telltale droppings on a table. Thereafter, the damper on the upstairs fireplace was closed to prevent further intrusions.[21]

Like their predecessors, the Deals use the mansion to promote Georgia and Georgia products. The Deals had lived for most of their lives on small farms where they grew fresh fruits and vegetables and raised their own meat. They are proud of Georgia-grown products, especially the internationally competitive wines and olive oils. Joy Forth, the mansion manager, noted, "This also reflects a popular trend, the farm-to-table movement." Ember added, "The Deals proudly serve Georgia products and want others to enjoy them. Even in their daily lives, they support the communities that grow and produce them."[22] The Deals have continued their tradition of maintaining a garden and a small orchard on the grounds, but they needed a little help with keeping the chipmunks and squirrels from running off with the bounty.

Two cats, Bill and Veto, who came to the mansion through the governor's chief of staff, Chris Riley, have become part of the family and have jobs of their own—to ward off the animals that want to eat the garden. Chris described their arrival and impact: "They were the unexpected gift of my nine-year-old son's cat, Cinnamon. We brought them to the mansion at eight weeks, and Doug, one of the trusties, became their caretaker. He had been at the mansion for some time and had not spoken very much. The cats became his project, and he built them a home and fed and cared for them. The next thing we knew, he was talking and opening up to the governor and the first lady and to the rest of the staff."[23] The cats have become a source of constant entertainment. Sandra explained, "One day, I saw the cats on the pool cover. They were watching the water move under it. They would jump around as it moved. They were fun to watch. Their job was to catch chipmunks, and they have become very efficient."[24]

The Deals have made three important additions to the grounds that have improved safety, increased the capacity for events, and streamlined operations. During the inauguration weekend's snowstorm, the Deals had a full house, including additional staff members and troopers. When Governor Deal visited their quarters in the red barn, he was surprised. Chris Riley described his reaction: "He walked out to where they were staying and saw the poor condition of the barn, which included the gaps in the walls to the outside, and the department of corrections beds they were using. He immediately decided that they deserved better. He sent the troopers to his home in Gainesville to retrieve newer mattresses and brought them to the red barn, and he started planning and approving construction for what we now call the mini-mansion. The ribbon was cut in the fall of 2011." Also that year, Chris and Steve Stancil, head of the Georgia Building Authority, decided to build a helipad to make landings at the mansion safer. Before this addition, pilots had to land in the grass on the front lawn, without lights. Chris, a pilot, knew that the mansion needed both a safer landing area and a site that could be useful in case of an emergency. In addition, he worked with Steve Stancil and Joy Forth, the mansion manager, to install a permanent tent over the west porch. A guest had passed out after a red carpet tour because of the heat, so besides being an important safety feature, this addition made the space more usable.[25]

Since the duties of the first lady and the mansion staff include caring for and interpreting the mansion's collection, they spent a few months familiarizing themselves with the furnishings, artwork, silver, and other pieces. To help protect the collection, Sandra continued the tradition of selecting an Executive Fine Arts Committee, a group of ten with representatives from

The helipad, 2012. *Courtesy Ember Bishop.*

The mini-mansion for the state troopers, 2014. *Courtesy Jennifer Dickey.*

Renovated guest bathroom, 2014. *Courtesy Andrea Briscoe.*

around the state to assist with restoration and preservation of the entire collection. As with the Fine Arts Committees that came before it, this one reviewed each room and helped prioritize what needed conservation or repair. While Mary Perdue had focused on renovating the kitchen and conserving collection pieces on the main floor, Sandra focused her efforts on the second floor. Four of the rooms had been given attention, but four other rooms needed some work.[26] Noting that the bathrooms in the living quarters had not been updated since the mansion's opening in 1968, the committee recommended that the Formica countertops and the wallpaper be replaced, along with bedspreads and draperies in the bedrooms. Richard Zimmerman, a well-known interior designer whose wife, Vicki Lynn, is a member of the committee, volunteered his expertise.

The library collection also became a special project for Sandra, and it reflects her love of history. As she explained, "Soon after becoming governor, Nathan was asked to speak at a Martin Luther King, Jr., holiday observance ceremony. In preparation for his speech, we searched the mansion library for a book about King. Unable to locate one, Nathan quoted from a book by his friend, U.S. Congressman John Lewis. Later we discovered the card catalog, which helped us find the King book."[27] Soon after, Lamar Veatch, the state librarian, invited Sandra to address a group of librarians at the National Archives branch in Morrow, Georgia. She talked about the mansion's collection, for which she had

great appreciation, and expressed her concern about the treasures hidden on the shelves. Dozens of librarians from across the state volunteered to digitize the library catalogue and, eventually, the books themselves, and to make them available on the Georgia Pines Catalog, the online database used throughout the state.[28] The project also generated some notable additions, including Hugh McCall's two-volume *The History of Georgia: Containing Brief Sketches of the Most Remarkable Events up to the Present Day, 1784* (1811, 1816), donated by the Georgia Daughters of the American Revolution, and a missing volume of *The Revolutionary Records of the State of Georgia*, edited by Governor Allen D. Candler, donated by Veatch. The library project reflects Sandra's commitment to literacy; her Read Across Georgia initiative has reached all 159 Georgia counties.

The volunteer docents who lead tours at the mansion three days a week are a significant part of the operations. As Sandra explained, "I was so grateful when they showed up after we took office. I was worried that each first lady had to recruit new docents. Imagine my relief when they came. I try to go down as often as I can to thank them, but I learned very quickly that they have their own stations and are serious about their work. One day, I was going to say something to an older docent, and she said, 'I'm sorry, Honey, I don't have time. I've got these people to talk to.'"[29] The docents often remark on how knowledgeable Sandra is and how much she enjoys being at the front door to greet her guests, especially children. Kathy Lovett, Sandra's longtime friend from Gainesville and mansion docent, observed, "I just want to say how enriching this experience has been to be a part of the mansion and their administration. Sandra and Nathan are such caring people. It is so exciting to be able to help them. We all feel such a real sense of gratitude about how much we have learned as docents and how much fun it is to share this knowledge with the public."[30] One of the docents, Pat Mutzberg, even contributed to the collection. During a tour of the living quarters as part of the annual docent luncheon, Pat noticed that two of the bedrooms did not have rugs, so she approached the first lady about donating rugs to the collection. The rugs are in the first couple's bedroom and another of the upstairs bedrooms.[31]

Like every governor and first lady before them, the Deals use the mansion to host a range of events, including legislative dinners, Christmas tree lightings, Easter egg hunts, and receptions focused on business

Georgia DAR members presenting
Sandra Deal with Hugh McCall's history
of Georgia, 2013. *Courtesy Ember Bishop.*

Sandra Deal reading to children in the mansion, 2014. *Courtesy Christopher Oquendo.*

and economic development. Special events included the fiftieth anniversary of the Governor's Honors Program and the centennial anniversary of the Girl Scouts. One of the most memorable events supported the Tons of Fun program, which was a statewide fitness challenge by the Department of Natural Resources (DNR) to help combat obesity through good nutrition and an active lifestyle. A highlight of the event, which was hosted on the mansion lawn, came when the first lady and DNR commissioner Mark Williams rappelled off one of the mansion's trees. Joy Forth, the mansion manager, noted that the Deals enjoy these events: "At Christmas, the Easter egg hunt, and Valedictorian Day, they will stand and take pictures with everyone who attends. It is a way to make each visitor feel important. It also reflects their personality. They are tireless and really want to make people feel welcome." That level of hospitality has not gone unnoticed. Joy explained that the staff from the Atlanta Ritz-Carlton wanted to visit the mansion to study its level of service: "I certainly welcomed them but explained that the tone is set by the first lady. We don't measure how far a fork is from the end of the table. We're not Buckingham Palace. Our hospitality is personal. We look to Mrs. Deal, and she gives everyone five-star treatment. The special thing about this house is the people who live in it."[32]

Some events are focused specifically on the staff, which reflects the Deals' tendency to view them as family. Sandra observed, "My husband enjoys hiring young people and takes great pride in watching them develop their talents. He encourages them to participate in group activities outside the office. In August 2012, we hosted ballroom dance lessons for the staff at the mansion. We hired an instructor, and the staff learned the waltz, fox-trot, and the shag. The ballroom was filled with diligent learners who did lots of counting."[33] Two staff members in the governor's office, Erin Hames and Lonice Barrett, pitched the idea of creating a professional development program for the staff. The yearlong program focused on leadership development through seminars, workshops, and guest speakers. The final program ended in June 2014 with an event in the ballroom at the mansion. Chris Riley described the goals of the program: "I have always believed that if you're going to

Cast from Springer Opera House's *A Christmas Carol*, 2013. *Courtesy Christopher Oquendo.*

Easter egg hunt at the mansion, 2014. *Courtesy Christopher Oquendo.*

Hostess luncheon under the tent on the west porch, 2014. *Courtesy Andrea Briscoe.*

Christmas tree delivery to the mansion by the Poppell Family of Jesup, Georgia, 2012. *Courtesy Ember Bishop.*

Nathan's Knuckleballers, 2014. *Courtesy Andrea Briscoe.*

Deal grandchildren: Cordelia, Noah, Fallin, Rosemily, Ethan, and Dawson, at the mansion, December 2011. *Courtesy Nathan and Sandra Deal.*

be in a fox hole with someone, you want to trust them and for them to trust you. You have to come together outside of the office to facilitate those relationships."[34] The Deals also host staff events off-site, including cookouts on the Chattahoochee River in North Georgia, golf outings at Lake Lanier, and softball games pitting Nathan's Knuckleballers against teams from Chick-fil-A, Coca-Cola, Georgia Power, and AGL Resources. All these events reflect the Deals' spirit of good cheer.

Because spending time with their grandchildren can be a challenge, Sandra instituted a tradition that has become a much-loved annual celebration at the mansion—the annual Grandma's Camp. The Deals' six grandchildren are invited to stay at the mansion without their parents for a week each July. Sandra and the grandchildren spend time at the mansion but also venture farther afield. As she explained, "We often see our family one group at a time, and I wanted the six grandchildren to have time together. I want them to have fun, but also to learn something. We have visited sites in Atlanta such as Stone Mountain, Fernbank Museum of Natural History, and the Georgia Aquarium as well as Historic Westville, the Little White House, and various state parks."[35] The governor participates in the festivities when his schedule allows, making it truly a family affair.

Each year for Sandra's birthday in February, members of her prayer group, who also volunteer as docents, are invited to spend the night at the mansion. She said, "We have a spend-the-night party. They come in the afternoon, and we visit a historic site, have dinner and breakfast, and then tour the city again. We have been to the Wren's Nest, the High Museum of Art, the Atlanta History Center, the Margaret Mitchell House, the Carlos Museum at Emory, and Rhodes Hall. It is a wonderful fellowship time and is a great way to celebrate each year."[36]

The Deals also focus on outreach, especially the first lady, through her With a Servant's Heart platform. In addition to hosting groups at the mansion, Sandra has focused on visiting each county in the state to encourage early reading and to learn about organizations that help strengthen their communities. Consistent with that theme, at Christmas 2013, Nathan and his chief of staff, Chris Riley, proposed an alternative to a traditional staff holiday party at the mansion. The staff elected to go to the Atlanta Transitional Center, which houses the trusties who work at sites throughout the state, including the mansion, the airport, the capitol, and state patrol posts. The governor, first lady, and staff members served the trusties a Christmas dinner featuring fried chicken, green beans, and macaroni and cheese. As Ember Bishop observed, "We wanted to show them how much we appreciate everything they do for us. The governor's leadership in establishing a reentry program demonstrates a belief in second chances. Once you've paid your debt to society, we want you to be successful. The guys who work at the mansion knew us and were very comfortable. The others did not know quite what to think. The old saying rings true. Actions speak louder than words."[37] Chris Riley, the governor's chief of staff, added, "The mansion trusties were relaxed and joking at the luncheon. I heard John tell one of the other men, 'I told you how nice the Deals are.' The men who work at the mansion were proud, and I know the staff got a lot out of the event as well."[38] Reflecting on the trusties and the work they do, Nathan commented:

> The trusties are very hardworking people. They never complain. Even though they've committed horrible crimes, Sandra and I appreciate that they would be willing to serve other people, including us. You would not judge them as somebody dangerous. If that were the case, they would not be here. If we have an event, they'll be in their tuxedos, serving the guests. I think it's a simple thing, just respecting human dignity. Prison takes their dignity away from them. If, in some way, their experience at the mansion can help restore that dignity, their

chances of being successful when they are released are greatly enhanced. They try to do the job they are asked to do, even if it is menial. That means a lot. Quite honestly, their display of good character is part of the motivation for planning the third leg of our criminal-justice system, which is transition, support, and reentry.[39]

To a person, the seventeen trusties working at the mansion describe the Deals as "caring and compassionate." When Sandra or Nathan inquires after his day, John replies with a sentiment that is widely shared: "I am blessed because I'm working for you."[40]

Like the first families before them, Nathan and Sandra have their own favorite things at the mansion. Sandra admires the French porcelain Benjamin Franklin vase from about 1800, a mahogany card table owned by the granddaughter of George Walton (Georgia's fourth governor and a signer of the Declaration of Independence), and a painting of the Old Governor's Mansion in Milledgeville by the well-known Atlanta artist and historian Wilbur Kurtz. The painting hung for many years on the family floor of the mansion, but Sandra moved it into a place of prominence in the ballroom on the ground floor so that guests could see it. "I went to college in Milledgeville, and that makes the governor's mansion there really special," Sandra explained, adding, "The dormitory I lived in was on

Wilbur Kurtz's painting of the Old Governor's Mansion in Milledgeville, 2014. *Courtesy Christopher Oquendo.*

the other side of the mansion, so for two years I would walk in front of it every day to go to class."[41]

The governor's favorite spot in the mansion is his leather recliner in the family sitting room. It is there that he feels most comfortable and can relax and watch television. But he does have a great appreciation for the mansion's proximity to his office. "One of my favorite things about the mansion is its convenience," he said. "It's the closest I've lived to work since we moved out into the country in 1973." Nathan also appreciates the value of the mansion as a symbol of the state. The Deals have used the mansion for economic development, much as their predecessors did, with the green carpet and red carpet tours. They have also used it to entertain foreign guests, to sponsor community events that benefit charitable causes, and to promote education through the ever-popular Valedictorian Day. "We use it for the kinds of things you'd expect a mansion to be used for," said Nathan, explaining, "It was planned by Carl and Betty Sanders with that in mind. It is very suited for public entertainment."[42] The Deals have become dedicated caretakers of this extraordinary resource that serves the state of Georgia and its citizens, a role that they will play for another four years following Nathan's reelection on November 4, 2014.

Joy Forth, Alyssa Botts, Ember Bishop, and Sandra Deal at the mansion, 2015. *Courtesy Andrea Briscoe.*

CHAPTER TWELVE

Manning the Mansion

Eight first families have left an imprint on the mansion; so, too, have the dozens of people who have worked there since 1968. In addition to functioning as a home for the first family, the mansion serves as a venue for dozens of events throughout the year. As Marie Barnes explained, "The mansion staff did a marvelous job of putting together the events. Basically, thank goodness, all we had to do was show up."[1] The staff and volunteers maintain the building and its collection of furnishings and fine arts as well as the expansive grounds and gardens. Running the mansion takes a team of people with a vast range of skills and experience. This army of people—the first lady, who sets policy; the mansion manager, who oversees the day-to-day operations and special events; the Atlanta Transitional Center residents, who maintain the house and grounds; the chef and kitchen staff, who plan and prepare all the meals; the volunteer docents, who lead the guided tours; the Georgia State Patrol troopers, who provide security—all work together to make the mansion the pride of Georgia. An additional team, including members of the committees that help oversee the mansion's collections, has helped ensure that it remains in good condition and accessible to the public. Finally, several animals, from the bomb-sniffing dogs to Bill and Veto, the mansion's two cats, also serve the mansion.

First Lady

The first lady is the captain of the ship; she sets the tone for life in the mansion both publicly and privately. In the transition manual given to the governor after the election, there is a short, two-page section titled "The Role of the First Lady and the Management of the Executive Mansion." Though she did not run for election or apply for the position, the first lady inherits a full-time, unpaid job to oversee the daily operations of what is "both a private residence and a public facility" fondly called the "people's house." One of the first lady's main duties is to establish "a schedule and agenda for management of the executive residence." This includes setting policies for who can use the mansion. Most of the eight families who have lived in the mansion have allowed nonprofit organizations and charities to use it as an event venue, but that is a decision made by each first family. The first lady also plays a role in distinguishing between official functions (paid for by the state) and personal functions (paid for by the first family). As the manual explains, "The need for separating the personal expenses from public expenses requires very stringent record-keeping

The first ladies of Georgia at Marie Barnes's home, December 2012. *Courtesy Sandra and Nathan Deal.*

and accounting from the start. It is the responsibility of the Governor and First Lady to ensure that these records are accurately prepared and maintained." A third major area of responsibility is to resolve "any management or policy problems that arise at the mansion compound." While each first family is free to hire whom they choose, many have retained staff members and staff positions from the previous administrations. This has helped with efficiency and continuity. The section of the manual dealing with the first lady concludes with an important warning: "The demands on the time and energies of a First Lady are tremendous. She will almost certainly face a loss of privacy and a corresponding need for security precautions." As a result, she can find "herself dealing with a greater share of day-to-day decisions than prior to her husband's election."[2] While the first lady is the captain of the ship, she has a dedicated crew that helps things run smoothly.

Mansion Manager and First Lady's Executive Assistant

Two positions that are instrumental to the smooth running of the mansion are the mansion manager and the first lady's executive assistant. They work together, in conjunction with the first lady, to keep everything happening on time and under budget.

If the first lady is the ship's captain, the mansion manager is the first mate. A number of talented people have held this job, including Mary Page Dwozan, Caroline Ballard Leake, Amy Huckaby, Maurice "Mo" Perron, Sharon Burrow, and Joy Forth. This job requires the skill of a diplomat, the energy of a jackrabbit, the patience of Job, and the humor of Groucho Marx. The position has evolved over the years, and it is so complex that there is no formal job description. As the current manager, Joy Forth, explained:

The best thing about the job is that every day is different. I might be overseeing an event, dealing with a plumbing issue, researching an issue related to protocol, or making sure I have the right supplies. I oversee tours, maintenance of the house and the fine arts collection, and special events. I work hand in hand with the rest of the staff—Kirk Talgo on grounds, Chris Riley in the governor's office, and chef Holly Chute and her assistant, Simon, in the kitchen. I have to make sure no details are overlooked. My goal is to ensure that the governor and first lady are the best hosts they can be and that the guests all have a lovely time. I have to do all of this without overspending our budget.[3]

She explained, "If we have a big event, it's an all-skate. Everybody skates. We do what is required to make it all work. We all want it to be a success. Everyone works so hard that when you hear compliments about the food, the flowers, or the hospitality, it can bring you to tears of joy in a hurry."[4]

The first lady's executive assistant keeps an office at the mansion and is also a key member of the crew. He or she maintains the first lady's schedule, coordinates appearances, oversees public relations and social media, keeps records, answers correspondence, processes mail, and assists with events at the mansion. Like the mansion manager, "this person has almost unlimited access to the First Lady and the private areas of the mansion, and must be someone who has the implicit trust and confidence of the First Lady."[5] As Ember Bishop, Sandra Deal's assistant, explained, "It is a very intimate relationship. I am amazed how much I know about Mrs. Deal—what she likes to eat, when she is tired, and what kinds of clothes she enjoys wearing. If we were thousands of miles away, I could probably pull it all together. If I don't trust my own decision, I can say to her, 'This is how I'm feeling about this. What do you think?' We talk about everything and trust each other."[6]

Ember Bishop and Governor Deal's photographer, Andrea Briscoe, 2013.
Courtesy Jennifer Dickey.

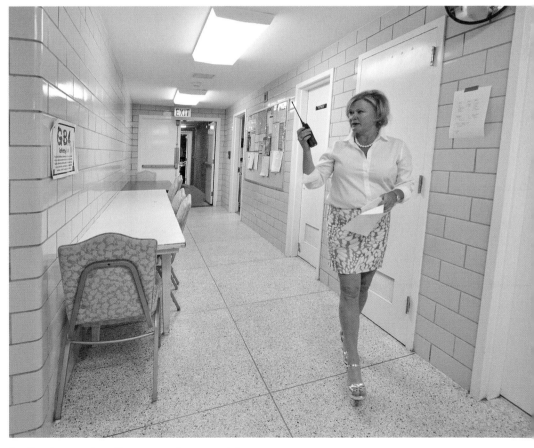

Joy Forth, mansion director, on the ground floor, 2014.
Courtesy Jennifer Dickey.

Landscape Manager

The Georgia Building Authority (GBA) has three positions—two assistant managers and one manager—who oversee the landscaping at the GBA's three dozen buildings. Kirk Talgo holds the position of landscape manager at the mansion, and his main role is to create a landscape plan, oversee the grounds, and manage the team of Atlanta Transitional Center (ATC) residents (trusties) who maintain the grounds. Part of Kirk's duties includes training the trusties to use the right techniques and to learn a new trade. Kirk focuses on preserving the original design of the landscaping as well as trying new things such as composting, introducing native species, planting an organic garden, and using the greenhouse to grow flowers, fruits, or plants that can be used in the house and on the grounds. Kirk, who has worked at the mansion for two years, oversees eight of the men from the ATC and noted, "It was a pleasant surprise to see how motivated the guys are, how willing they are to do just about anything necessary to be done. They have a great work ethic, and the whole team coordinates really well. It's a very collaborative situation."[7]

Trusties

Many visitors are surprised to learn that the majority of the workers at the mansion are prisoners serving life sentences. The ATC program commonly known as the Trusty Program has been part of the Department of Corrections' reentry effort for more than half a century and is also used in other states. Inmates in Georgia work at the mansion, the capitol, the Atlanta airport, and state trooper posts. The seventeen men who make up the crew onsite at the mansion, all ATC residents, work at the mansion five days a week and offer support for events on evenings and weekends. Upon arriving early in the morning, they are divided into the grounds and house crews. Many of the grounds-crew members are also trained to help with events and don tuxedos when required. Larry, one of the trusties, explained, "We know ahead of time if we have a function. We shower and change out, and Joy does a good job of giving everyone their assignment. We have a system to keep things running smoothly. We have all really learned a lot."[8] Another trusty, John, who has become a master pruner, added that the events can make for a long day: "I get up

Kirk Talgo in the mansion orchard, 2014. *Courtesy Christopher Oquendo.*

Cleaning the chandelier, 2014. *Courtesy Christopher Oquendo.*

The organic garden, 2014. *Courtesy Jennifer Dickey.*

at 3:30 in the morning. There are nights when some of us get three hours' sleep. But we love it. Joy and Kirk will work with you. They let us take breaks and appreciate all the help."

The mission of the thirteen Georgia transitional centers is to "protect the public by providing community residential services to inmates prior to their discharge or parole from incarceration."[9] The Deals and the mansion staff respect the men and their work but never lose sight of how their acts of violence affected the families of the victims. This balance and the desire to help the men lead more productive lives have been part of what has made the program so successful. As Warden Steven Perkins explained, "They have been in prison an average of twenty-two years and are on what we call long-term maintenance. Their work helps them transition back into society, and we work hard to help them learn basic skills."[10] The mansion detail is reserved for residents who have had no major disciplinary problems, have completed a number of programs in prison that demonstrate a willingness to help other prisoners, and have demonstrated a positive outlook. As Perkins added, "The mansion assignment is a highly desirable position if your record in prison is good enough to get you there."[11] Sergeant Frank Pfirman explained the relationship between the residents and the state troopers: "We treat them just like anybody else. If we have an

issue, it's addressed quickly. We know they have a violent past, but we hope they have put it behind them and they keep focused on their work. They know what they have to do; they know what they are working toward."[12]

The trusties work on a vast range of projects and are on hand to deal with whatever is required. Joy Forth oversees the men in the house, and Kirk Talgo supervises the grounds crew. While Forth and Talgo each oversee a particular area, they are also prepared for the unexpected. Merrill, one of the trusties, tells a story that on the Deals' election night, "A six-point buck jumped the fence. I joked that it was a Democratic deer that was trying to get back into the mansion. We also caught a hawk one day, and the troopers transported it to a wildlife center."[13] Doug, a trusty who cares for Bill and Veto, has worked with the troopers to keep the raccoons away from the cats' food.

The mansion runs like a well-oiled machine. Terry oversees the magic laundry basket that is so popular among the first families, and Joy Forth claims that "he is better at getting out stains than any drycleaner in this city."[14] She also urged Bill and Larry, who work on the grounds crew, to embrace a very special assignment—to keep the grounds free of snakes, especially copperheads. Bill is a talented mechanic who keeps all the equipment on the grounds in good order and helps the other residents maintain the organic garden. Curtis, another trusty, cooks for the men and plans a menu each week with food that is provided by the Department of Corrections. He has become known for his cornbread and tuna casserole. The residents also do basic repairs around the mansion. As Carla Blanks of the Georgia Building Authority commented, "As with any aging building, there are a number of small repairs that need attention. There are constant demands for maintenance."[15] Steve Stancil, head of the GBA, further explained that there are three tiers of repairs: those that Kirk or the residents can do, those that require the GBA staff, and those that need outside contractors. Several former trusties, including Matt O'Donnell, David Camp, and Russell Jones, have returned to the mansion to admire some of the permanent features that they helped construct while working there, including the gazebo, the walkways through the woods, the dog pen, and the playground.

All the men talk about how the Deals have helped them feel comfortable with their roles at the mansion. "When I arrived," a trusty named Aldridge explained, "the Deals asked me to come and meet with them in the

Mansion maintenance tools, 2014.
Courtesy Christopher Oquendo.

top kitchen. They asked me to tell my story, to explain how I got here. After we finished talking, Mrs. Deal gave me a hug and a warm smile. That meant a lot. They know everyone's name and always speak to us."[16] As Joy explained, the transitional program is important to both the men and the mansion. "Most of these men are very anxious to work," she noted, adding, "They want to have some responsibility, and their good behavior has caught the attention of the warden. The mansion's operations would come to a screeching halt without them. Many people admire the mansion, but the men really make it run. The work they do here is also a way for them to regain their humanity."[17]

Chef's Team

The kitchen is the heartbeat of the mansion, and for many years it was the domain of Holly Chute. She started on April 1, 1981, and worked through the Busbee administration before leaving to work with her husband for several years. She returned to the mansion at the beginning of the Barnes administration. In all, she served as the mansion's chef for more than thirty years. In 2014, Holly left the mansion to work for the Department of Agriculture, and Simon, a former trusty who served as Holly's assistant for more than two years, assumed the

position as cook. The kitchen is rarely quiet; staff members and ATC residents are either preparing meals for the Deals or developing and implementing complex menus for special events. Holly's food was widely praised—her signature dishes were creamy Vidalia onion soup and collard green wontons. Her favorite thing to do was to prepare a five-course meal for fifteen to twenty guests. Holly has many stories about the mansion, but one of her most memorable experiences came during the Busbee administration during the Snow Jam of 1982. Holly recalled:

> I worked the dinner shift until 8:00 p.m. The butler was from Florida, and was looking out at the flakes of snow. I commented that they weren't that big and were not going to accumulate. Boy, was I was wrong. The troopers went out to pick up friends and family who were stranded. I started a pot of vegetable soup and grilled-cheese sandwiches. I had to stretch the food because people kept coming. We were here for three days, and slept wherever we could. I slept in Jeff Busbee's room, and after a couple of days, the troopers, who had tire chains, took me back to my house to get clothes.[18]

Working in the kitchen is not simply a job—it is an opportunity to show gratitude and express hospitality. Simon, the former trusty who was hired by the Georgia Building Authority as a sous-chef, explained, "The governor took a chance with me. In prison, you have no choice and no responsibility. Here you are given some, and it means a lot. I try to do all I can for

Chef Holly Chute sharing Easter cookies with Emma Companiotte, 2014. *Courtesy of Kathy Knapp.*

Stanley Simon in the kitchen, 2014. *Courtesy Jennifer Dickey.*

A funny incident for the kitchen staff during the Perdue administration involved the elevator, which serves all three floors of the mansion. The trusties would often hang the governor's suits on the hook in the elevator, and he would retrieve them when the elevator arrived at the third floor. One day as the governor stepped into the elevator to pick up his suit, Hope Godinich, the sous-chef, summoned the elevator to the basement. The door closed on him, and the elevator descended into the basement with the governor, dressed in a T-shirt and boxer shorts, on board. The elevator opened, and "Hope was mortified to see the governor hiding behind his suit. Everyone laughed, but they were both pretty surprised," recalled the former mansion manager Sharon Burrow.[21]

The elevator has been a source of entertainment as well as aggravation over the years. Amy Carter loved to ride in it. The staff often put C.C., the Barneses' dog, in it. Zell Miller once got trapped inside it. As Bob Satterfield, an electrician, remembered, "During the Christmas open house, Zell went missing. Everyone was searching for him, and it turned out that he had gotten stuck for nearly an hour on the elevator. He was pretty mad when they finally got the doors open."[22]

Troopers

The troopers of the Georgia State Patrol, charged with providing executive security under Georgia statute, are a key part of the mansion's operations. The Executive Security Team reports directly to the deputy commissioner of public safety—currently, Lieutenant Colonel Russell Powell. Sergeant First Class David Herring leads the Deals' security detail. The plainclothes troopers provide security for the governor, the first lady, the Speaker of the House, the chief justice of the supreme court, and the lieutenant governor. Uniformed troopers provide security for the mansion in a range of capacities, depending on the day or event.

The transition to public office can sometimes be a surprise for the first family. Early in the Busbee administration, the governor needed a gallon of milk, so he jumped in his car, saluted the trooper at the gate, and drove to the grocery store. The troopers quickly intervened, reminding him that he could not travel alone.[23] Marie Barnes recalls that on the morning after they won the election, she awoke and intended to walk to the hotel vending machine to get ice. She was greeted in her pajamas by two state troopers outside her door. David

the Deals. I come in on the weekends, just in case they need something. My job is to serve them when they are hungry. I want to make sure everyone is happy."[19] Holly reflected on what made the mansion so special: "I loved driving through the gates every day. It's a beautiful place with great people. When you get to know the governor and his family, you become part of their family. Food speaks to everybody. When you feed somebody, you see a different side of them. It's been an honor. I leave the mansion with a heavy heart. I am humbled by how much support they have given me as I plan to leave."[20]

Herring recalls the few days after the Deals' election: "We had a couple of functions and then traveled to their river house. The next day, the security detail was outside, and I turned my back for a minute and Governor Deal was on the ladder. I said to him, 'With all due respect, you have to get off that ladder. I'll do that. We cannot let something happen to you.'"[24] The troopers complete executive-protection training or dignitary-protection training with the Louisiana State Police or the North Carolina Highway Patrol.[25] Executive security requires a specific kind of discretion, as the commissioner of public safety, Mark McDonough, detailed: "David and his team are part of an inner circle and are privy to private conversations. We respect that. Our job is to supervise and support them. You have to have mature people who can control themselves and understand the importance of privacy."[26]

Sergeant Frank Pfirman, who oversees the uniformed troopers at the mansion, explained that the greatest challenge his team faces is to keep up "with the diversity of people that visit." It is a balancing act: "We don't want to be too intrusive. We want to provide adequate security but also want visitors to feel welcome."[27] While the troopers' primary role is to provide security, they also embrace their responsibility to serve as ambassadors for the Deals and the state of Georgia, as troopers Jody Taylor and Olin Lundy explained. Mark McDonough clarified the philosophy that guides mansion security: "Our mindset is [that] if we secure the building for the kids, everyone is safe. That is a different frame of mind. We start with our responsibility [for] the children who might be on the grounds."[28] David Herring explained, "That is the great thing about the Deals—it's not like a job; it's like a family. I have told Governor Deal that he sets a great example. It is nice to have people who are so cordial. It is a great team."[29] The troopers at the mansion are supported by Linda Jackson, who serves as secretary for the Department of Public Safety and joined the mansion staff in February 2014. Her duties include maintaining the gate roster, distributing policy updates, and coordinating the docent schedule. She says of the work, "I still can't believe I'm here. This is the best job I've ever had. It is quite interesting to work with the troopers, and the Deals are like a godsend."[30]

Trooper James Brown checking in a guest, 2014.
Courtesy Christopher Oquendo.

Marie and Roy Barnes with their security detail, 2000.
Courtesy Marie and Roy Barnes.

Docent Appreciation Luncheon at the mansion, ca. 2000s. *Courtesy Governor's Mansion Collection.*

Docents

The mansion docents are a dedicated group of volunteers, mostly retired women, who come each month to help lead tours for the public. Some have served in this capacity since the Harris administration (1983–91). Many are former teachers, like Brenda Bedinfield, from Pickens County, who started volunteering during the Barnes administration. "I started doing this as a Chi Omega service project," explained Brenda, adding, "When I retired as a schoolteacher, one of my friends said you have to start doing this. So, I retired in May and started as a docent in June of 1999."[31] Three days a week, between eight and twelve docents arrive at 9:30 a.m. to gather for the tours that begin at 10:00 in the morning and run until noon. Tour groups schedule their visits in advance, but the mansion allows walk-in visitors during regular tour days, which are currently Tuesday through Thursday. The mansion cook, Simon, prepares coffee and pastries for the docents during their half hour of fellowship. When the tours start, each docent reports to a particular station on the main floor, where she provides visitors information about the room and its notable antiques. Although the docents are given written details about the rooms and the collection, they often learn more from one another and the first lady.

As Barbara D'Emilio explained, "I mostly learned on the job. I have listened to other docents and Mrs. Deal, and now feel pretty knowledgeable about the collection."[32] Carleen O'Toole joked, "I have been doing this for twenty-six years, and I'm just beginning to get the hang of it."[33]

The docents field a range of questions. What kind of grass grows on the mansion lawn? Who has the key to the front door? Children are often curious about why are there no televisions on the main floor and where they can meet the governor. They also frequently want to know what they have to do to be able to live in the mansion. Margie Bowyer tells them, "You can be governor. You can have a cook and a chauffeur and live like this. Just work hard, and do what your parents and your teachers say."[34] Because the mansion attracts a large number of international visitors, brochures are available in Spanish, French, German, Japanese, Portuguese, and Chinese. Cynthia Day was excited about the variety of visitors: "I was an international flight attendant, and I particularly enjoy the international guests that we get. People from countries like Japan do not get to see an enormous house like this. So they are amazed. The concierges at prominent hotels often encourage guests to visit. At Christmas there is a Georgia Tech professor who brings colleagues from China. They love to take pictures with the state troopers."[35] The docents often have to deal with unexpected surprises, as Carleen O'Toole detailed: "We have to be nimble. We have had as few as three volunteers. One of the worst days I remember was when Mo Perron was the mansion manager. We had a busload of children, and it was really cold outside. We didn't have room to let them all inside at once. So we created a plan that rotated every fifteen minutes. We finished in under an hour, and Mo was surprised at how well it worked."[36] Each fall, to honor the hundreds of hours of volunteer service, the mansion hosts an appreciation luncheon for the docents. Margie Bowyer loves the occasion: "This is an annual event for those of us who have worked quite a bit during the year.

The first lady often shows us the family quarters upstairs and talks about the changes that have been made to the mansion. It's a real treat for us."[37]

Friends of the Mansion, Fine Arts Committee, Book Committee

In addition to the docents, an additional corps of volunteers serves the mansion. First Lady Mary Perdue created Friends of the Mansion, Inc., to raise private funds to refurbish and renovate the mansion in 2005. The committee has evolved over the years, and Wendy Leebern and Rayna Casey currently oversee its operations. The first Fine Arts Committee, created in the late 1960s, was chaired by Henry D. Green and was responsible

Friends of the Mansion pamphlet. *Courtesy Kenan Research Center at the Atlanta History Center.*

Mansion Book Committee: Amy Huckaby, Henry Turner, Sandra Deal, Mary Hart Wilheit, Katherine Farnham, and Alice Jepson, 2014. *Courtesy Jennifer Dickey.*

for assembling the extraordinary collection that today graces the mansion. That committee was disbanded under Governor Lester Maddox. Recognizing the need for a permanent committee to oversee the protection and care of the mansion collection, Governor Jimmy Carter introduced legislation in 1974 to create a new Executive Center Fine Arts Committee whose members would be appointed by the governor and would serve rotating terms. In 1975, under the administration of Governor George Busbee, the Georgia General Assembly approved the formation of a permanent Executive Fine Arts Committee, which continues to oversee the care of the collection. Under the Deals, the committee includes Beverly Allen, Norma Edenfield, Helen Rice, Gloria Norwood, Linda McWhorter, Gena Tarbutton, Mary Hart Wilheit, Vicki Zimmerman, Rayna Casey, and Wendy Leebern. First Lady Sandra Deal established an additional committee in 2013 to serve as advisers as she was working on the book that would document the mansion's history. Henry Turner, Kitty Farnham (the mansion's first curator), Alice Jepson, Amy Huckaby (a former mansion manager), and Mary Hart Wilheit are all members of the Mansion Book Committee. First Lady Betty Sanders, who deserves credit for helping build and furnish the mansion, is an honorary member of the group.

Fred and Trooper Smith, 2014. *Courtesy Christopher Oquendo.*

Four-Legged Staff Members

Some members of the mansion's workforce have four legs. Atom and Fred, the bomb-sniffing dogs handled by Officers Michael Diggs and Scott Smith, are an important part of the mansion's operations. On-site regularly, especially around tours and special events, Atom and Fred patrol the grounds to ensure that the first family, the staff, volunteers, and guests are safe. The two dogs keep a full schedule. As Officer Jody Taylor noted, "They have double duty: they work at the capitol and help the county and city. They are constantly going somewhere."[38]

Bill and Veto, the mansion cats, arrived in the spring of 2013. The hope was that their presence would help reduce the chipmunk population, which was wreaking havoc with the garden. According to Doug, the trusty who cares for them: "[They are] quite lovable, people-oriented cats. They are almost like dogs; they will follow me around. Their collars have their names and 'Governor's Mansion' on the back in case they get lost.

Veto and Bill, 2014. *Courtesy Jennifer Dickey.*

They have a house in the garage, and I have a heating pad for them when it gets cold. At Christmas, I have a Santa blanket for them. They come when called, and I so look forward to seeing them every morning."[39]

A Public and Private Place

A large, dedicated team serves the mansion; its members are also witnesses to the history of Georgia in a way that few others are. Matt O'Donnell, a former trusty and now a supervisor at the Georgia Building Authority, offered a personal reflection on his experience of working at the mansion:

> I suppose what people need to know about their governors is that they are just regular people. We expect a lot out of them without considering the cost to their families. While they live at the mansion, it is never really a home. I often wondered what it would be like to have hundreds of visitors walking through my house every day. I saw myself as having a dual role—to make the mansion a showpiece for the people of Georgia and to help the governor and his family be as comfortable as possible. The public saw the politician; we saw the person. We saw the tears of Governor Miller when he returned from touring devastating tornado damage in 1994. We saw a troubled Governor Barnes pacing around the pool worrying over the flag issue while protestors shouted obscenities from West Paces. We saw a concerned Governor Perdue mourning at a broken section of fence where two people died in a car crash the night before. I cannot imagine the burden of office.

> I was never happier than at Christmas when after all the monumental work put into decorating, I got to see the faces of the children light up as we lit the big tree. There were hard times, but so much joy, too. I remember the Barnes' daughter getting married at the mansion, Zell Miller rolling around the grass with the dogs, the Perdues' grandson Jack riding around behind me in his little truck helping me put out mulch.

> We were never treated with anything but love and respect, no matter who the governor was. The whole staff worked hard and made the possible out of the impossible. I feel blessed to have been able to serve. I met presidents, prime ministers, actors, and musicians. I would see the faces of the people who were so excited just to catch a glimpse of the governor and first lady, and here I talked to them every day. Our efforts never went unnoticed or unappreciated. During one event for Jimmy Carter, he left his guests to come back to the kitchen and personally thank each of us working behind the scenes. That's what I am really getting at. The Mansion is so much—a grand display of the leadership of this state, but more importantly the embodiment of home, family, friendship, and love.[40]

The Georgia Governor's Mansion is indeed all these things. It is a symbol of the state, a public building, and a family home. It is a hub of almost constant activity. The banker Mills Lane once prophesied that the mansion "would be a showplace to put the South's best foot forward—an investment in Georgia's future."[41] After almost fifty years, the mansion still serves as a showplace for Georgia and the South. It has proved to be a wise investment.

Residents of the Georgia Governors' Mansions

Residents of the Old Governor's Mansion

MILLEDGEVILLE (1839–68)

Charles J. McDonald (1839–43)

George W. Crawford (1843–47)

George W. B. Towns (1847–51)

Howell Cobb (1851–53)

Herschel Johnson (1853–57)

Joseph E. Brown (1857–65)

Charles Jones Jenkins (1865–68)

General Thomas Ruger, provisional governor
(January–July 1868)

Residents of the Second Governor's Mansion

CAIN AND PEACHTREE STREETS, ATLANTA (1870–1921)

Rufus B. Bullock (1868–71)

Benjamin Conley, president of Senate (1871–72)

James M. Smith (1872–77)

Alfred H. Colquitt (1877–82)

Alexander H. Stephens (1882–83)

James S. Boynton, president of Senate (1883)

Henry D. McDaniel (1883–86)

John B. Gordon (1886–90)

William J. Northen (1890–94)

William Y. Atkinson (1894–98)

Allen D. Candler (1898–1902)

Joseph M. Terrell (1902–7)

Hoke Smith (1907–9)

Joseph M. Brown (1909–11)

Hoke Smith (1911)

John M. Slaton, president of Senate (1911–12)

Joseph M. Brown (1912–13)

John M. Slaton (1913–15)

Nathaniel E. Harris (1915–17)

Hugh M. Dorsey (1917–21)

Residents of the Third Governor's Mansion

205 THE PRADO, ATLANTA (1925–68)

Clifford M. Walker (1923–27)

Lamartine G. Hardman (1927–31)

Richard B. Russell, Jr. (1931–33)

Eugene Talmadge (1933–37)

Eurith D. Rivers (1937–41)

Eugene Talmadge (1941–43)

Ellis G. Arnall (1943–47)

Herman E. Talmadge (1947)

Melvin E. Thompson (1947–48)

Herman E. Talmadge (1948–55)

S. Marvin Griffin (1955–59)

S. Ernest Vandiver, Jr. (1959–63)

Carl E. Sanders (1963–67)

Lester G. Maddox (1967–71)

Residents of the Current Governor's Mansion

391 WEST PACES FERRY ROAD NORTHWEST, ATLANTA
(1968–PRESENT)

Lester G. Maddox (1967–71)

James E. Carter (1971–75)

George Busbee (1975–83)

Joe Frank Harris (1983–91)

Zell Miller (1991–99)

Roy E. Barnes (1999–2003)

Sonny Perdue (2003–11)

Nathan Deal (2011–18)

Fine Arts Committee, 1968

General chairman: Henry Green

Books, Manuscripts, and Memorabilia Committee

Chairman: Franklin Garrett
Cochairman: Holcombe T. Green
Cochairman: F. Clason Kyle

COMMITTEE MEMBERS

Eugene Black
Hal Clarke
Beverly DuBose
Miss Carroll Hart
Mrs. James G. Kenan
Mrs. Baxter Maddox
Mrs. E. N. McKinnon
Harold T. Patterson
Roy Richards

Furniture and Furnishings Committee

Chairman: Mrs. Albert E. Thornton
Cochairman: Mrs. James W. McCook Jr.
Cochairman: Mrs. Floyd W. McRae Sr.

COMMITTEE MEMBERS

Mrs. Francis L. Abreau
Mrs. Jack Adair
Mrs. Phillip Alston Jr.
Mrs. Joe E. Birnie
David R. Byers III
Mrs. Frank V. Carmichael
Mrs. Julian S. Carr
Mrs. Rueben Clark
Mrs. George S. Craft
Mrs. Frank Ferst
Ben W. Fortson Jr.
Mrs. J. B. Fuqua

Henry Green
Mrs. R. Irving Gresham Jr.
Granger Hansell
J. D. Harris
Mrs. James R. Hedges
Mrs. Albert Howell
Miss Isabel Johnston
Edward V. Jones
Mrs. Gordon Jones
Mrs. Thornton Kennedy
Thomas E. Martin Jr.
Mrs. Bernard N. Neal Sr.
Lucien Oliver
Norman P. Pendley
Mrs. Jas. D. Robinson Jr.
Robert H. Smalley
Charles B. Townsend
Mrs. W. R. Woodruff

Garden and Grounds Committee

Chairman: Mrs. Mills B. Lane Jr.
Cochairman: Mrs. Arthur Montgomery
Cochairman: Mrs. William Morris

COMMITTEE MEMBERS

Mrs. Ivan Allen Jr.
Mrs. John O. Chiles
Edward Daugherty
J. B. Fuqua
Mrs. Jack P. Glenn
Mrs. Martin Kilpatrick
Peter S. Knox
Mrs. Howell Newton
Hubert S. Owens
Mrs. Carl E. Sanders
Mrs. Edward Smith
W. S. Stuckey
Mrs. Elwyn W. Tomlinson

Georgia's Archival Collections

The authors used numerous archival collections when researching this book. They would like to acknowledge the assistance provided by the following archives and to encourage readers and other scholars to become familiar with the diverse resources available to the public throughout the state of Georgia.

James G. Kenan Research Center, Atlanta History Center

The James G. Kenan Research Center (at 130 West Paces Ferry Road, Atlanta, Georgia, 30306) is the research component of the Atlanta History Center's exhibitions, education, and public programs. The 42,000-square-foot center is dedicated to James G. Kenan as a tribute to his lifelong philanthropic support of historical scholarship and literature. Resources at the Kenan Research Center include over 1,700 collections from individuals, families, businesses, charities, civic organizations, and city and county governments. The majority of the collection dates from the Civil War to the mid-twentieth century. The visual arts collections contain images relating to local and regional topics from the antebellum South to the present: photographic prints, negatives, postcards, maps, architectural drawings, films, and video recordings. Kenan Research Center holdings include over twenty thousand books, pamphlets, and periodicals about Atlanta and Georgia history, the Civil War, architecture and decorative arts, genealogy, and garden history. Rare book collections include the Beverly M. DuBose and Thomas S. Dickey Civil War collections; the Philip Trammell Shutze and Harvey Smith collections of architecture, design, and decorative arts; the Shillinglaw Cookbook Collection (southern cookbooks); the Bobby Jones Golf Library; and the Franklin M. Garrett Library. Available online are the Kenan Research Center's online catalogue, Terminus; finding aids (collection inventories); Album (digitized database of photographs,

video recordings, and audio recordings); an architecture database; and the Franklin Garrett Necrology genealogy database. All are accessible at www.AtlantaHistoryCenter .com/Research. The center is free and open to the public from 10:00 a.m. to 5:00 p.m., Wednesday–Saturday. Patrons must register and provide photo identification to obtain a research card. For more information about the Kenan Research Center, visit www.AtlantaHistoryCenter .com/Research, call 404–814–4040, or e-mail Reference @AtlantaHistoryCenter.com.

Georgia Archives

The Georgia Archives (at 5800 Jonesboro Road, Morrow, Georgia, 30260) was established in 1918 as the Georgia Department of Archives and History. In 2013, the Georgia Archives became part of the University System of Georgia. The mission of the archives is to identify, select, preserve, and make available documents that constitute Georgia's recorded history, to increase the efficiency of state government through effective records management, and to improve the quality of records and archives management throughout the state. The archives building (opened in 2003) houses over seventy thousand cubic feet of materials, including the official records of Georgia dating from 1732 to the present and a smaller collection of business records, private manuscript collections, and photographs. The Archives Reference Library is open Tuesdays through Saturdays from 8:30 to 5:00. Researchers may use original materials or consult a reference collection of twenty-five thousand books (primarily state, local, and family histories and published laws), state and local records on microfilm, and online databases. The Georgia Archives website, www .GeorgiaArchives.org, has a section called the Virtual Vault, which contains images of original documents, photographs, and maps. For more information, visit www.georgiaarchives .org/ or call 678–364–3710.

Georgia State University, Special Collections and Archives

Georgia State University Library's Special Collections and Archives (located on the eighth floor of the University Library South building, 103 Decatur Street, SE, Atlanta, Georgia 30303) collects and preserves unique and rare historical materials in select subject areas with the goal of advancing scholarship and furthering the educational, research, and service missions of the university. Many of the collections consist of records of organizations or papers of individuals documenting the twentieth- and twenty-first-century American South. Subject strengths include the heritage of workers and their unions in the South and elsewhere (Southern Labor Archives, Archives of the International Association of Machinists and Aerospace Workers), American popular music and culture (Johnny Mercer Collection, Popular Music & Culture Collection), efforts to ratify the Equal Rights Amendment (ERA) in Georgia and the second wave of the women's movement (Donna Novak Coles Georgia Women's Movement Archives), regional and national efforts to ratify the ERA and the second wave of the women's movement (Lucy Hargrett Draper U.S. Equal Rights Amendment [1921–82] Research Collection), women-centered and LGBTQ activist and advocacy activities in Georgia and the Southeast (Archives for Research on Women and Gender), and other social movements, especially in Georgia (Social Change Collection). Georgia's political heritage is documented in several of the collections as well as in the Georgia Government Documentation Project. The collection also houses the Georgia State University Archives, consisting of records of university offices, deliberative bodies, and organizations, as well as resources on GSU history. In addition to manuscripts and organizational records, many of the collections listed above contain visual resources, sound recordings, and moving images. Special Collections and Archives houses millions of historical photographs documenting twentieth-century Atlanta and Georgia (Photograph Collections, Atlanta Journal-Constitution Photographic Archive). Oral histories, containing personal accounts of people's lives and events they observed or participated in, are another strength of Special Collections and Archives. Active oral-history programs are a feature of many of the collections. Finally, the University Library's Rare Book Collection is housed in Special Collections and Archives. For more information, visit http://library.gsu.edu/search-collections/special-collections-archives, call 404–413–2880, or e-mail archives@gsu.edu.

New Georgia Encyclopedia

Originally launched in 2004, the *New Georgia Encyclopedia* (NGE, www.georgiaencyclopedia.org) is the first state encyclopedia designed exclusively for publication online. This authoritative resource contains original content and helps users understand the rich history and diverse culture of Georgia. The NGE includes more than two thousand articles and six thousand images. The NGE is a program of the Georgia Humanities Council in partnership with the University of Georgia Press, the University System of Georgia/GALILEO, and the Office of the Governor.

University of Georgia, Special Collections Libraries

The Hargrett Library (in the Russell Special Collections Building, 300 South Hull Street, Athens, Georgia, 30602) focuses on Georgia history and culture. It holds rare books and Georgiana, historical manuscripts, photographs, maps, broadsides, and UGA archives and records. Other areas of emphasis include the performing arts and natural history. Holdings date from the fifteenth century to the present. For more information, visit www.libs.uga.edu/hargrett or call 706–542–7123.

The Richard B. Russell Library for Political Research and Studies is Georgia's repository of record for political and public policy collections. The second-largest modern congressional papers research center in the United States, the Russell Library houses the papers of over fifty members of Congress from Georgia. Comprehensive collections, services, and programs have earned the library a national reputation as a model program. In four decades, the Russell Library has acquired over 350 collections of historically important documents and artifacts, which occupy twenty thousand linear feet. The Russell Library's dynamic oral history program captures the memories of public officials, community leaders, activists, farm families, businessmen, immigrants, and others. Annually, Russell Library archivists work with nearly 1,200 public school students and nineteen departments at UGA to provide instruction to over thirty classes in a variety of disciplines. As a premier destination for cultural tourism, the Russell Library is committed to developing and presenting exhibits and public programs that educate and inspire visitors of all ages about how Georgia and its citizens have shaped the political life of their communities, the state, their nation, and the world. No matter what the featured exhibit or program, there are opportunities throughout the museum galleries and public spaces to participate and view documents, artifacts, film, and photographs that describe political life and events. All researchers must create an online Special Collections Research Account to use materials in the collections, www .libs.uga.edu/scl/research/policies.html; for Russell Library searchable finding aids, visit www.libs.uga.edu/russell, call 706–542–5788, or e-mail russlibs@uga.edu. The Russell Library's reading room is open 8:00 to 4:30, Monday–Friday; galleries are open 8:00 to 5:00, Monday–Friday, and 1:00 to 5:00 on Saturday. Access is free and open to all.

The Walter J. Brown Media Archives and Peabody Awards Collection is the only public archive in Georgia devoted solely to the preservation of audiovisual materials. The collection, started in 1995, preserves over 250,000 titles in film, video, audiotape, transcription disks, and other recording formats dating from the 1920s to the present. The mission is to preserve, protect, and provide access to the moving image and sound materials that reflect the collective memory of broadcasting and the history of the state of Georgia and its people. The Peabody Awards Collection is the flagship of the archives and contains nearly every entry for the first major broadcast award given in the United States. The judging for the Peabody awards is conducted by the Peabody Awards Office in the Grady School of Journalism by a panel of distinguished television scholars, critics, and media professionals.

Georgia history is highlighted in three newsfilm collections in the Walter J. Brown Media Archives. The wsb Newsfilm Collection contains raw news footage from 1949 to 1981. More than five million feet of film clips show the history of Atlanta and the Southeast, span the entire civil rights movement, and cover such social and cultural events as the desegregation of the University of Georgia. Major leaders and political figures, including Julian Bond, Jimmy Carter, Maynard Jackson, Martin Luther King Jr., Lester Maddox, Richard Russell, Carl Sanders, Herman Talmadge, George Wallace, and Andrew Young, are featured in the collection. The walb Newsfilm Collection contains raw news footage from Albany and surrounding areas dating from 1961 to 1978. The collection covers the Albany Movement of 1961–62, which is considered the first mass movement to desegregate an entire community in the modern civil rights era, as well as the people and events that affected South Georgia. Recordings from Augusta, Georgia, can be found in the wrdw Newsfilm Collection, which features footage from 1961 to 1976. Amateur films, videos, and audiotapes highlighting Georgia people, places, and musicians are also part of the collection. The Arnold Michaelis Collection of Living History features interviews with social, political, and cultural headliners from the 1950s to the 1980s. For more information, visit www.libs.uga.edu /media/# or call 706–542–4757.

Notes

Unless otherwise noted, all interviews for this book were conducted by Catherine Lewis, Jennifer Dickey, and/or Sandra Deal.

Introduction

1. Elizabeth Harris, Joe Frank Harris, and Joe Frank Harris Jr., interview, July 9, 2014.
2. Ibid.

CHAPTER ONE. From the Tent to the Granite Mansion

1. From the time of its construction in the 1960s, Governor's Mansion on West Paces Ferry Road has been described as a Greek Revival mansion. Although the correct term for twentieth-century adaptations of this style of architecture is "Neoclassical Revival," the term "Greek Revival" is used throughout the book to reflect the description commonly given to the mansion.
2. The 1732 Charter, which gave the British trustees control of Georgia, forbade Oglethorpe from holding office, so he was never called "governor"; see Edwin L. Jackson, "James Oglethorpe," *New Georgia Encyclopedia*, last modified September 15, 2014, accessed October 31, 2014, www.georgiaencyclopedia.org/articles/history-archaeology/james-oglethorpe-1696–1785.
3. Jack Spalding, "Georgia's Governors Had Many Homes But Oglethorpe's Tent Most Unusual," *Atlanta Journal and Constitution*, April 12, 1953.
4. Edwin L. Lawson, "The History of Georgia's Capitols and Capital Cities," Carl Vinson Institute of Government, Georgia State University and Frank Daniel, "That Miserable Mansion," *Atlanta Journal and Constitution*, January 27, 1957.
5. Spalding, "Georgia's Governors Had Many Homes."
6. Bernice McCullar, "How Early Governors Were

Chosen," *Atlanta Journal and Constitution Magazine*, March 28, 1971.
7. Edwin L. Jackson, "Georgia's Historic Capitals," *New Georgia Encyclopedia*, last modified June 5, 2014, accessed October 31, 2014, www.georgiaencyclopedia.org/articles/government-politics/georgias-historic-capitals.
8. Spalding, "Georgia's Governors Had Many Homes."
9. Jackson, "Georgia's Historic Capitals."
10. Ibid.
11. Ibid.; Spalding, "Georgia's Governors Had Many Homes."
12. Robert J. Wilson, "Milledgeville," *New Georgia Encyclopedia,* last modified September 16, 2014, accessed October 31, 2014, www.georgiaencyclopedia.org/articles/counties-cities-neighborhoods/milledgeville.
13. James C. Turner, Matthew Davis, and Travis Byrd, *The Old Governor's Mansion: Georgia's First Executive Residence* (Macon, Ga.: Mercer University Press, 2013), 13.
14. Leola Selmon Beeson, *The One Hundred Years of the Governors' Mansion, Milledgeville, Georgia, 1838–1938* (Macon, Ga.: Burke, 1938), 2–3.
15. Ibid., 4.
16. Spalding, "Georgia's Governors Had Many Homes."
17. Beeson, *One Hundred Years*, 15.
18. Turner, Davis, and Byrd, *Old Governor's Mansion*, 13.
19. Quoted in Andrew Sparks, "Governors Lived Here," *Atlanta Journal Constitution Magazine*, October 20, 1968.
20. Steven Moffson, "Charles B. Cluskey (ca. 1808–1871)," *New Georgia Encyclopedia*, last modified September 3, 2014, accessed October 31, 2014, www.georgiaencyclopedia.org/articles/arts-culture/charles-b-cluskey-ca-1808–1871; Old Governor's Mansion National Register Nomination, May 13, 1970, 3.
21. Photograph of the Gordon-Porter-Ward-Beall-Cline-O'Connor House, 311 West Greene Street, Milledgeville, available at the Vanishing Georgia Collection, Georgia State Archives, accessed July 1, 2014, http://cdm.sos.state.ga.us:2011/cdm/singleitem/collection/vg2/id/4158/rec/1.

22. James C. Bonner, *Milledgeville: Georgia's Antebellum Capital* (Macon, Ga.: Mercer University Press, 1985), 128.

23. James C. Turner, "Old Governor's Mansion," *New Georgia Encyclopedia*, last modified August 7, 2013, accessed October 15, 2013, www.georgiaencyclopedia.org/articles /history-archaeology/old-governors-mansion.

24. Turner, Davis, and Byrd, *Old Governor's Mansion*, 5.

25. Ibid., 14.

26. Sparks, "Governors Lived Here," 21, and Turner, "Old Governor's Mansion."

27. Quoted in Turner, Davis, and Byrd, *Old Governor's Mansion*, 9.

28. Ibid., 20.

29. Ibid., 25–26.

30. Ibid., 27.

31. Ibid., 30–31.

32. Mary Eleanor Wickersham, "The Mansion at Milledgeville," *Outdoors in Georgia*, 9:1 (January 1979): 22.

33. Ibid.

34. Turner, Davis, and Byrd, *Old Governor's Mansion*, 36.

35. Ibid., 42.

36. William T. Sherman, *Memoirs of General William T. Sherman*, 2nd ed. (New York: Appleton, 1889), 2:188.

37. Turner, Davis, and Byrd, *Old Governor's Mansion*, 44–45.

38. Ibid., 45–47.

39. Sparks, "Governors Lived Here," 21.

40. Quoted in ibid.

41. Wickersham, "Mansion at Milledgeville," 23.

42. Today, the college is known as Georgia College and State University.

43. Mary Burdell, "Sharing Henry Green," in *Georgia Inside and Out: Architecture, Landscape, and Decorative Arts; Proceedings from the Second Henry D. Green Symposium of the Decorative Arts* (Athens: Georgia Museum of Art, University of Georgia, 2003), 71.

44. Turner, Davis, and Byrd, *Old Governor's Mansion*, 6; Lord, Aeck & Sargent, press release, March 3, 2005, www. lordaecksargent.com/assets/news_releases/OGM_e-version _fnl_2005.pdf.

45. Wright Marshall, "Georgia's Governors' Mansions," *The Georgian Revival* (blog), October 26, 2009, http ://thegeorgianrevival.wordpress.com/2009/10/26 /georgias-governors-mansions/.

46. Diane Hopper Schmidt, *A Century of Better Care: 100 Years of Piedmont Hospital* (Atlanta: Piedmont Hospital, 2004), 16–17.

47. Garrett quoted in Frank Daniel, "Mansion Troubles in 1916," *Atlanta Journal and Constitution*, May 19, 1963.

48. "Two Rooms in an Executive Mansion," *Carpet and Upholstery Trade Review*, March 15, 1894.

49. Quoted in Daniel, "Mansion Troubles in 1916."

50. Ibid.

51. Ibid.

52. Wright Marshall, "Georgia's Governors' Mansions."

53. Frank Daniel, "That Miserable Mansion," *Atlanta Journal and Constitution*, January 27, 1957.

54. Andrew Sparks, "Governors' Families Her Neighbors for 40 Years," *Atlanta Journal and Constitution Magazine*, March 12, 1967, 7, 42, 45.

55. Daniel, "That Miserable Mansion."

56. Quoted in Sparks, "Governors' Families Her Neighbors," 7.

57. Ibid.

58. Ibid., 42.

59. Ibid., 45.

60. Quoted in Agnes Fahy, "Georgia's State Garden," *Atlanta Constitution*, June 24, 1928.

61. Ibid.

62. Untitled article in Governor's Mansion Subject Files on 205 The Prado at the Atlanta History Center. Arnall was the resident of the mansion during part of the "three governors controversy" of 1946–47. Herman Talmadge occupied the mansion for about two months in early 1947 before being told to vacate it following a ruling by the State Supreme Court that designated lieutenant governor–elect M. E. Thompson governor following the death of governor-elect Eugene Talmadge in December 1946.

63. Daniel, "That Miserable Mansion."

64. Phil Smith, "Stone Prison for Our Governors?" *Atlanta Journal*, June 28, 1961.

65. Betty Sanders, interview, January 21, 2014.

66. Betty Sanders to Ben Fortson, April 9, 1963, Carl E. Sanders Collection, series 7, box 1, folder: Mansion Present, Richard B. Russell Library for Political Research and Studies, University of Georgia Libraries (this archive hereafter cited as Sanders Collection); Paul Valentine, "Expenses for Governor's Mansion Total $124,165 for Fiscal 1964, *Atlanta Journal*, August 6, 1964.

67. Walker Lundy, "Governor's Ceiling Slips; Squirrels Enliven Attic," *Atlanta Journal*, February 8, 1965.

68. O. P. Hanes, "Mansion Proposal Began in '53, *Columbus Ledger*, April 23, 1963.

69. Quoted in Charles Pou, "Mansion Forced on Sanders?," *Atlanta Journal*, April 24, 1963.

70. "State Panel Approves Plans for New $750,000 Mansion," *Savannah News*, April 20, 1963.

71. Ibid.; Sanders interview.

72. Quoted in "State Panel Approves Plans"; Sanders interview.

CHAPTER TWO. A New Mansion

1. Andrew Sparks, "Site of New Governor's Mansion Is an Atlanta Showplace," *Atlanta Journal and Constitution Magazine*, November 25, 1962, 50.

2. Ibid., 48.

3. Sanders interview.

4. Quoted in Sparks, "Site of New Governor's Mansion," 50.

5. "A Cheaper Mansion to Get Okay," *Atlanta Constitution*, May 7, 1963.

6. "State Buys $225,000 Site for Governor's Mansion," *Atlanta Constitution*, March 26, 1964.

7. O. P. Hanes, "Low Bid for Governor's Mansion Too High for State," *Augusta Chronicle*, December 23, 1964.

8. "State to Pay Cash, Saving $300,000," *Atlanta Journal*, November 26, 1964.

9. William O. Smith, "Governor's Mansion Decision Due Shortly," *Atlanta Journal and Constitution*, June 27, 1965.

10. Quoted in "New Governor's Home Gets Go-Ahead Signal in Atlanta," *Augusta Chronicle*, July 3, 1965.

11. Sam Hopkins, "Mansion Gets Green Light with $1 Million Contract," *Atlanta Journal*, July 3, 1965.

12. "New Mansion in Prospect By November," *Macon Telegraph*, May 16, 1966.

13. William O. Smith, "Mansion Ready in February?," *Atlanta Journal and Constitution*, November 20, 1966.

14. Sanders interview; Katharine Farnham, "Classicism Returns to Georgia: Shaping a Collection of American Federal Period Furniture for the Governor's Mansion in Atlanta," in *The Third Henry D. Green Symposium of the Decorative Arts*, edited by Ashley Callahan (Athens: Georgia Museum of Art, University of Georgia, 2006), 47.

15. Draft letter from Mrs. Carl Sanders and Ernest Davis, June 8, 1966, series 7, box 1, Sanders Collection.

16. Carl E. Sanders, executive order, July 14, 1966, series 7, box 1, Sanders Collection.

17. "The New Mansion," *Atlanta Journal and Constitution*, November 6, 1966, 30.

18. Smith, "Mansion Ready in February?" A complete list of the members of the Fine Arts Committee is presented in appendix B.

19. Quoted in Farnham, "Classicism Returns to Georgia," 50.

20. *Portrait of Georgia: Paintings by Georgia's First Lady, Mrs. Carl E. Sanders*, May 1966; "Mrs. Sanders Raises $20,000 with Exhibit," *Atlanta Journal*, December 6, 1966; H. M. Cauley, "Betty Sanders' Milestone Art; Former First Lady Puts on a Show," *Atlanta Journal-Constitution*, July 31, 2006.

21. "That's Not Fair Pool," *Atlanta Constitution*, August 15, 1980.

22. Elizabeth Sawyer, "Landscape to Be a Dixie Jewel," *Atlanta Journal*, April 10, 1968.

23. Ibid.

24. Sam Hopkins, "This Caretaker Comes with Mansion," *Atlanta Constitution*, September 6, 1967.

25. William R. Mitchell, Jr., *Edward Vason Jones: Architect, Connoisseur, and Collector* (Savannah: Martin–St. Martin, 1995), 17.

26. Duane Riner, "$116,000 Fence to Ring Mansion," *Atlanta Constitution*, June 29, 1967.

27. Ibid.

28. Quoted in Philip Gailey, "Quips and Clay Fly on Mansion Tour," *Atlanta Constitution*, August 31, 1967, 6.

29. Ibid.

30. Ibid.

31. Ibid.

32. Elizabeth Sawyer, "Executive Mansion Palatial Palace," *Atlanta Journal and Constitution*, October 22, 1967.

33. "Art and Government Share a Home," *Southern Living*, April 1984, 4.

34. Katharine Farnham, interview, December 30, 2013.

35. Mrs. Lester G. Maddox, "The Georgia Governor's Mansion," in *Executive Mansions and Capitols of America*, ed. Jean Houston Daniel and Price Daniel (Waukesha, Wisc.: Country Beautiful, 1969).

36. Elizabeth Sawyer, "Mansion's Her Charge," *Atlanta Journal*, May 22, 1968.

37. Larry Shealy, "Antiques Give Young'uns a Glimpse into the Past," *Atlanta Journal*, June 23, 1972.

38. "$76,520 Bid for Mansion," *Atlanta Journal*, July 10, 1969.

39. Gene Stephens, "Old Mansion Nets $100,000," *Atlanta Constitution*, July 26, 1969.

40. Hugh Nations, "Mansion Rocks to Phooey Party," *Atlanta Journal*, September 9, 1969.

41. Farnham, "Classicism Returns to Georgia," 53.

CHAPTER THREE. Behind the Velvet Ropes

1. Edward Daugherty, interview, June 20, 2014.

2. Quoted in Gailey, "Quips and Clay Fly."

3. Roy Wyatt, "Homage to Mansion's Gardens of Yesteryear," *Atlanta Journal-Constitution*, July 28, 1985.

4. Harris, Harris, and Harris interview.

5. Daugherty interview.

6. Ibid.

7. Elsie Crutchfield Moses, *The Georgia Governor's Mansion* (Atlanta, 1975).

8. Beth Wassell, interview, June 19, 2014.

9. Roderick Hardy of Hardy-Halpern, Inc., interview, June 5, 2014.

10. *Still Life with Fruit, Goblet, and Canary (Nature's Bounty)*, by Severin Roesen, 1851; see White House Historical Association, http://www.whitehouseresearch.org /assetbank-whha/action/viewHome.

11. Caroline Ballard Leake, interview, January 2, 2014.

12. Steve Stancil and Paul Melvin of the Georgia Building Authority, interview, June 26, 2014; Joy Forth, interview, June 25, 2014.

13. Forth interview.

14. Ibid.

15. David O'Connell, *The Art and Life of Atlanta Artist Wilbur G. Kurtz* (Charleston, S.C.: History Press, 2013), 89–91.

16. Forth interview.

CHAPTER FOUR. Opening the People's House

1. Jack Anderson, "Will Governor Maddox Fall Off His Political Bicycle," *Palm Beach Post*, May 30, 1970.

2. Justin Nystrom, "Lester Maddox (1915–2003)," *New Georgia Encyclopedia*, last modified September 15, 2014, accessed October 31, 2014, www.georgiaencyclopedia.org /articles/government-politics/lester-maddox-1915–2003.

3. Quoted in Bob Short, *Everything Is Pickrick* (Macon, Ga.: Mercer University Press, 1999), 102.

4. Quoted in "Georgia Governor's Wife One of a Vanishing Breed," *Meriden (CT) Morning Record*, February 20, 1967.

5. Larry Maddox, interview, December 19, 2013; Larry Maddox to the authors, e-mail, May 27, 2014.

6. Short, *Everything Is Pickrick*, 104.

7. Ibid., 107.

8. Quoted in "4 Escapees Surrender to Maddox," *Toledo Blade*, April 17, 1967.

9. Ibid.

10. Celestine Sibley, "Women Redeem Trading Stamps for Tablecloths for Mansion," *Atlanta Journal*, October 30, 1967.

11. Ibid.

12. Quoted in Short, *Everything Is Pickrick*, 113.

13. Ibid.

14. Steve Ball Jr., "Things Buzzin' for Troopers at the Governor's Mansion," *Atlanta Journal and Constitution*, December 24, 1967.

15. Quoted in Short, *Everything Is Pickrick*, 114.

16. Quoted in Sparks, "New Governor's Mansion."

17. Ibid.

18. Bruce Galphin, "A 'Well Done' for the Mansion's Unsung Heroes," *Atlanta Constitution*, January 29, 1968.

19. Celestine Sibley, "Governor and His Lady Given Separate Rooms in New Home," *Atlanta Constitution*, January 15, 1968.

20. Ball, "Things Buzzin' for Troopers."

21. Bob Cohn, "Maddox Boiling Mad—Couldn't Find Hot Water," *Athens Banner-Herald*, July 1, 1968.

22. "Maddox Asks Flag Donation," *Atlanta Journal*, July 2, 1968.

23. Quoted in ibid.

24. Quoted in Don Winter, "Senior Citizens Tour Mansion," *Atlanta Journal*, May 18, 1968.

25. Virginia "Ginny" Maddox Carnes and George Carnes, interview, January 3, 2014.

26. "Ride with the Governor Dec. 25," *Atlanta Constitution*, December 18, 1969.

27. Maddox interview.

28. Quoted in Kathryn Johnson, "Virginia Will Succeed Him," *Eugene (OR) Register*, December 29, 1968.

29. Quoted in Margaret Hurst and Duane Riner, "Maddox Ousts Mansion Fine Arts Committee," *Atlanta Constitution*, June 16, 1968.

30. Ibid.

31. Ibid.

32. Quoted in Mary Utting, "Elegant Mansion Built for Georgia Governor," *Charlotte Observer*, May 8, 1968.

33. Ibid.

34. Carnes and Carnes interview.

35. Maddox interview.

36. "Maddox Is Given a White Goose," *New London (CT) Day*, June 3, 1968.

37. Elizabeth Sawyer, "Wife of Governor Makes Mansion Feel like Home," *Atlanta Journal*, July 30, 1969.

38. Katharine Farnham to Jennifer Dickey, July 31, 2014.

39. Sawyer, "Wife of Governor."

40. Ibid.

41. Quoted in Selby McCash, "Mansion Reflects Maddox' Tastes," *Macon Telegraph*, June 22, 1969.

42. Maddox interview.

43. Quoted in McCash, "Mansion Reflects Maddox' Tastes."

44. Utting, "Elegant Mansion Built."

45. Maddox interview.

46. "Maddox Gets Big Farewell," *Daytona Beach Morning Journal*, January 4, 1971.

47. Short, *Everything Is Pickrick*, 153.

48. Peter Applebome, "In Georgia Reprise, Maddox on Stump," *New York Times*, January 14, 1990.

49. Maddox interview.

1. Georgia Southwestern College was renamed Georgia Southwestern State University.

2. Gary M. Fink, "Jimmy Carter (b. 1924)," *New Georgia Encyclopedia*, last modified September 15, 2014, accessed October 31, 2014, www.georgiaencyclopedia.org/articles /government-politics/jimmy-carter-b-1924.

3. Jimmy and Rosalynn Carter, interview, April 10, 2014.

4. "New Day A'Coming in the South," *Time*, May 31, 1971, 15.

5. Kenneth Morris, *Jimmy Carter: American Moralist* (Athens: University of Georgia Press, 1996), 181.

6. E. Stanly Godbold Jr., *Jimmy and Rosalynn Carter* (New York: Oxford University Press, 2010), 17.

7. Bruce Mazlish and Edwin Diamond, *Jimmy Carter: A Character Portrait* (New York: Simon and Schuster, 1979), 177.

8. Jimmy and Rosalynn Carter interview.

9. Ibid.

10. Rosalynn Carter, *First Lady from Plains* (Boston: Houghton Mifflin, 1984), 75.

11. Ibid.

12. Ibid., 76.

13. Ibid., 77.

14. Ibid., 78.

15. Ibid.

16. Ibid.

17. Ibid., 79.

18. Ibid., 91.

19. Ibid., 79.

20. "Inaugural Balls Draw Thousands," *Atlanta Constitution*, January 13, 1971.

21. Jimmy and Rosalynn Carter interview.

22. Quoted in Sarah Booth Conroy, "Toward Comfort for Some, Grandeur for All," *Washington Post*, December 3, 1978.

23. Phil Gailey, Memoirs of a Political Partner," *New York Times*, April 15, 1984.

24. Carter, *First Lady from Plains*, 80.

25. Ibid., 80.

26. Godbold, *Jimmy and Rosalynn Carter*, 220–21.

27. Ibid., 221–22.

28. Jimmy and Rosalynn Carter interview.

29. Ibid.; Ambassador Anne Cox Chambers, interview by Ann Miller Morin, October 23, 1985, Association for Diplomatic Studies and Training, Foreign Affairs Oral History Project, Women Ambassador Series, www.adst.org/OH%20TOCs/Chambers,%20Anne%20Cox .toc.pdf.

30. Carter, *First Lady from Plains*, 83.

31. Ibid., 83.

32. Quoted in Sarah Booth Conroy, "Rosalynn Carter: Turning the Page," *Washington Post*, April 25, 1984.

33. Carter, *First Lady from Plains*, 91.

34. Betty Glad, *Jimmy Carter: In Search of the Great White House* (New York: Norton, 1980), 143.

35. Godbold, 218–19.

36. Austin Scott, "A Governess for Amy: Amy and Her Governess Reunited at White House," *Washington Post*, February 5, 1977.

37. Quoted in Clare Crawford, "A Story of Love and Rehabilitation: The Ex-Con in the White House," *People*, March 14, 1977.

38. Ibid.

39. Quoted in Mike Christensen, "Amy's Friend in the White House," *Atlanta Journal*, January 21, 1977.

40. Crawford, "Story of Love and Rehabilitation."

41. Quoted in Scott, "A Governess for Amy."

42. Scott Kaufmann, *Rosalynn Carter: Equal Partner in the White House* (Lawrence: University Press of Kansas, 2007), 23.

43. Carter, *First Lady from Plains*, 84.

44. Godbold, *Jimmy and Rosalynn Carter*, 172.

45. Jimmy and Rosalynn Carter interview.

46. Carter, *First Lady from Plains*, 85.

47. Ibid., 81.

48. Ibid., 89.

49. Jimmy and Rosalynn Carter interview.

50. Carter, *First Lady from Plains*, 89–90.

51. Gailey, "Memoirs of a Political Partner."

52. Quoted in Conroy, "Toward Comfort for Some."

53. Ibid.

54. Carter, *First Lady from Plains*, 81.

55. Ibid., 82.

56. Ibid., 81.

57. Ibid., 106.

58. Jimmy and Rosalynn Carter interview.

59. Carter, *First Lady from Plains,* 106.

60. Jimmy and Rosalynn Carter interview.

61. Kaufmann, *Rosalynn Carter*, 19.

62. Ibid.

63. Carter, *First Lady from Plains*, 88–89.

64. Glad, *Jimmy Carter*, 150.

65. Jimmy and Rosalynn Carter interview.

66. Glad, *Jimmy Carter*, 151.

67. Carter, *First Lady from Plains*, 87.

68. Godbold, *Jimmy and Rosalynn Carter*, 213.

69. Carter, *First Lady from Plains*, 90–91. Jack married Judy Langford, daughter of family friend and state senator

Beverly Langford, in 1971. Chip married Caron Griffin, an intern at the state capitol, in 1973.

70. Godbold, *Jimmy and Rosalynn Carter*, 193.

71. Jimmy and Rosalynn Carter interview.

72. Carter, *First Lady from Plains*, 86.

73. Ibid.

74. Ibid., 81.

75. Ibid., 93.

76. Ibid. In an interview in 1982, Jimmy Carter mentioned that he had begun to plan to run as early as 1971 (Jimmy Carter, interview, Miller Center Interviews, Carter Presidency Project, vol. 19, November 29, 1982, 2, Jimmy Carter Library).

77. Jimmy and Rosalynn Carter interview.

78. Ibid.

CHAPTER SIX. Southern Hospitality with an International Flair

1. Mary Beth Busbee and Jan Busbee Curtis, *Guess Who's Coming to Dinner: Entertaining at the Governor's Mansion; Menus, Recipes, and Anecdotes* (Atlanta: Peachtree, 1986), 3. The authors would like to extend a special thanks to Jan Busbee Curtis, Jeff Curtis, Buz Busbee, and Mary Beth Kindt for their assistance with this chapter.

2. Jeff Busbee and Jan Curtis, interview, January 25, 2014.

3. Ibid.; Busbee and Curtis, *Guess Who's Coming to Dinner*, 3.

4. Quoted in Jim Tharpe, "Busbee, Workhorse Governor, Dies at 76," *Atlanta-Journal Constitution*, July 17, 2004.

5. Ibid.

6. James F. Cooke, "George Busbee (1927–2004)," *New Georgia Encyclopedia*, last modified, September 9, 2014, accessed October 31, 2014 www.georgiaencyclopedia.org /articles/government-politics/george-busbee-1927–2004.

7. Ibid.

8. Jeff Busbee and Jan Curtis interview.

9. Ibid.

10. George Busbee Jr. to Catherine Lewis, e-mail, February 24, 2014.

11. Ron Martz, "Memories of the Mansion," *Atlanta Journal-Constitution*, January 9, 1983.

12. Quoted in Sharon Bailey, "Running State's Top Mansion: A Stately Chore," *Atlanta Journal*, October 14, 1982.

13. Ibid.

14. Ibid.

15. Jeff Busbee and Jan Curtis interview.

16. Ibid.

17. Martz, "Memories of the Mansion"; Beth Busbee Kindt, interview, February 19, 2014.

18. Beth Busbee Wiggins Kindt, "Life in the Georgia Governor's Mansion," unpublished paper, January 2014, in Catherine Lewis's possession.

19. Busbee and Curtis, *Guess Who's Coming to Dinner*, 3.

20. Ibid., 4.

21. Cecil Phillips, interview, February 5, 2014.

22. Ibid.

23. Quoted in Martz, "Memories of the Mansion."

24. Busbee and Curtis, *Guess Who's Coming to Dinner*, 9–10.

25. Quoted in Bailey, "Running State's Top Mansion."

26. Busbee and Curtis, *Guess Who's Coming to Dinner*, 106.

27. Ibid.

28. Ibid., 57–58.

29. Phillips interview.

30. Jimmy Carter, *Keeping Faith: Memoirs of a President* (Fayetteville: University of Arkansas Press, 1995), 51.

31. Busbee and Curtis, *Guess Who's Coming to Dinner*, 73.

32. Ibid., 25–27.

33. Jeff Busbee and Jan Curtis interview.

34. Busbee and Curtis, *Guess Who's Coming to Dinner*, 43–44.

35. Ibid., 115.

36. Ibid., 15.

37. Ibid., 39.

38. George Busbee Jr. to Catherine Lewis, e-mail, February 24, 2014.

39. Ibid.

40. Ibid.

41. Martz, "Memories of the Mansion."

42. Busbee and Curtis, *Guess Who's Coming to Dinner*, 65.

43. Jeff Busbee and Jan Curtis interview.

44. Quoted in Prentice Palmer, "Mansion 'Prettier' after Repairs," *Atlanta Journal*, April 9, 1975.

45. Ibid.

46. Kindt interview.

47. Jeff Busbee and Jan Curtis interview.

48. Busbee and Curtis, *Guess Who's Coming to Dinner*, 95.

49. Quoted in Tom Crawford, "Governor Gets His Own Backyard Pool," *Atlanta Journal*, August 15, 1980.

50. Phillips interview.

51. "That's Not Fair Pool," *Atlanta Constitution*, August 15, 1980.

52. Jeff Busbee and Jan Curtis interview.

53. Phillips interview.

54. Holly Chute, interview, January 25, 2014.

55. Jeff Busbee and Jan Curtis interview.

56. Ibid.

57. Martz, "Memories of the Mansion."

58. Cook, "George Busbee (1927–2004)."

59. Tharpe, "Busbee, Workhorse Governor."

60. Phillips interview.

61. Quoted in Tharpe, "Busbee, Workhorse Governor."

CHAPTER SEVEN. Not in Our Wildest Dreams

1. Joe Frank Harris, *Personal Reflections on a Public Life* (Macon, Ga.: Mercer University Press, 1998), 35.

2. Jingle Davis, "Georgia Inaugurals Up Close and Personal," *Atlanta Journal and Constitution*, January 10, 1999.

3. Celestine Sibley, "Harris Shares Golden Advice for Guvs-To Be," *Atlanta Constitution*, November 16, 1998.

4. Harris, *Personal Reflections*, 105.

5. Ibid., 97.

6. Ibid., 104.

7. Elizabeth Harris, interview, February 6, 2014.

8. Ibid.

9. Harris, *Personal Reflections*, 106.

10. Ibid., 223.

11. Elizabeth Harris interview.

12. Ibid.

13. Scott Peacock, "Southern Recipe Restoration Project," *Atlanta Journal-Constitution*, November 2, 2006.

14. Elizabeth Harris interview; Harris, Harris, and Harris interview.

15. Elizabeth Harris interview.

16. Ibid.

17. Harris, Harris, and Harris interview.

18. Quoted in Andy Johnston, "State Writer Collection Catalogued," *Atlanta Journal and Constitution*, September 25, 2012.

19. Elizabeth Harris interview.

20. Harris, Harris, and Harris interview.

21. Harris, *Personal Reflections*, 106.

22. Elizabeth Harris interview.

23. Ibid.

24. Quoted in Roy Wyatt, "First Lady of the Gardens," *Atlanta Journal and Constitution*, July 28, 1985.

25. Harris, *Personal Reflections*, 108.

26. Ibid., 107.

27. Wyatt, "First Lady of the Gardens."

28. Ibid.

29. Ibid.

30. Harris, Harris, and Harris interview.

31. Brooke Harris, interview, July 9, 2014.

32. Rhonda Cook, "Harris Era Ends," *Atlanta Journal and Constitution*, January 7, 1991.

33. Elizabeth Harris interview.

34. Ibid.

35. Ibid.

36. Ibid.

37. Harris, *Personal Reflections*, 223.

38. Ibid., 224–25.

39. Ibid., 225.

40. Ibid., 225–26.

CHAPTER EIGHT. From the Mountains to the Mansion

1. Zell and Shirley Miller, interview, April 1, 2014.

2. Ibid.

3. Alan Patureau, "Shirley Miller: First Lady of Georgia," *Atlanta Journal and Constitution*, January 14, 1991; Jeanne Cummings, "Incoming Governor Brings Outgoing Style to Inaugural," *Atlanta Journal and Constitution*, January 14, 1991.

4. Zell Miller, interview by Bob Short, October 24, 2006, Reflections on Georgia Politics Series, Richard B. Russell Library for Political Research and Studies, University of Georgia Libraries.

5. Maria Sapporta, "'Having Writ,' Miller Content to Be Home," *Atlanta Journal and Constitution*, July 4, 1999.

6. Chris Grant, "Zell Miller (b. 1932)," *New Georgia Encyclopedia*, last modified September 25, 2014, accessed October 31, 2014, www.georgiaencyclopedia.org/articles /government-politics/zell-miller-b-1932.

7. Zell and Shirley Miller interview.

8. Shirley Miller, interview, January 7, 2014.

9. Ibid.

10. Leake interview.

11. Zell and Shirley Miller interview.

12. Quoted in Patureau, "Shirley Miller."

13. Shirley Miller interview.

14. Patureau, "Shirley Miller."

15. Ibid.

16. Amy Huckaby, interview, January 2, 2014.

17. Zell and Shirley Miller interview.

18. Ibid.

19. Tinah Saunders, "At Home with Zell and Shirley," *Atlanta Journal Constitution*, September 30, 1991; Huckaby interview.

20. Saunders, "At Home with Zell and Shirley."

21. Shirley Miller interview.

22. Jeanne Cummings, "Inaugural Ceremonies to Reflect Miller's Experiences, Personality," *Atlanta Journal and Constitution*, January 13, 1991.

23. Beverly Messer, notes about the Governor's Mansion, February 17, 2014, in possession of Catherine Lewis.

24. Russ DeVault, "Zell Miller: Packing Up, Heading Home," *Atlanta Journal and Constitution*, January 3, 1999.

25. Jeanne Cummings, "A Gathering of Governors," *Atlanta Journal and Constitution*, January 26, 1991.

26. Ibid.

27. Charles Walston, "Catching Up with Shirley Miller," *Atlanta Journal and Constitution*, September 14, 1994.

28. Saunders, "At Home with Zell and Shirley."

29. Shirley Miller interview; Zell and Shirley Miller interview.

30. Shirley Miller interview.

31. Walston, "Catching Up with Shirley Miller."

32. Keith Mason, interview, February 5, 2014.

33. Ibid.; Steve Wrigley, interview, January 17, 2014.

34. Zell and Shirley Miller interview.

35. Phil Kloer, "Mysteries, Movies, and the Mansion," *Atlanta Constitution*, May 22, 1991.

36. Leake interview.

37. Quoted in Tinah Saunders, "Open House: Step Right Up to the Governor's Mansion," *Atlanta Journal and Constitution*, September 29, 1991.

38. Ibid.

39. Helen C. Smith, "Georgia Artists to Be Lauded at the Governor's Mansion," *Atlanta Journal and Constitution*, March 10, 1992.

40. Colin Campbell, "Lost and Found at the Governor's Mansion," *Atlanta Journal and Constitution*, March 28, 1992.

41. Mason interview.

42. Zell and Shirley Miller interview.

43. Ibid.

44. Shirley Miller interview.

45. Ibid.

46. Wrigley interview.

47. Zell and Shirley Miller interview.

48. Leake interview.

49. Shirley Miller interview.

50. Leake interview.

51. Shirley Miller, interview by Bill Short, December 16, 2008, Reflections on Georgia Politics Series, Richard B. Russell Library for Political Research and Studies, University of Georgia Libraries.

52. Shirley Miller interview.

53. Ibid.

54. Shirley Miller, interview by Bill Short.

55. Wrigley interview.

56. Ibid.

57. Zell and Shirley Miller interview.

58. Colin Campbell, "Our First Lady: Sweet Antidote to Ugly Politics," *Atlanta Journal Constitution*, August 23, 1998.

59. Dick Pettys, "Miller Bids Emotional Farewell to Staff," Associated Press, December 30, 1998.

60. Ibid.

61. Quoted in Kathey Pruitt, "Zell Miller: Packing Up, Heading Home," *Atlanta Journal and Constitution*, January 2, 1999.

62. Ibid.

63. "Miller's One of a Kind," editorial, *Atlanta Journal and Constitution*, January 4, 1999.

64. Colin Campbell, "All's Well with Zell in Mountain Life Return," *Atlanta Journal and Constitution*, April 27, 1999.

65. Grant, "Zell Miller (b. 1932)."

CHAPTER NINE. Come On In

1. Dick Pettys, "Barnes: Less Spit-and-Polish than Miller, More Fun Loving," Associated Press, November 7, 1998.

2. Quoted in Elizabeth Lee, "Just Call Her Marie, Not May-ree Barnes," *Atlanta Journal-Constitution*, January 27, 1999.

3. F. Erik Brooks, "Roy Barnes (b. 1948)," *New Georgia Encyclopedia*, last modified May 14, 2013, accessed November 12, 2014, www.georgiaencyclopedia.org/articles /government-politics/roy-barnes-b-1948.

4. Marie Barnes, interview, January 6, 2014.

5. Lee, "Just Call Her Marie."

6. Roy and Marie Barnes, interview, April 8, 2014.

7. Ibid.

8. Marie Barnes, interview by Bob Short, January 29, 2009, Richard B. Russell Library for Political Research and Studies, University of Georgia Libraries.

9. Lori Johnston, "Governor-Elect's Wife Focused on Family," Associated Press, December 25, 1998.

10. Roy and Marie Barnes interview.

11. Chute interview, January 25, 2014.

12. Roy and Marie Barnes interview.

13. Ibid.

14. Quoted in Johnston, "Governor-Elect's Wife Focused on Family."

15. Marie Barnes interview; Johnston, "Governor-Elect's Wife Focused on Family."

16. Marie Barnes interview.

17. Ibid.

18. Quoted in Celia Sibley, "Welcoming Day at the Mansion," *Atlanta Journal and Constitution*, January 10, 1999.

19. Justine Bachman, "Despite Chill, Football, Crowds Turn Out to Meet Barnes, Tour Mansion," Associated Press, January 9, 1999.

20. Quoted in Sibley, "Welcoming Day at the Mansion."

21. Marie Barnes interview.

22. Ibid.

23. Ibid.

24. Ibid.

25. Ibid.

26. Johnston, "Governor-Elect's Wife Focused on Family."

27. Marie Barnes interview.

28. Ibid.

29. Ibid.

30. Johnston, "Governor-Elect's Wife Focused on Family."

31. Marie Barnes interview.

32. Ibid.

33. Ibid.

34. Lee, "Just Call her Marie."

35. Marie Barnes interview.

36. Ibid.

37. Marie Barnes, interview by Bob Short.

38. Marie Barnes interview.

39. Ibid.

40. Ibid.

41. Ibid.

42. Marie Barnes interview; Roy and Marie Barnes interview.

43. Marie Barnes, interview by Bob Short.

44. Marie Barnes interview.

45. Ibid.

46. Ibid.; Marie Barnes, interview by Bob Short.

47. Roy and Marie Barnes interview.

48. Marie Barnes interview.

49. Ibid.

50. Jim Galloway, "Flag Foes Bid Barnes Noisy Adieu," *Atlanta Journal-Constitution*, January 6, 2003.

CHAPTER TEN. Down-Home Style

1. Matthew C. Hulbert, "Sonny Perdue (b. 1946)," *New Georgia Encyclopedia*, last modified August 22, 2013, accessed April 15, 2014, www.georgiaencyclopedia.org /articles/government-politics/sonny-perdue-b-1946.

2. Quoted in Mia Taylor, "Georgia's New First Lady— Mary Perdue," *Atlanta Journal-Constitution*, November 11, 2002.

3. Sonja Lewis, "Down-Home, Perdue-Style," *Atlanta Journal-Constitution*, January 12, 2003.

4. Ibid.

5. Kristen Wyatt, "Perdue to Become First Republican Governor in 130 Years," *Associated Press*, January 13, 2003.

6. Taylor, "Georgia's New First Lady."

7. Mary Perdue, interview, January 16, 2014.

8. Jen Bennecke, interview, May 1, 2014.

9. Quoted in Mia Taylor, "The Governor's Inauguration," *Atlanta Journal-Constitution*, January 10, 2003.

10. Ibid.

11. Ibid.

12. Ibid.

13. Ibid.

14. Mary Perdue interview.

15. Taylor, "Georgia's New First Lady."

16. Holly Chute, quoted in Helena Oliviero, "Governors Change, but First Chef Keeps Cooking," *Atlanta Journal-Constitution*, January 9, 2012.

17. Joyce White, interview, April 30, 2014.

18. Chute, quoted in Oliviero, "Governors Change."

19. White interview.

20. Bennecke interview.

21. Mary Perdue interview.

22. Lewis, "Down-Home, Perdue-Style."

23. Mary Perdue interview.

24. Ibid.

25. Ibid.

26. Quoted in Brandon Larrabee, "Friends of Mansion Takes Funds but Isn't Registered," *Augusta Chronicle*, October 11, 2005.

27. Bennecke interview.

28. Mary Perdue interview.

29. Bennecke interview.

30. "Fire at Georgia Governor's Mansion," Associated Press, September 12, 2008.

31. Quoted in "Governor Highlights Conservation Benefits for All," States News Service, October 31, 2008.

32. "Governor Perdue Welcomes Aga Khan to Georgia," States News Service, April 18, 2008.

33. "Governor and Mrs. Perdue Host U.N. Secretary-General at State Luncheon," States News Service, May 8, 2008.

34. Bennecke interview.

35. Mary Perdue interview.

36. White interview.

37. "Georgia Governor Stumping for 'Favorite Daughter' in Idol Vote," Associated Press, May 24, 2004.

38. Ken Sugiura, "The Governor Grooves: Perdue Opens Mansion to Safe Party after Prom," *Atlanta Journal-Constitution*, May 15, 2006.

39. Ibid.

40. Ibid.

41. Ibid.

42. Greg Bluestein, "Hundreds Take After-Prom Party to Georgia Governor's Front Lawn," Associated Press, May 15, 2006.

43. "First Lady Perdue Hosts Foster Family Appreciation Night," *U.S. State News*, June 7, 2007. "Wednesday's Child" is a segment on WAGA-TV that profiles children awaiting adoption.

44. "Governor Perdue, First Lady Host Little League Celebration at Governor's Mansion," *U.S. States News*, November 17, 2007.

45. White interview.

46. Andrea Jones, "Eggs Go Fast, Like a Bunny," Cox News Service, April 5, 2007.

47. Ibid.

48. Ibid.

49. Alma E. Hill, "First Lady's Holiday Style: Down-to-Earth," *Atlanta Journal-Constitution*, December 6, 2003.

50. Ibid.

51. Ibid.

52. Teresa Stepzinski, "Kids Craft Official Decorations," *Florida Times-Union*, December 3, 2004.

53. Mary Perdue interview.

CHAPTER ELEVEN. Georgia Grown

1. Ember Bishop and Joy Forth, interview, January 2, 2014.

2. Jackie Kennedy, "From Rural Georgia to the Governor's Mansion," *Georgia Magazine*, September 2013, 18.

3. Quoted in "A New Deal for Georgia: A Special Celebration Section," *Gainesville (GA) Times*, January 2011, 4.

4. Sandra Deal, interview, February 6, 2014.

5. Sandra Deal and Ember Bishop, interview, June 4, 2014.

6. Deal and Bishop interview; Carolyn Crist, "Movin' On Up," *Gainesville (GA) Times*, January 7, 2011.

7. Deal and Bishop interview.

8. Nathan and Sandra Deal, interview, June 16, 2014.

9. Lori Johnston, "The Governor's Mansion," *Atlanta Journal-Constitution*, March 17, 2013; Deal and Bishop interview; Ember Bishop to Catherine Lewis, e-mail June 2, 2014.

10. Crist, "Movin' On Up."

11. Ember Bishop to Catherine Lewis.

12. Nathan and Sandra Deal interview.

13. Larry Peterson, "Snow Prompts Savannahians to Watch Nathan Deal Inauguration from Afar," *Savannah Morning News*, January 11, 2011.

14. Johnston, "The Governor's Mansion."

15. Nathan and Sandra Deal interview.

16. Deal and Bishop interview.

17. Ibid.

18. Nathan and Sandra Deal interview.

19. Ibid.

20. Ibid.

21. Sandra Deal interview.

22. Deal and Bishop interview.

23. Chris Riley, interview, June 24, 2014.

24. Sandra Deal interview.

25. Riley interview; Stancil and Melvin interview.

26. Bishop and Forth interview.

27. Sandra Deal interview.

28. The librarians who worked on the project include Peggy Chambliss, Dawn Dale, Bill Davis, Patricia Dollisch, Carolyn Fuller, Thelma Glover, Teresa Harris, Elaine Hardy, Stephen Hart, Christina Hodgens, Nancy Holmes, Dustin Landrum, Chris Lester, Bin Lin, Vicki Marshall, Elizabeth McKinney, Deborah McLaughlin, Davis Moore, Kathy Pillatzki, Nathan Rall, Barbara Sanders, Judy Serritella, Chris Sharp, Christy Southard, Leslie St. John, Peiling Su, Linh Uong, Diana Very, Susan White, Daniel Zeiger, and Shelley Zhang. A committee of the Georgia Library Association also worked on expanding and cataloguing the mansion library in the years 1970–83 under the leadership of David E. Estes. They worked with First Lady Rosalyn Carter; Mrs. W. J. "Cissy" Dolvin, Governor Carter's aunt; First Lady Mary Beth Busbee; and First Lady Elizabeth Harris. Others on the committee were John W. Bonner, Lynn Bradley, Ira Lois Brown, Tony Dees, Holcombe Green Sr., Adrienne Lunsford, Virginia McJenkin, John Pattillo, Gaynell Richardson, and Ken Thomas. Over the years, the extensive library collection has been catalogued and supervised by Claudia Medori, Nancy Newman, and Sandy Candler.

29. Sandra Deal interview; Ember Bishop to Catherine Lewis.

30. Kay Kunzer, Helen Pirkle, Susan Jessup, Marty Owens, Tina McDaniel, Elaine Childers, Kathy Lovett, Joan Yearwood, and Barbara Lawson, interview, June 18, 2014.

31. Deal and Bishop interview.

32. Bishop and Forth interview.

33. Sandra Deal interview.

34. Riley interview.

35. Deal and Bishop interview.

36. Ibid.

37. Ibid.

38. Riley interview.

39. Nathan and Sandra Deal interview.

40. Governor's Mansion trusties, interview, June 4, 2014.

41. Deal and Bishop interview.

42. Nathan and Sandra Deal interview.

CHAPTER TWELVE. Manning the Mansion

1. Marie Barnes interview.

2. *Governor's Transition Manual*, "The Role of the First Lady and the Management of the Executive Mansion," in author's possession, 27–28.

3. Forth interview.

4. Ibid.

5. *Governor's Transition Manual*, "The Role of the First Lady," 27–28.

6. Deal and Bishop interview.

7. Kirk Talgo, interview, May 22, 2014.

8. Atlanta Transitional Center residents, interview, June 4, 2014. For security reasons, the trusties are referred to by first name only.

9. Georgia Department of Corrections, "Probation, Detention and Transitional Centers," fact sheet, provided by Joan Heath, in author's possession.

10. Steven Perkins, interview, June 8, 2014.

11. Ibid.

12. Frank Pfirman, interview, June 30, 2014.

13. Atlanta Transitional Center residents interview.

14. Ibid.

15. Carla Blanks, interview, June 26, 2014.

16. Atlanta Transition Center residents interview.

17. Forth interview.

18. Holly Chute, interview, May 22, 2014.

19. Simon, interview, June 25, 2014.

20. Chute interview, May 22, 2014.

21. Sharon Burrow, interview, June 26, 2014.

22. Bob Satterfield, interview, June 26, 2014.

23. Gordy Wright, interview, February 7, 2014.

24. David Herring, interview, January 7, 2014.

25. Wright interview.

26. Mark McDonough, interview, February 25, 2014.

27. Pfirman interview.

28. McDonough interview.

29. Herring interview.

30. Linda Jackson, interview, July 9, 2014.

31. Cynthia Day, Brenda Bedinfield, Margie Bowyer, Barbara Fussell, Janet Robertson, Beth Wassell, Pat Valz, Patricia Chandler, Gayle Hollinger, and Shirley Townsend, interview, June 19, 2014.

32. Carleen Toole, Suzanne Decker, Barbara D'Emilio, Jane Mitchell, Julia McDonald, Joan Kennel, and Madge Babich, interview, June 25, 2014.

33. Ibid.

34. Day et al., interview.

35. Ibid.

36. Toole et al., interview.

37. Day et al., interview.

38. Jody Taylor and Olin Lundy, interview, June 26, 2014.

39. Doug, ATC resident, interview, December 17, 2013.

40. Matthew, e-mail, June 11, 2014, in author's possession.

41. Quoted in "State Panel Approves Plans for New $750,000 Mansion," *Savannah News*, April 20, 1963.

Acknowledgments

This project was a partnership in the every sense of the word. A number of books have been published about Georgia's governors over the years, but there is no single volume devoted to the mansion and its history. The authors express their deep gratitude to the many friends and colleagues throughout the state who helped make this book possible.

All the first families who lived in the West Paces Ferry Road mansion agreed to assist with the book. We owe special thanks to Betty Foy Sanders for her special devotion to the project. Although her family never lived in the current mansion, she and her husband, Governor Carl Sanders, were instrumental in shaping its form and the nature of its furnishings, and she cheerfully shared her memories of that process. The children of Virginia and Lester Maddox, Lester Maddox Jr., Larry Maddox, Virginia Maddox Carnes, and her husband, George Carnes, were among our first interviewees, in December 2013. Jimmy Carter and Rosalynn Carter kindly agreed to meet us at the Carter Center, and they were ably assisted by Beth Davis, Lauren Gay, Melissa Montgomery, Polly Nodine, Sara Mitchell, Amanda Pellerin, and Carla Ledgerwood. Jan Busbee Curtis, Jeff Busbee, George "Buz" Busbee Jr., and Beth Busbee Kindt, the children of George and Mary Beth Busbee, and Cecil Phillips, a former member of Governor Busbee's staff, and Sharon Green provided rich material for chapter 6. Elizabeth Harris, Joe Frank Harris, Joe Frank Harris Jr., and Brooke Harris consented to multiple meetings and regaled us with stories of their time in the mansion. We met Shirley Miller and Zell Miller at the mansion and at their home in Young Harris. Their former staff members Amy Huckaby, Caroline Ballard Leake, Keith Mason, and Beverly Messer also kindly assisted us. Marie and Roy Barnes hosted us in their home, and Sharon Holt helped us manage their schedule. We also thank Mary Perdue, Sonny Perdue, and their former staff member Joyce White and Jen Bennecke for several lively conversations. Chris Riley and Andrea Briscoe, from Nathan Deal's office, were particularly helpful, and we owe special thanks to Governor Deal for his enthusiasm for the project.

So many people at the mansion helped make this book possible. Joy Forth and Ember Bishop were instrumental in the book's success and deserve special recognition. They helped us at every step of the way and were wonderful ambassadors for the project. Holly Chute, Stanley Simon, Kirk Talgo, Linda Jackson, Alyssa Botts, and Katie McCreary were all key players. Former mansion team members Freda Martin Amrod, Matt O'Donnell, Russell Jones, David Camp, and Sharon Burrow agreed to share their memories with us. The men at the Atlanta Transitional Center lent their voices to the project and provided a welcome behind-the-scenes view of the mansion's daily operations.

The state troopers and members of the Department of Public Safety were valuable members of our team. We thank Mark McDonough, Gordy Wright, David Herring, Frank Pfirman, James Andrews, Tony Henry, Michael Coverson, Danny Hall, Keith Jones, Vince Mooney, Jimmy Sumner, Chris Wigginton, Alton Wilkins, Bobby Mathis, David Phillips, Scott Ogle, James Brown, J. S. Carroll, J. S. Joiner, Hoa Lauridson, Olin Lundy, Timothy McRae, Darin Rice, Samuel Taylor, and Moses Little. We owe special thanks to the volunteers who agreed to serve on the book committee, including Kitty Farnham, Amy Huckaby, Henry Turner, Alice Jepson, Mary Hart Wilheit, and Betty Foy Sanders. Wendy Leebern and Rayna Casey, who currently oversee the operations of Friends of the Mansion, deserve special thanks for their support. We also acknowledge the efforts of the members of Atlanta Chapter 24 of the National Association of Watch and Clock Collectors, including Brooks Coleman, George Waterhouse, Donna Kalinkiewicz, Christian Brown,

Bernie and Carol Tekippe, Warren and Kathy Brook, Randy Grunwell, Richard Mangum, Kathi Edwards, Martha Smallwood, Pete Schreiner, Chris Martin, and Mike Mellard.

A number of the mansion docents agreed to be interviewed for the book, and we acknowledge Carleen Toole, Suzanne Decker, Barbara D'Emilio, Jane Mitchell, Julia McDonald, Joan Kennel, Madge Babich, Cynthia Day, Brenda Bedinfield, Margie Bowyer, Barbara Fussell, Janet Robertson, Beth Wassell, Pat Valz, Patricia Chandler, Gayle Hollinger, Shirley Townsend, Kay Kunzer, Helen Pirkle, Susan Jessup, Marty Owens, Tina McDaniel, Elaine Childers, Kathy Lovett, Joan Yearwood, and Barbara Lawson.

A range of state employees, scholars, archivists, museum professionals, and others assisted us with this book, including Matt Davis (Old Governor's Mansion); Ellen Johnston (Georgia State Libraries); Trey Gaines and Sandy Moore (Bartow History Museum); William Gray Potter, Toby Graham, Ruta Abolins, Jill Severn, and Sheryl Vogt (University of Georgia Libraries); Dale Couch (Georgia Museum of Art); Jamil Zainaldin (Georgia Humanities Council); Michael Rose, Don Rooney, Sheffield Hale, and Staci Catron (Atlanta History Center); Christopher Davidson, Ann Smith, Steven Engerrand, and Gail DeLoach (Georgia Archives); Steve Stancil, Paul Melvin, Linda Eidson, and Carla Blanks (Georgia Building Authority); Brian Owens, Steven Perkins, and Joan Heath (Department of Corrections); Hank Huckaby and Steve Wrigley (University System of Georgia Board of Regents); Edward L. Daugherty; Benjamin Vinson (McKenna Long & Aldridge LLP); Roderick Hardy (Hardy Halpern, Inc.); and Mary Miley Theobald.

Much of the new photography in the book is credited to Christopher Michael Oquendo, our photographer. He became a critical member of our team and worked diligently to capture the beauty of the mansion, the collections, and the grounds.

Many of our colleagues at Kennesaw State University deserve recognition, including Daniel Papp, Randy Hinds, David Parker, Ashley Bailey, Patricia Mosier, Julia Brock, Richard Harker, Zoila Torres, Tony Howell, Teresa Reeves, Justin Rabideau, Anna Tucker, James Newberry, and the other staff members in the Department of Museums, Archives & Rare Books. Additionally, we appreciate the support of Paula Strange, Charles Amlaner, Carolyn Elliott-Farino, and Alice Pate.

We extend a warm and hearty thanks to Ouida Dickey and Richard Lewis for their valuable edits to the manuscript. They labored for many hours, and we are grateful for their keen attention to detail and good humor. Our families deserve credit for helping make this book possible. Jennifer would like to thank Kathy Knapp; Catherine would like to recognize John and Emma Companiotte; and Sandra would like to thank Nathan Deal.

Finally, the authors owe quite a debt to the editorial staff at the University of Georgia Press, led by its director, Lisa Bayer. Her team—which included Elizabeth Crowley, Amanda Sharp, Erin New, John Joerschke, and Sean Garrett—helped bring this book to fruition. We are thankful for their wisdom, dedication, and hard work.

About the Authors

SANDRA D. DEAL, the daughter of educators, has dedicated her life to encouraging childhood education. After teaching for more than fifteen years, she retired as a sixth-grade middle school teacher in Hall County. As first lady of Georgia, she has focused her energies on a range of issues. Through Read Across Georgia, she has visited all 159 counties in the state to encourage reading for children. Her With a Servant's Heart platform has encouraged statewide community service programs and volunteerism events. She serves as chair of the Governor's Office for Children and Family and cochair of the Georgia Children's Cabinet. Sandra grew up in Gainesville and graduated from Georgia College and State University.

JENNIFER W. DICKEY is an associate professor at Kennesaw State University (KSU) and coordinator of the Public History Certificate Program. She has a master's degree in heritage preservation and a PhD in public history from Georgia State University. She is the author of *A Tough Little Patch of History: "Gone with the Wind" and the Politics of Memory* (2014) and coeditor of *Museums in a Global Context: National Identity, International Understanding* (2013). Before coming to KSU, she served as the campus preservation specialist and the director and curator of Historic Berry at Berry College in Rome, Georgia. She has worked as a historian for the National Park Service and for the Historic Preservation Division of the State of Georgia.

CATHERINE M. LEWIS is the assistant vice president of Museums, Archives & Rare Books, the director of the Museum of History and Holocaust Education, and a professor of history at Kennesaw State University. She is also a guest curator and special projects coordinator for the Atlanta History Center. She completed a BA in English and history with honors at Emory University and an MA and PhD in American Studies at the University of Iowa. She has curated more than thirty exhibitions throughout the nation and has authored, coauthored, or edited ten books, including *The Changing Face of Public History: The Chicago Historical Society and the Transformation of an American History Museum* (2005), *Don't Ask What I Shot: How Eisenhower's Love of Golf Helped Shape 1950s America* (2007), and four documentary collections with the University of Arkansas Press.

Index

family, 37; volunteer docents, 34, 46, 64, 87–88, 125, 175, *192*, 192–93

red barn, 42, *45*, 174
Redding, Otis, 89
Reed, Jerry, 99, 101, 102
Regan, Jerry, 140
renovations: Deal administration, 175; guest bathroom, *175*, 175; guest bedroom, 157; kitchen, 35, 58, 157, 160, *160*, 175; major renovations, 65; Perdue administration, 35, 58, 65, 156–57, 160, 175; red barn, 42; second floor, 175; storage areas, 65; tennis courts, 42. *See also* Friends of the Mansion
repairs and improvements: Aubusson carpet, 54–55; dining room table, 89; furnishings and interior decoration, 35, 37, 156–57, 160, *160*; Granite Mansion, 20–21; mirror, 59; Old Governor's Mansion, 13; tornado damage, 105, 107. *See also* renovations
Revolutionary War period, 6, 8
Reynolds, Burt, 99, 101
Reynolds, Herbert, 17
Reynolds, John, 6
Reynolds, Nannie, 17
Rice, Darin, 172
Rice, Helen, 194
Rich, Dick, 20
Rich's Department Store, 20
Richt, Mark, 154
Riley, Chris, 174, 177, 179, 180, 185
Riley, Dick, 130
Rivers, E. D., *18*
Robinson, J. Mack, 125
Robinson, Nita, 125
Rockefeller, Nelson, 73
Rodgers, William F., *18*
Roesen, Severin, 52, 57
Ruger, Thomas H., 13
Rusk, Dean, 102S
Russell, Richard B., 17

safety and security, 35, 91, 96–97, 112, 172, 174, 190–91. *See also* security gate and fence; state troopers
Salter, Allison Barnes, 151. *See also* Barnes, Allison
Salter, John, 151
Sams, Ferrol, 130
Sanders, Betty Foy, *21*, *31*, *40*, *125*; Christmas card, *3*; documentary film, 150–51; Granite Mansion repairs, 20–21; mansion construction and furnishing,

27, 29, 31, 70; mansion tours, 37; new mansion search, 23; and Shirley Miller, 125
Sanders, Carl, *21*, *125*; documentary film, 150–51; Granite Mansion repairs, 20–21; gubernatorial elections, 7; and Henry D. Green, 130; and Lester Maddox, 79; mansion construction, 27; Old Governor's Mansion restoration, 13; oral history project, 128; and Shirley Miller, 125
Satterfield, Bob, 190
Sawyer, Elizabeth, 31, *75*
Schley, William, 9
Schott, Marguerite, 69
Schreiner, Pete, 158
Scott, John, 8
Scott, Robert W., 84
security gate and fence, *34*, 39, 69–70
Selznick, David O., *18*
Seymour, John, 52
Shaw, Robert, 88
Sherman, William Tecumseh, 12
Shipp, Bill, 107, 120
Short, Bob, 69, 78
Shorter, Edward, 27
Shutze, Philip, 23
Sibley, Celestine, 69, 70, 115
Simon, Stanley, 172, *173*, 185, 189–90, *190*, 192
Slaton, John, 64
Slemons, Margaret, *19*
Smallwood, Martha, 158
Smith, Edward, 42
Smith, Eric, 172
Smith, Frances Allethea Murray, 81
Smith, Laura Maddox, 42
Smith, Priscilla, *90*
Smith, Scott, 194, *194*
Smith, Wilburn Edgar, 81
Smith, William Armstrong, *90*
Sorrells, Keith, 135
Sorrel-Weed House, 9
South, Joe, 127
Southern Living, 34
Spalding, Jack, 6
special events: Barnes family, 140, 143, 148, 151; Busbee family, 99, 101, 104; Carter family, 88–90; Deal family, 175, 177, *177–78*, 179–80; Harris family, 112, 114, 115, 117; Maddox family, 72–73, 77–78, 83, 124; Miller family, 125, 128, 130, 132–35; Perdue family, 154, 162–63, 165
Springer, Billy, 11
Stancil, Steve, 174, 188

state capital, 8, 13
state constitutions, 7, 13
state patrol headquarters, 35, 42, 45
state troopers, 190–91, *191*, *194*, 194
Steele, Leslie J., 18
Stephanopoulos, George, 130
Stephens, Alexander H., 15
Stitt, Mike, 77
Strickland, Troy, 31
Sumner, Jimmy, 172
Swan House, 23
swimming pool, 45–46, 69–70, 107, *108*

Talbot, Mary Beth. *See* Busbee, Mary Beth
Talgo, Kirk, 185, 186, *186*, 188
Talmadge, Betty, 17
Talmadge, Clara Bryant, *18*
Talmadge, Eugene, 17, *18*
Talmadge, Herman, 17, 128, 150
Talmadge, Mattie, 17, 18, 20
Tanksley, Charles, 151
Tanner, Bonnie Kessler, 167
Tarbutton, Gena, 194
Taylor, Jody, 191, 194
Taylor, Mark, 150
Taylor, Mia, 155
Tekippe, Bernie, 158
Tekippe, Carol, 158
tennis courts, 42, 69–70, 86, 148
Third Military District, 13
Thomas, Danny, 73
Thompson, M. E., 20
Thornton, Edna, 27
Tomochichi, 5
tornado damage, 35, 105, *105*, *106*, 107
Towns, George W. B., 12
Troup, George M., 7, 9
Trumbull, John, 51
trusty program: Barnes family, 143; Busbee family, 104; Carter family, 87, 91; Deal family, 173, 174, 179–80; functional role, 186, 188–89; garden benches, 42; Harris family, 112; Miller family, 128; Perdue family, 161, 190; personal reflection, 195
Turner, Henry, *193*, 194
Turner, James, 8
Turner, Joseph Mallord William, 61, 63

Uhry, Alfred, 130
U.S. Supreme Court decisions, 7

valedictorian event, 134–35, 148
Vandiver, Betty, 140, 150
Vandiver, Ernest, 20, 21, 128, 150
van Loo, Charles-Amédée-Philippe, 48